THE EUROPEAN UNION AND SOCIAL SECURITY LAW

The aim of this book is to examine how EU law relates to and impacts on the national social security systems of the Member States. It asks three key questions. Firstly, it looks at how the internal market and its developments have eroded Member States' sovereignty over their social security systems, despite the fact that the EU has limited competence in the field. It then explores, secondly, how the Union Citizenship and, thirdly, the Charter of Fundamental Rights has affected the coordination of these regimes.

Volume 77 in the Series Modern Studies in European Law

Modern Studies in European Law
Recent titles in this series:

The European Union's External Action in Times of Crisis
Edited by Piet Eeckhout and Manual Lopez-Escudero

The Legitimacy of Family Rights in Strasbourg Case Law:
Living Instrument or Extinguished Sovereignty?
Carmen Draghici

Strengthening the Rule of Law in Europe:
From a Common Concept to Mechanisms of Implementation
Edited by Werner Schroeder

The Pluralist Character of the European Economic Constitution
Clemens Kaupa

Exceptions from EU Free Movement Law
Edited by Panos Koutrakos, Niamh Nic Shuibhne and Phil Syrpis

Reconceptualising European Equality Law: A Comparative Institutional Analysis
Johanna Croon-Gestefeld

Marketing and Advertising Law in a Process of Harmonization
Edited by Ulf Bernitz and Caroline Heide-Jörgensen

The Fundamental Right to Data Protection:
Normative Value in the Context of Counter-Terrorism Surveillance
Maria Tzanou

Republican Europe
Anna Kocharov

Family Reunification in the EU
Chiara Berneri

EU Liability and International Economic Law
Armin Steinbach

The EU and Nanotechnologies: A Critical Analysis
Tanja Ehnert

Human Rights Between Law and Politics:
The Margin of Appreciation in Post-National Contexts
Edited by Petr Agha

For the complete list of titles in this series, see
'Modern Studies in European Law' link at
www.bloomsburyprofessional.com/uk/series/modern-studies-in-european-law

The European Union and Social Security Law

Jaan Paju

•HART•
PUBLISHING
OXFORD AND PORTLAND, OREGON
2017

Hart Publishing
An imprint of Bloomsbury Publishing Plc

Hart Publishing Ltd
Kemp House
Chawley Park
Cumnor Hill
Oxford OX2 9PH
UK

Bloomsbury Publishing Plc
50 Bedford Square
London
WC1B 3DP
UK

www.hartpub.co.uk
www.bloomsbury.com

Published in North America (US and Canada) by
Hart Publishing
c/o International Specialized Book Services
920 NE 58th Avenue, Suite 300
Portland, OR 97213-3786
USA

www.isbs.com

HART PUBLISHING, the Hart/Stag logo, BLOOMSBURY and the Diana logo are trademarks of Bloomsbury Publishing Plc

First published 2017

British Library Cataloguing-in-Publication Data
A catalogue record for this book is available from the British Library.

ISBN: HB: 978-1-50991-157-8
ePDF: 978-1-50991-155-4
ePub: 978-1-50991-156-1

Library of Congress Cataloging-in-Publication Data

Names: Paju, Jaan, author.

Title: The European Union and social security law / Jaan Paju.

Description: Portland, Oregon : Hart Publishing, 2017. | Series: Modern studies in European law ; volume 77 | Includes bibliographical references and index.

Identifiers: LCCN 2017018589 (print) | LCCN 2017022675 (ebook) | ISBN 9781509911561 (Epub) | ISBN 9781509911578 (hardback : alk. paper)

Subjects: LCSH: Social security—Law and legislation—European Union countries.

Classification: LCC KJE3387 (ebook) | LCC KJE3387 .P35 2017 (print) | DDC 344.2403—dc23

LC record available at https://lccn.loc.gov/2017018589

Typeset by Compuscript Ltd, Shannon
Printed and bound in Great Britain by Lightning Source UK Ltd

In loving memory of my father Otto Paju (1926–2016)

Preface

This monograph would never have come about, had not my (now) former supervisor, Professor Ulf Bernitz, encouraged me to get in touch with Hart Publishing for a discussion on publishing my thesis in an edited form.

It takes two to tango: thank you Sinead Moloney at Hart Publishing for believing in the project. I owe debts of gratitude to Emily Braggins at Hart Publishing for all support when completing the monograph, as well as to Peggy Oskarsson for improving the language of the initial manuscript. Their contributions have been invaluable; however, of course, any errors remain my own. The law is as it stands as of 1 January 2017.

Thanks and love to my sons Villem and Hannes. My world.

The monograph was made possible thanks to the Stockholm Centre for Commercial Law enabling my stay at Christ Church College and the Institute of European and Comparative Law at Oxford University as the Stockholm Centre Oxford Fellow 2015–16. Generous financial support for editing and proofreading the monograph was provided by Stiftelsen Juridisk Fakultetslitteratur and Emil Heijnes Stiftelse för rättsvetenskaplig forskning.

Stockholm,
May 2017

Contents

Table of Cases

1

Introduction: Starting Points, Purpose and Methodology

1.1. PURPOSE AND QUESTIONS

THE PURPOSE OF this monograph is to analyse how EU law relates to and impacts on the national social security systems of Member States. The monograph contributes to a deeper understanding of the transformation of national social security models brought about as an inevitable result of EU law.

When the first regulation in the field of social security within the European Economic Community, Regulation 3/58,[1] was passed, the question of harmonisation of the social security systems of Member States was subject to discussion and analysis. Harmonisation was, however, not considered to be necessary, since it was assumed that the economic development within the European Economic Community would lead to a natural convergence of the national social security systems.[2] For this reason, the Regulation was limited to coordination of Member States' social security systems, while the Member States' legislative competence remained unrestricted:

> In the absence of harmonisation at Community level, it is for the legislation of each Member State to determine both the conditions concerning the right or duty to be insured with a social security scheme … and the conditions for entitlement to benefits.[3]

However, with the development of the Economic Community into a Union, coordination of EU Member States' social security systems has increasingly evolved

[1] Regulation 3/58 of 25 September 1958, OJ No 30, 16 December 1958.

[2] See the Ohlin Report; 'Social aspects of European economic co-operation: Report by a group of experts', Studies and Reports, New Series No 46, ILO, Genève, 1956; chs IV and V and the report's conclusions p 115 ff.

[3] Case C-158/96 *Raymond Kohll v Union des caisses de maladie* [1998] ECR I-1931, 18. Cf Case 266/78 *Bruno Brunori v Landesversicherungsanstalt Rheinprovinz* [1979] ECR 2705; Case C-275/96 *Anne Kuusijärvi v Riksförsäkringsverket* [1998] ECR I-3419, 29; Case C-227/03 *AJ van Pommeren-Bourgondiën v Raad van bestuur van de Sociale verzekeringsbank* [2005] ECR I-6101, 33; Case C-388/09 *Joao Filipe da Silva Martins v Bank Betriebskrankenkasse-Pflegekasse* [2011] ECR I-5737, 71; Joined Cases C-611/10 and C-612/10 *Waldemar Hudzinski v Agentur für Arbeit Wesel—Familienkasse* (C-611/10) and *Jaroslaw Wawrzyniak v Agentur für Arbeit Mönchengladbach—Familienkasse* (C-612/10) EU:C:2012:339, 42.

into a legal framework in which Member States' legislative competence 'must be exercised in compliance with Community law'.[4]

This context constitutes the core of this monograph: how EU law has influenced and continues to influence national social security models, regardless of the fact that, on paper, the EU competence has been limited to coordination.

For the purpose of the monograph, three questions are addressed.

The first question is how the internal market and its development through the years has had an impact on national social security models, even though the EU competence has been limited to coordination. The legal situation in 2017 is very different from what it was in 1958. The EU aims to implement the Lisbon Treaty leading to a social market economy and rights-based union. There are currently three parallel frameworks that can influence the national social security systems in the Member States when EU law is brought to the fore. These frameworks can have a parallel as well as joint influence. They can strengthen the EU law, but are also capable of pushing it to new directions. Therefore, the second and third questions, respectively, are how Union citizenship and the EU Charter of Fundamental Rights have influenced the coordination of national social security systems.

This monograph addresses these three questions, both from the perspective of the Member States and from the perspective of the individual, since these are integrated in such a way that greater individual freedom usually leads to a Member State's competence being limited, and vice versa.

1.2. THE THEORETICAL FRAMEWORK

The purpose of this monograph gives rise to the question of whether there is a possible erosion of sovereignty of national competence with respect to social security systems.[5]

The starting point for sovereignty erosion is that Member States are the 'masters of the Treaties' and the situation is observed from a purely national standpoint.[6]

[4] Case C-158/96 *Raymond Kohll v Union des caisses de maladie* [1998] ECR I-1931, 19. See also Case 275/81 *GF Koks v Raad van Arbeid* [1982] ECR 3013, 10 and Case C-137/11 *Partena ASBL v Les Tartes de Chaumont-Gistoux SA*, EU:C:2012:593, 59.

[5] I assume the Westphalian concept of sovereignty with an absolute internal authority without the possibility of external actors intervening; Brown talks about 'establishing a State centered system that was based on principles of equal State sovereignty and the absolute right to internal self-determination without external interference', G Brown, 'State Sovereignty, Federation and Kantian Cosmopolitanism' [2005] *European Journal of International Relations* 495, 498. Cf M Isenbaert, *EC Law and the Sovereignty of the Member States in Direct Taxation* (Amsterdam, IBFD Publications, 2010) ch 2.

[6] This approach does not take into account the fact that, early on with Case 6/64 *Costa v ENEL* [1964] ECR 585 the CJEU created a Community law, 'a special legal system', with its own legal framework and principles. For a review of the concept of sovereignty in the EU legal context see M Isenbaert, *EC Law and the Sovereignty of the Member States in Direct Taxation* (Amsterdam, IBFD Publications, 2010) ch 2 and T Schilling, 'The Autonomy of the Community Legal Order: An Analysis of Possible Foundations' [1996] *Harvard International Law Journal* 389. See also K Lenaerts, 'Constitutionalism and the Many Faces of Federalism' [1990] *American Journal of Comparative Law* 205; GF Mancini, 'The Making of a Constitution for Europe' [1989] *CMLR* 595; J Weiler, 'The Transformation of Europe'

Therefore, a transfer of legislative competence under EU cooperation is based on active actions on the part of a Member State. For example, the Danish constitutional law mentions abandonment of sovereignty, while in the Swedish case it is a matter of transfer of authority.[7]

Sovereignty erosion is characterised by a situation where EU law substantially influences national legislations without the Member States having agreed to a formal transfer of competence.[8]

There are cases where, seemingly exclusive, national legislative competence are in conflict with the EU law and the latter takes precedence.[9] Ferrera observes:

> 'It is clear that the principles of direct effect and of EC law supremacy as well as the transformation of the preliminary ruling system significantly eroded the Member States' Westphalian sovereignty, that is, their ability to exclude external authority structures from their jurisdictional space.'[10]

Sovereignty erosion is not a new phenomenon within EU law and this is not surprising; as a general principle, EU law takes precedence in case of a conflict.[11] Leibfried and Pierson discuss a situation in which EU law has led to significant sovereignty erosion with regard to national legislative competences when the welfare systems of the Member States conflicted with the market theories of the EU law.[12]

With regard to social security, it is a case of EU coordination, as mentioned above in section 1.1; a coordination where EU law respects Member States' legislative

[1990–91] *The Yale Law Journal* 2403. For a critical assessment, H Rasmussen, *On Law and Policy in the European Court of Justice. A Comparative Study in Judicial Policymaking* (Dordrecht, Martinus Nijhoff Publishers, 1986). Cf MP Maduro, *We, the Court, the European Court of Justice & the European Economic Constitution* (Oxford, Hart, 1998).

[7] Hartig Danielsen talks about a possibility of abandonment of sovereignty: J Hartig Danielsen, *Suverænitetsafgivelse* (Copenhagen, Jurist- og Økonomforbundets Forlag, 1999). The Danish Constitution § 20, The Swedish Constitution, Regeringsformen 10:6.

[8] Walker talks about a 'late sovereignty', a developed sovereignty in a new multi-dimensional order that is characterised by openness to the idea that the concept of sovereignty has developed beyond the Westphalian concept of sovereignty, and that there is no return. N Walker, 'Late Sovereignty in the European Union', in N Walker (ed) *Sovereignty in Transition* (Oxford, Hart, 2003) 19 ff.

[9] Leanerts finds that 'There simply is no nucleus of sovereignty that the Member States can invoke, as such, against the Community.' K Lenaerts, 'Constitutionalism and the Many Faces of Federalism' [1990] *American Journal of Comparative Law* 205,220.

[10] M Ferrera, *The Boundaries of Welfare, European Integration and the New Spatial Politics of Social Protection* (Oxford, Oxford University Press, 2005) 99.

[11] In the preliminary rulings in *Costa v ENEL*, *Internationale Handelsgesellschaft* and *Simmenthal II*, the CJEU determined that the EU law has precedence where there is a conflict of norms, regardless of the form of national legislation or if it was adopted at a later date. See Case 6/64 *Costa v ENEL* [1964] ECR 585; Case 11/70 *Internationale Handelsgesellschaft mbH v Einfuhr- und Vorratsstelle für Getreide und Futtermittel* [1970] ECR 1125 and Case 106/77 *Amministrazione delle Finanze dello Stato v Simmenthal SpA* [1978] ECR 629. Cf. M Isenbaert, *EC Law and the Sovereignty of the Member States in Direct Taxation*, which is based on similar ideas about sovereignty erosion to those expressed in this monograph, but takes into account Member States' competence when it comes to income taxation.

[12] P Leibfried and P Pierson, 'Semisovereign Welfare States: Social Policy in a Multitiered Europe', in P Leibfried and P Pierson, (eds), *European Social Policy: Between Fragmentation and Integration* (Washington DC, Brookings Inst Press, 1995) 44.

competence. According to the doctrine, there is, however, also an erosion of sovereignty in the field of social security. Watson mentions how 'the sovereignty of the Member States has been subject to a degree of erosion'.[13] Knorpel observes, in connection with the Court's decision in Patteri,[14] that 'the Court has now firmly rejected the long held but increasingly eroded notion that the Community law of social security has not gone beyond the stage of co-ordination of autonomous national legislations'.[15] Also see Dougan, who describes how the CJEU reduces the sovereignty of political bodies when it does not base its rulings on the Regulation.[16]

It can also be considered an erosion of sovereignty with regard to national welfare systems when Member States preclude the erosion by changing or refraining from legislation. When Sweden became an EU member in 1995, there was awareness that, in the EU legal environment, residence-based benefits were vulnerable to a greater degree than work-based benefits. The social security legislation then in force was therefore divided into work-based benefits, with reimbursement rates calculated on the basis of income, and residence-based benefits for everyone residing in Sweden. Furthermore, a basic pension was introduced, that was conditional, depending on the qualification period, to replace the state pension which had been based on residence. A Member State can also decide not to go through with certain legislation. For example, Germany decided in the 1990s, in order to avoid future potential export of the social security benefit, to bury a legislative initiative (the Fink model) for an additional state pension for low-income people, regardless of the fact that there was a political consensus about the need for such a benefit.[17]

However, in order to be able to speak about sovereignty erosion, first there has to be sovereignty. Wrange had posed the question 20 years earlier, whether the term sovereignty could in the future properly be used to describe reality.[18] MacCormick describes in his famous work *Questioning Sovereignty*[19] how understanding of sovereignty has changed through the centuries: in ancient times there were city-states like Athens and Sparta, followed by the Roman Empire that was certainly a controlled area but where groups of the population retained a degree of independence; in Scotland, the clan system had been prevalent well into the Middle Ages, and in Germany small feudal states thrived, where a person received

13 P Watson, *EU Social and Employment Law*, 2nd edn (Oxford, Oxford University Press, 2014) 71.

14 Case 242/83 *Caisse de compensation pour allocations familiales du bâtiment, de l'industrie et du commerce du Hainaut v Salvatore Patteri* [1984] ECR 3171.

15 H Knorpel, 'Social Security Cases in the Court of Justice of the European Communities' [1986] *CMLR* 359, 380.

16 M Dougan, 'Expanding the Frontiers of EU Citizenship by Dismantling the Territorial Boundaries of the National Welfare States', in C Barnard and O Odudu (eds), *The Outer Limits of European Union Law* (Oxford, Hart, 2009) 149 ff.

17 For the latter situation see L Conant, *Justice Contained, Law and Politics in the European Union* (Ithaca NY, Cornell University Press, 2002) 194.

18 P Wrange, 'The Concept of Sovereignty—Alive and Kickin'' [1994–95] *Juridisk Tidskrift* 350.

19 N MacCormick, *Questioning Sovereignty—Law, State, and Practical Reason* (Oxford, Oxford University Press, 1999).

patronage in exchange for services. Only later did these societies develop into the states that we know today.[20]

The national state is generally considered a sovereign state that encompasses all political functions and fields. As a sovereign state, it is based on a legal system, with a constitution and defined separation of powers between national political authorities.[21]

For states that are members of the EU, there is an additional legal dimension.[22] An EU Member State must rely not only on its national constitution, but also on EU Treaties and secondary EU law. This is a constitutional pluralism, with two parallel constitutional systems functioning side by side.[23]

However, it is difficult to imagine a harmonious constitutional pluralism in cases where the EU legal system takes precedence over national legislation. Rossa Phelan proposes instead a constitutional situation resembling revolution or revolt for Member States: a revolution at home when EU law takes precedence, and a revolt on the basis of the idea that the national law or the constitution should take precedence over EU law.[24]

Areas of constitutional conflict have emerged mainly within the internal market, but later on have also appeared in the field of Union citizenship and the Charter of Fundamental Rights. The institution that makes these conflict areas visible is the CJEU, which can only tear them apart. In other words, the Court rules—it does not legislate.[25]

MacCormick determines two ways of resolving these conflict areas that are left open. Either the situation can be resolved by radical pluralism, where there is awareness that the two constitutional systems are not always easy to reconcile, that the EU law does not always take precedence,[26] or it can be resolved by a legal balancing act, which is usually subject to a political solution. Where legal systems

[20] ibid, 17.

[21] G Poggi, *The State—Its Nature, Development and Prospects* (Cambridge, Polity Press, 1990).

[22] N MacCormick, *Questioning Sovereignty—Law, State, and Practical Reason* (Oxford, Oxford University Press, 1999) 97 ff. See also Wrange, 'The Concept of Sovereignty—Alive and Kickin'', 362.

[23] The preliminary ruling in Case 26/62 *Van Gend en Loos v Nederlandse Administratie der Belastingen* [1963] ECR 1 introduced a new constitutional situation by stating: 'The Community constitutes a new legal order of international law for the benefit of which the states have limited their sovereign rights, albeit within limited fields, and the subjects of which comprise not only Member States but also their nationals. Independent of the legislation of Member States, Community law therefore not only imposes obligations on individuals but is also intended to confer upon them the rights which become a part of their legal heritage.'

[24] D Rossa Phelan, *Revolt or Revolution: The Constitutional Boundaries of the European Community* (London, Round Hall/Sweet & Maxwell, 1997) 413 ff.

[25] However, the Court's case law can lead to a positive integration in the long run, if its judicial function makes the Member States consolidate their applicable laws. Cf the Patient Directive which consolidates the case law on the cross-border health care; Directive 2011/24/EU of the European Parliament and of the Council of 9 March 2011 on the application of patients' rights in cross-border healthcare, [2011] OJ L88/45.

[26] cf RD Kelemen, 'On the Unsustainability of Constitutional Pluralism: European Supremacy and the Survival of the Eurozone' [2016] *Maastricht Journal of European and Comparative Law* 136.

interact in a common legal environment, MacCormick foresees general principles and rules of international law providing an outer framework.[27]

As long as we cannot free ourselves from the prevailing concept of sovereignty, the issue of sovereignty erosion—where one side gains sovereignty at the expense of another—will continue.[28] It is within this prevailing constitutional context that the three questions of this monograph are based.

1.3. MATERIALS AND METHOD

For the purpose of the monograph, it can be observed that the EU legal doctrine in the field of social security is relatively limited, despite the importance of social security systems in the national context.[29] The basis of the monograph consists therefore mainly of approximately 600 cases that the CJEU has dealt with over the years.

The monograph analyses the influence of the internal market in a more substantial way in comparison to the Union citizenship and the Charter of Fundamental Rights. This can be explained by the initial need for coordination of Member States' social security systems as a result of cross-border movements of the labour force. Therefore, free movement of workers constitutes a foundation for the Regulation. In addition, the internal market generates the majority of the preliminary rulings.

Abstraction and generalisation of the extensive case law in the field can reveal structural patterns, which in turn can clarify the legal structures.[30] The approach making a division into three acting legislative powers—the internal market, Union citizenship and the Charter of Fundamental Rights—provides an explanation for the phenomenon of sovereignty erosion, and why one Member State's welfare model is exposed while another may not be influenced at all.

1.4. CONCEPTS

A welfare state and its social security system is built on solidarity among those who reside (and/or are citizens) within a territorially limited area (a state). Four concepts—state, citizenship, solidarity and social security—therefore are central to the subject of this monograph.

[27] N MacCormick, *Questioning Sovereignty—Law, State, and Practical Reason* (Oxford, Oxford University Press, 1999) 116 ff.

[28] Wrange: 'Until we learn to think about the European Union as something completely different from everything we know today,' sovereignty' seems to be a necessary part of our vocabulary.' Wrange, 'The Concept of Sovereignty—Alive and Kickin'' 364.

[29] In the case of Sweden, more than one billion SEK a day is paid in benefits, not counting unemployment benefits.

[30] cf K Tuori, *Critical Legal Positivism* (Aldershot, Ashgate, 2002) 154 ff.

The first concept of a state can be traced back to the Greek city-states.[31] However, it is only towards the close of the nineteenth century that we see a more structured national state as it is understood today.[32] The monograph relies on Tilly's definition of a state: 'State building provided for the emergence of specialized personnel, control over consolidated territory, loyalty, and durability, permanent institutions with a centralized and autonomous state that held the monopoly of violence over a given population'.[33]

The concepts of citizenship and solidarity are closely intertwined and indeed interdependent. Citizenship can also be traced back to the Greek city-states.[34] Citizenship is normally given to natural persons by a sovereign state and provides them with various rights and obligations towards the state. The conditions for the acquisition and loss of citizenship are in a state's competence, and their contents are ultimately defined by the respective state.[35] Citizenship has usually been a precondition for solidarity. In *Rottmann*, the CJEU defined 'the special relationship of solidarity and good faith between it and its nationals'.[36] This definition has traces of Habermas' theory that describes citizenship as 'an abstract, legally mediated solidarity between strangers'. Citizenship therefore leads to solidarity.[37]

The third concept, solidarity, according to Derpmann, can best be described as an obligation or a feeling of obligation to act for another person's (citizen's) well-being, even in situations where one may thereby deny oneself of material position or one's own well-being.[38] This solidarity can arise as a result of free will, or through laws that form the basis for social security.[39]

[31] FH Hinsley, *Sovereignty*, 2nd edn (Cambridge, Cambridge University Press, 1986) 28 ff.

[32] C Tilly, 'Reflections on the history of European state-making', in C Tilly (ed), *The formation of national states in Western Europe* (Princeton NJ, Princeton University Press, 1975) esp 608 ff.

[33] ibid, 70 ff.

[34] D Heater, *Citizenship: The Civic Ideal in World History, Politics and Education*, 3rd edn (Manchester, Manchester University Press, 2004) 3 ff.

[35] See for instance Case C-200/02 *Kunqian Catherine Zhu, Man Lavette Chen and Secretary of State for the Home Department* [2004] ECR I-9925, 37.

[36] Case C-135/08 *Janko Rottmann v Freistaat Bayern* [2010] ECR I-1449, 51.

[37] J Habermas, 'Why Europe Needs a Constitution' [2001] *New Left Review* 16.

[38] P Derpmann, 'Solidarity and Cosmopolitanism' [2009] *Ethical Theory and Moral Practice* 303, 304. Cf K Tuori, 'European Social Constitution: Between Solidarity and Access Justice', in K Purnhagen and P Rott (eds), *Varieties of European Economic Law and Regulation, Liber Amicorum for Hans Micklitz* (Cham, Springer, 2014) 374 ff, where Tuori creates an image of solidarity that is built on common history, values and identity. Pieters talks about 'circles of solidarity' which are not necessarily territorially limited: D Pieters, *Social Security: An Introduction to the Basic Principles*, 2nd edn (Haag, Kluwer, 2006) 21.

[39] cf D Schiek, 'Perspectives on social citizenship in the EU—from status positivus to status socialis activus via two forms of transnational solidarity', in D Kochenov (ed), *EU Citizenship and Federalism: The Role of Rights* (Cambridge, Cambridge University Press, 2016); N Nic Shuibhne, 'Limits Rising, Duties Ascending: the Changing Legal Shape of Union Citizenship' [2015] *CMLR* 889. Ross describes 'we and they' as a set that characterises citizenship and solidarity and that both include and exclude groups of people. M Ross, 'The Struggle for EU Citizenship: Why Solidarity Matters', in A Arnull, C Barnard, M Dougan and E Spaventa (eds), *A Constitutional Order of States? Essays in EU Law in Honour of Alan Dashwood* (Oxford, Hart, 2011) 284.

The fourth concept, social security, depends on one's understanding of what that term implies, so the definition can differ depending on whom one asks. Most national definitions of social security provide a list of what it includes, but not what is really meant by social security. Since there is no generally accepted definition, and no possibility of formulating one, social security is defined by the respective state and therefore differs from one state to another.[40]

Furthermore, there is no international definition of what is meant by social security.[41] The ILO defines the concept, in *Into the 21st Century: The Development of Social Security*,[42] as follows:

> social security has wider aims than the prevention or relief of poverty. It is the response to an aspiration for security in its widest sense. Its fundamental purpose is to give individuals and families the confidence that their level of living and quality of life will not, in so far as is possible, be greatly eroded by any social or economic eventuality. This involves not just meeting needs as and when they arise but also preventing risks from arising in the first place.[43]

According to the above, Regulation 883/2004 does not include a definition of the concept of social security; instead it lists the areas that are encompassed by the Regulation. Hence there is an outer framework. The limits of this framework have been developed by the CJEU in its judicial capacity, so that an independent EU judicial area has emerged.

1.5. DISPOSITION

This monograph consists of eight chapters, including this introductory method chapter and concluding with Chapter 8.

Chapter 2 provides both background and context. It notes that national security systems differ, but that they have one thing in common: territorial limitation. This limitation makes cross-border movement more difficult, in that a person can lose earned rights by moving or not having these rights acknowledged in the other

[40] cf P Watson, *EU Social and Employment Law*, 2nd edn (Oxford, Oxford University Press, 2014) 71.

[41] UN Universal Declaration of Human Rights describes in Art 22 how everyone has the right to social security, without explaining in detail what social security includes. The explanatory Art 25 clarifies the term to a certain extent by naming a list of benefits that should be included: Art 25 para 1: 'Everyone has the right to … security in the event of unemployment, sickness, disability, widowhood, old-age or other lack of livelihood in circumstances beyond his control.' Art 25, para 2: 'Motherhood and childhood are entitled to special care and assistance.' UN Universal Declaration of Human Rights, resolution 217A(III) of 10 December 1948. ILO Convention Concerning Minimum Standards of Social Security also does not offer a legal definition of the term. The Social Security (Minimum Standards) Convention, 1952 (No.102), UN Doc, www.ilo.org/dyn/normlex/en/f?p=NORMLEXPUB:12100:0::NO:12100:P12100_INSTRUMENT_ID:312247:NO.

[42] ILO Publications, *Into the Twenty-First Century: The Development of Social Security* (Genève, ILO, 1984).

[43] ibid, 19.

state, giving rise to the need of coordinating the social security systems, thereby introducing Regulation 883/2004.

The analytical approach of this monograph is introduced in Chapter 3, which explores how the CJEU's methods of legal interpretation have led to the expansion of both material and personal scope. In turn, a larger material and personal scope has meant more cases and therefore more preliminary rulings that have strengthened the impact of EU law.

Chapter 4 describes the evolution of non-discrimination in the field of social security from direct discrimination to market access. This chapter analyses how the CJEU has developed the principle of non-discrimination, where the assimilation of facts forms an important part. Assimilation of facts from previously earned qualification periods from different Member States may seem obvious from the internal market perspective, but not for national social security systems.

Chapter 5 analyses how the CJEU has made use of primary law in cases where the Regulation is not applicable. The analysis focuses on the preliminary rulings in *Öberg*[44] and *Rockler*,[45] as well as the case law in the field of cross-border healthcare, starting with the preliminary ruling in *Kohll*.[46]

Chapter 6 looks into how the Union Citizenship and Directive 2004/38[47] influence and affect the national social security systems. The chapter focuses mainly on the question of whether EU citizenship can lead to access to national social security systems' residence-based benefits.

The EU's Charter of Fundamental Rights (Charter of Rights)[48] is a new basis for Union law that has developed on grounds other than the purely economic ones upon which EU cooperation was previously established. Chapter 7 analyses how the Charter of Rights can influence the social security systems of Member States within the EU legal context. In this regard, the chapter studies the directly applicable Article 34 as well as adjacent basic rights.

Chapter 8 summarises the monograph's analysis and conclusions and draws a closing comprehensive conclusion. The chapter also discusses the existing legal position from a sovereignty perspective and possible de lege ferenda solutions.

[44] Case C-185/04 *Ulf Öberg v Försäkringskassan* [2006] ECR I-1453.

[45] Case C-137/04 *Amy Rockler v Försäkringskassan* [2006] ECR I-1441.

[46] Case C-158/96 *Raymond Kohll v Union des caisses de maladie* [1998] ECR I-1931.

[47] Directive 2004/38/EC of the European Parliament and of the Council of 29 April 2004 on the right of citizens of the Union and their family members to move and reside freely within the territory of the Member States amending Regulation (EEC) No 1612/68 and repealing Directives 64/221/EEC, 68/360/EEC, 72/194/EEC, 73/148/EEC, 75/34/EEC, 75/35/EEC, 90/364/EEC, 90/365/EEC and 93/96/EEC, [2004] OJ L158.

[48] Charter of Fundamental Rights of the European Union, [2010] OJ C83/389.

2

Social Security, the Territorial Aspect and Regulation 883/2004

2.1. INTRODUCTION

SOCIAL SECURITY IS based on systems of insurance that cover the entire life cycle. It follows a person through life, when a person is born, gets sick, becomes a parent, perhaps becomes disabled, and finally retires. Of all the social security benefits, the most significant are the forms of parental insurance, that include parental benefit and child allowance; health insurance; rehabilitation insurance; insurance for occupational accidents and injury; insurance for the disabled; unemployment benefits; housing benefits and the pension system.

Social security has been based throughout history on a collective solution[1] and since the 1870s, when the first regulations were adopted in Prussia, has mainly been organised on a national basis in Europe. Social security is built upon the idea that the citizens of a state take part in national or nationally regulated social security benefits by paying taxes and making social contributions. It can be regarded as a social contract that is concluded between the state and its subjects. This contract usually does not go beyond a state's borders, nor does it automatically include those who have arrived from other states.[2]

The social security of a state is built upon a historical development characterised by initially basic (matter of survival) and religious foundations, and later political and cultural arrangements.[3] The Member States developed their social security systems over time and on the basis of circumstances that were specific to

[1] N Rennuy, 'The Emergence of a Parallel System of Social Security Coordination' [2013] *CMLR* 1221, 1222; H Verschueren, 'European (Internal) Migration Law as an Instrument for Defining the Boundaries of National Solidarity Systems' [2007] *European Journal of Migration Law* 307; D Pieters, *Social Security: An Introduction to the Basic Principles* (Haag, Kluwer, 2008) 21.

[2] F Pennings, *European Social Security Law*, 6th edn (Cambridge - Antwerp - Portland, Intersentia, 2015) 4 ff; P Roberts, 'A Short History of Social Security Coordination', in Y Jorens (ed), *50 Years of Social Security Coordination—Past, Present, Future* (European Union Publications Office, 2010) 8 ff; V Paskalia, *Free Movement of Persons and Social Security* (Stockholm, Stockholm University Press, 2004) 48 ff; P Watson, *Social Security Law of the European Communities* (London, Mansell Publishing, 1980) 4 ff.

[3] D Sindbjerg Martinsen, 'Social Security in the EU: The De-Territorialization of Welfare', in G de Búrca (ed), *EU Law and the Welfare State, In Search of Solidarity* (Oxford, Oxford University Press, 2005) 99; V Paskalia, *Free Movement of Persons and Social Security* (Stockholm, Stockholm University Press, 2004) 48 ff.

the state; therefore these systems represent the innermost essence of the national state. These standpoints are confronted with entirely different starting points that are common for the European Union project.[4]

What makes social security different from other types of insurance, such as home insurance, motor insurance or travel insurance, is that it is obligatory, uniform, and public.[5] The reason why most EU Member States are guarantors for the social security insurance is that private insurance firms do not usually include the whole population. Therefore the state needs to act as an insurer if the entire population is to be covered. Furthermore, the state gains thereby control over the development and distribution of the welfare.[6]

Depending on how one defines or classifies various national social security laws, one can identify two or more social-political models.[7] In general, there are the classic Bismarck and Beveridge models, complemented with the Nordic model.

The Bismarck model considers employment as a prerequisite to qualifying for social security benefits. These benefits depend on income and paid contributions. Financing is provided through social partners by means of their own contributions and employer contributions, and in some cases state contributions. The employee and employer organise and manage the insurance under the state's supervision. Those who do not work, or are not members of the employee's family, are directed

[4] D Sindbjerg Martinsen, 'Social Security in the EU: The De-Territorialization of Welfare', in G de Búrca (ed), *EU Law and the Welfare State, In Search of Solidarity* (Oxford, Oxford University Press, 2005) esp 98 ff. Cf M Ross, 'Solidarity—A New Constitutional Paradigm for the EU?' in M Ross and Y Borgmann-Prebil (eds), *Proving Solidarity in the European Union* (Oxford, Oxford University Press, 2010); M Ferrera, 'Towards an "Open" Social Citizenship? The New Boundaries of Welfare in the European Union', in G de Búrca (ed), *EU Law and the Welfare State, In Search of Solidarity* (Oxford, Oxford University Press, 2005); AP Van der Mei, *Free Movement of Persons within the European Community—Cross Border Access to Public Benefits* (Oxford, Hart, 2003) 3 ff and 11 ff.

[5] For a detailed review of the respective Member States, see: www.missoc.org. MISSOC is an initiative by the Commission by which all Member States, EFTA states and Switzerland report changes in their systems twice a year and these reports then update databases so that citizens of the Union can find current and relevant legislation on all Member States.

[6] For a macroeconomic analysis see N Barr, *Economics of the Welfare State*, 5th edn (Oxford, Oxford University Press, 2012). For political science theories, see JE Roemer, *Theories of Distributive Justice* (Boston MA, Harvard University Press, 1996); B Rothstein and S Kumlin, 'Making and Breaking Social Capital: The Impact of Welfare State Institutions' (2005) 38 (4) *Comparative Political Studies* 339–65; B Rothstein and E Uslaner, 'All for All: Equality and Social Trust' [2005] *World Politics* 41–72.

[7] cf G Bonoli, 'New social risks and the politics of post-industrial social policies' in K Armingeon and G Bonoli (eds), *The Politics of Post-Industrial Welfare States* (Abingdon, Routledge, 2006). Esping-Andersen describes three ways of organising national welfare: conservative, liberal and socio-democratic. His categorisation is based on the evaluation of a number of parameters used to create national welfare models. G Esping-Andersen, *The Three Worlds of Welfare Capitalism* (London, Polity Press, 1990) 23 ff. Berge et al have instead developed five ideal types of social security models, created on the basis of the right to compensation, principles for compensation levels and how social security is managed: 1. a means-tested model with minimal amounts or lump sums in line with needs assessment; 2. a voluntary state-subsidised model; 3. a state-corporate model built on the loss of income principle; 4. a basic protection model that targets the entire population with low amounts; and 5. a general model with basic protection for everyone while working receive compensation on the basis of previous income. A Berge, W Korpi, J Palme, S-Å Stenberg and K Åmark, 'Välfärdsstat i brytningstid: historisk-samhällsvetenskapliga studier om genus och klass, ojämlikhet och fattigdom' [1999] *Sociologisk Forskning*, Supplement (with an English summary).

to seek the more limited benefits provided by local institutions, such as the church or the local authority. In this way the system distinguishes between those who are encompassed by it, namely those who work, and those outside of it, who receive less protection.

Unlike the Bismarck model, the Beveridge model, developed in Great Britain, extends to all people within a given territory, providing them with all-embracing benefits.[8] These benefits are financed by taxes but are relatively modest. To obtain benefits in excess of the subsistence minimum, one must be privately insured as well, and not everyone can afford this. This low basic protection requires an element of voluntary charity work, similar to the Bismarck model but on different grounds.

The Nordic model, developed in Sweden and other Nordic countries, is universal and financed by taxes. The benefits are connected to citizenship or residence; regardless of whether one works or not, everyone has the right to certain benefits. The main aim is redistribution and thereby greater equality in society.

These three welfare models are challenged in different ways by Union law and people moving between states.

2.2. CONSEQUENCE OF TERRITORIAL RESTRICTIONS FOR MIGRATION MOVEMENTS

As long as a person does not move from one state to another, the differences between states are irrelevant; as the person is part of one and the same system. When people move to another state, they leave behind their former social security affiliation that, normally, is territorially limited. Those who move permanently to another country may therefore lose their rights previously earned in the former country of residence. Those who move might, furthermore, face problems in joining the new state's social security system. Consider the example of a person who intends to retire and is granted a pension in a cold and dark country, but who wishes to spend his old age in a warmer place. Let us assume that the pension system of the cold country is territorially limited, so that pension is paid only within national borders. The pension authority follows the national legislation and ends the payment of pension because the person has moved to a warmer country. On the other hand, the pension system of the warmer country requires a person to have been a resident of that country for at least 10 years to receive the national state pension. This system also does not have any way of taking into account qualifying periods in another country. As a result, the person in question loses the pension rights from the cold country but is ineligible to receive a pension from the warmer country.

[8] However, these universal benefits may still have additional eligibility requirements such as an income below a certain threshold.

An employed person can end up in a situation of being completely uninsured, if this person commutes to work in a state having a social security system dedicated to all those residing in the country, while the person's country of residence has a system of contributions paid by the employers and employees and benefits are issued to those working in the same country. Since the employed person does not work in the country of residence, or live in the country of employment, neither country is providing insurance. The reverse scenario can also happen; the country of residence has an insurance system based on residence, and the country of employment has an insurance system based on an employee's contributions. The person in question will be included in both systems. There is now a paradoxical situation for national social security systems, where both states have to pay the person who may not have contributed at all with either taxes or contributions.

The high degree of uncertainty resulting from the territorial limits of social security systems naturally leads to reluctance to work in another country.[9] This reluctance is not beneficial for an individual personally considering moving, or for a state that cannot persuade its companies to expand beyond its national borders when the companies' employees hesitate to go to a new state to work.

These consequences became obvious when the labour force started to move between European states, and was especially acute in the border areas between states. The first bilateral convention on social security was concluded in 1827 between France and the Duchy of Parma, with the object of guaranteeing the payment of pensions in cross-border situations.[10] After Germany introduced its social security system at the end of the 1870s, international cooperation in this field intensified. A bilateral agreement of 1904 in the field of labour law between France and Italy represented the first modern approach to cross-border social security arrangements. The agreement included provisions on non-discrimination, export of pensions, and provisions regarding different working benefits. By the time of the First World War, 11 bilateral agreements had been concluded in Europe.[11] During the interwar period, 150 bilateral agreements were agreed upon.[12] Today, most European states have bilateral conventions with at least their neighbouring states and main trading partners.

In 1958 the six original EU members agreed to limit EU competence to coordination of national social security systems in cross-border worker-related cases.[13]

[9] cf D Wyatt, 'The Social Security Rights of Migrant Workers and Their Families' [1977] *CMLR* 411.

[10] See S Nickless and H Siedl, *Co-ordination of Social Security in the Council of Europe* (Strasbourg, Council of Europe, 2004) 14.

[11] WM Yoffee, *International Social Security Agreements*, Research Report No 43 (Washington, U.S. Department of Health, Education, and Welfare, 1973) 26.

[12] The agreements can be found in the International Labour Code, 1951, vol II, Appendix XII, Genève, ILO, 1952.

[13] Coordination is seen as a controlling construction where all the signatory states' social security systems are left untouched and where there is an effort to hook the systems together so that the people can rest assured that they are always a part of a national security system and that their insured periods

This coordination in the internal market today is implemented through Regulation (EC) no 883/2004 of 29 April 2004, on the coordination of social security systems (Regulation 883/2004).[14]

2.3. THE EU AND COORDINATION OF SOCIAL SECURITY

2.3.1. Legal Basis

In order for the EU to legislate in a certain material scope, this needs to be a part of the EU competence through a legally determined basis required for the legislative procedure.

Social security is not an independent field of competence that the Member States have transferred to the EU in order to have legislation on an intergovernmental level. Instead, the EU has competence partly through the EU social policy, and partly through the free movement of workers.

The EU social policy was introduced by the Treaty of Rome, Articles 117–22.[15] The policy was and is neither precise nor binding for Member States. The Treaty on the Functioning of the European Union (TFEU) states, in Article 151, that the Union should support employment, improve living and working conditions, provide adequate social protection and combat social exclusion. Article 153 TFEU specifies how these aims should be met and mentions that social security is also a part of the competence. However, the possibilities for the Union to act have been severely curtailed; any potential action can only support and complement the activities of the Member States, and the Council (which consists of the Member States' governments) decides unanimously on these measures in accordance with the special legislative procedure. In addition to these technical legal limitations, the Member States continue to shape their own social security without restrictions, under Article 153.4 TFEU. The margin for manoeuvre by the Commission to act in the social security field, in line with Part X of the Treaty on social policies, is therefore almost zero.

Thus the EU Social Policy respects the competence of the Member States to organise their social security systems. Since there is no harmonisation of Member States' social security systems at the Union level, the national legislators of the respective countries continue to determine the conditions under which the benefits are to be granted. However, this sovereignty of Member States over their own social security systems can have repercussions for the free movement of workers. As seen in the previous chapter, there are unexpected consequences

and rights will not be lost when moving to another country, cf F Pennings, *European Social Security Law*, 6 edn (Cambridge - Antwerp - Portland, Intersentia, 2015) 8 f.

[14] Regulation (EC) No 883/2004 of the European Parliament and of the Council of 29 April, 2004 on the coordination of social security systems, [2004] OJ L166.

[15] P Watson, *EU Social and Employment Law*, 2nd edn (Oxford, Oxford University Press, 2014) 38.

when a person moves from one country to another for work. It can be anything from difficulty in becoming a part of the other country's system, or not having one's previous insurance periods transferred, to payments from the initial country being frozen inside its borders. These consequences can influence the willingness of workers to move to another country to work. In a nutshell, national systems can influence and restrict the free movement of workers—a right which is considered to be fundamental to EU law. The EU's indirect competence in the field of social security is therefore based on the free movement of workers, Article 45 TFEU.

Article 48 TFEU strengthens the free movement of migrating workers by regulating the interaction of the Member States' social security systems by coordination of the Member States' social security systems through an EU Regulation; in the first year it was Regulation 3/58,[16] thereafter Regulation 1408/71[17] and since 1 May 2010, Regulation 883/2004.

2.3.2. The Historical Context

In the negotiations leading to the Treaty of Rome (the EEC Treaty), the original six Member States realised that there would not be a true common market unless social security was to be regulated one way or another at the Community level, in order to support the free movement of migrating workers. There was already a long tradition of concluding bilateral agreements in post-war Europe with regard to social security in cross-border situations, which supported the free movement of migrating workers.

On 7 November 1949, the Member States of the Brussels Treaty Organisation,[18] in parallel to the development of military cooperation, signed a convention to coordinate social security systems in cross-border situations.[19] The convention was based on the sovereignty of the signatory states and was mainly founded on the principle of aggregation. Where bilateral agreements were already concluded between the two signatories, the agreement would be applicable to other signatory states as well.[20] Four of the signatory states—Belgium, France, Luxembourg and the Netherlands—later became part of the founding countries of the European Community.[21]

[16] Amtsblatt der Europäischen Gemeinschaften Nr 30, 16.12.1958, Verordnung Nr 3 über die Soziale Sicherheit der Wanderarbeitnehmer.

[17] Regulation (EEC) No 1408/71 of the Council of 14 June 1971 on the application of social security schemes to employed persons and their families moving within the Community, [1971] OJ L149.

[18] The Brussels Treaty Organisation was later developed and replaced by the Western European Union.

[19] Convention on Social Security Schemes in the Member States of Western Union (Paris, 7 November 1949), International Labour Office, Legislative Series: 1949.

[20] See the preamble to the Convention. The Convention deals with the aggregation of the periods from three or more contracting states, determines the governing law with regard to maternity benefits and calculates pensions as well as how pension payments should be divided between the states in question.

[21] The signatory of the Convention on the part of France was Robert Schuman who already in 1949, saw the abstaining effects of the national social security systems on the free movement of workers.

The Rhine boatmen were, and are, a typical example of a highly mobile group that crosses national borders very frequently during their operations.[22] Passing in and out of different states' social security systems that had their border on the Rhine was not sustainable in the long run. For the purpose of coming to terms with this, there was another European parallel track at the end of the 1940s that aimed at reaching multinational regulation of the social security status of the Rhine ships' crews. The Agreement concerning the social security of Rhine Boatmen (Rhine Agreement),[23] concluded in 1950, and in force since 1953,[24] resulted in the ships' crews belonging to the social security system of the state where the shipping company had its headquarters. In the case of acute illness, the treaty foresaw that ships' crew members could receive healthcare in other countries that were the signatories of the treaty, at the cost of the competent state.[25]

At approximately the same time, Europe started an initiative to connect the previously conflicting parties in the coal and steel industries,[26] through an institutionalised cooperation in order to avoid recession in the sector. The result was the European Coal and Steel Community (ECSC).[27] This Treaty included rules on how much coal was to be produced during various time periods, as well as an overview of 'softer' issues that influenced the cooperation. As a result of this, the

[22] In some cases national borders run along the middle of rivers. This means that ships can cross national borders with every yaw. A person can also sleep in one state and have his morning coffee in another.

[23] ILO Official Bulletin: No 3, vol XXXIII, Nov 30, 1950.

[24] Signatory states were Belgium, France, the Netherlands, West Germany and Switzerland. Luxemburg became a signatory at the first revision of the treaty in 1961.

[25] Aside from the fact that the treaty was one of the first on the European level to coordinate social security, it has also introduced a form of cooperation that would characterise European cooperation. The Treaty, together with the ECSC Treaty, was namely the first to introduce an independent authority in the form of a special commission and administrative authority in charge of administering the Treaty. See also WM Yoffee, *International Social Security Agreements*, Research Report No 43 (Washington, U.S. Department of Health, Education, and Welfare, 1973) 37.

[26] After World War II the victorious Western countries started to dismantle the German coal and steel industry in order to rebuild their own coal and steel industries that were in ruins. This led to strong protests in Western Germany. In 1949–51 the Ruhr area was, instead, administered by a new authority established by the victorious parties called the International Authority for the Ruhr, IAR. This authority aimed at strengthening the coal and steel industry by, at first, setting prices below the world's market prices for steel and coal. The IAR also aimed to export a large part of the production, instead of it remaining in Germany and there representing a threat against Western powers. This extraordinary administration entered in 1951, into an equal cooperation with Western Germany through the Coal and Steel Community. See S Henze, 'The Inventory of Conflict & Environment (ICE), France, Germany and the Struggle for the War-making Natural Resources of the Rhineland', ICE Case Studies No 158, August, 2005, http://www1.american.edu/ted/ice/saar.htm.

[27] France, West Germany, Italy and the Benelux countries signed the ECSC treaty in 1951, in Paris and thereby created a community that would ensure free movement of coal and steel, as well as free access to the production sources. The Treaty included, naturally, technical provisions with regard to production and distribution of coal and steel, but it also included an independent institutional system, which turned out to be crucial for the Treaty's impact, a common high authority that managed administration and enforcement of the Treaty, without the Member States influencing it with their special interests. The Treaty expired on 23 July 2002, 50 years after its entry into force. See the Treaty establishing the European Coal and Steel Community (ECSC), [1992] OJ C191.

Member States at the time agreed to support the free movement of workers in several ways within the Treaty's scope. Chapter VIII dealt in detail with salaries and how the free movement of workers could be regulated. The signatory states also acknowledged the influence of different social security systems on the movement of the labour force. Article 69, para 4 talks about how:

> [the Member States] will work out amongst themselves any arrangements necessary so that social security measures do not stand in the way of the movement of labour.

With this legal basis and with regard to the Rhine Agreement, the ECSC started, in 1953, to work on the development of a joint convention for the coal and steel workers on social security. The convention was created by a task force that also included experts from the International Labour Organisation (ILO). The inputs from various Member States varied. France advocated for harmonisation in order to achieve the objectives. Other countries were more sceptical towards harmonisation.[28] A letter addressed to the negotiating delegation and lobbying conducted at the time show that the trade unions and other interest groups were also of the opinion that harmonisation was the way forward to counteract large differences in salaries.[29] Throughout the work that led to the Convention, three expert groups presented reports that rejected harmonisation in the field of social security.[30] Taking these reports into account, the activities in the social security committees created instead a convention that was built on coordination—a coordination that respected the differences among the Member States.

Following the Messina Conference held in June 1955, which reached the conclusion that the future common market should include the whole economies of the Member States, the scope of the final ECSC Convention was broadened to include all workers who were citizens of the Member States.[31]

[28] P Watson, *Social Security Law of the European Communities* (London, Mansell Publishing, 1980) 33 ff.

[29] For example, Jacques Doublet, the Chairman for Social Committee of the Intergovernmental Conference, informed the Chairman of the Intergovernmental Conference, the Belgian Foreign Minister Paul-Henri Spaak, in a letter dated 3 October 1955, of a meeting that he had had with the representatives of the International Confederation of the Christian Trade Unions (ICCTU), who had expressed their concerns about economic and social inclusion in Europe. Letter from Jacques Doublet, President of the Sub-Committee of Social Problems, to Paul-Henri Spaak, President of Intergovernmental Conference (Bruxelles, 3 October 1955), http://www.cvce.eu/obj/lettre_de_jacques_doublet_a_paul_henri_spaak_bruxelles_3_octobre_1955-fr-4bf95b18–432b-4089–9c49-acb75ae30cf5.html. Moreover, the European League for Economic Cooperation (ELEC) adopted a resolution on 14 December 1956 supporting the reinforcement of social insurance in the establishment of a common market. Resolution of the European League for Economic Cooperation on European integtration and Social security http://www.cvce.eu/search?q=R%C3%A9solution+de+la+Ligue+europ%C3%A9enne+de+coop%C3%A9ration+%C3%A9conomique+sur+l%E2%80%99int%C3%A9gration+europ%C3%A9enne+et+la+s%C3%A9curit%C3%A9+sociale.

[30] See also the so-called Ohlin report, 'Social aspects of European economic co-operation: Report by a group of experts, Studies and Reports', New Series No 46, ILO, Genève, 1956, chs IV and V, and the conclusions of the report p 115 ff.

[31] R Cornelissen, '50 Years of European Social Security Coordination' [2009] *European Journal of Social Security* 12.

The ECSC Convention on social security was signed on 9 December 1957, only a few weeks before the Treaty of Rome came into force in 1958. Despite taking years of work, the ECSC Convention never came into force, but was to emerge in another legal environment: the European Economic Community (EEC).

The background to this is that at the time, when the multilateral social security convention complementing the Treaty establishing the European Coal and Steel Community was being completed, a separate treaty on the EEC was being developed. Those working on the new treaty noticed early on, as in the case of the ECSC Treaty, that differences in the social security systems between the states could create potential obstacles to the free movement of workers. For this reason, Article 51 of the EEC at that time (currently Article 48 TFEU) determined that the legislative body should adopt a secondary legislation on social security, which would eliminate any obstacles to the free movement of workers. On 1 January 1958 the Treaty of Rome entered into force, foreseeing additional legislation in the field of social security. A few weeks earlier some of the Member States signed a multilateral convention with the same objective and contents. Instead of waiting for the international legal ratification process on the ECSC's social security convention on the one hand, and the opening of negotiations for a legislation in the social insurance field within the new Economic Community on the other hand, the negotiated ECSC Convention started to be implemented with minor adjustments in the form of a Regulation, Regulation no 3,[32] which together with its implementing Regulation no 4[33] entered into force on 1 January 1959.[34]

The ECSC Convention became in this manner the Economic Community's first substantive regulation, named Regulation 3/58. This was notwithstanding the fact that there were big differences between Article 69(4) of the ECSC Treaty and Article 51 of the Rome Treaty at that time; the former leaves it up to the signatories to agree to a convention that would be in force parallel to the ECSC Treaty, while the latter envisions a legal act in a completely new intergovernmental legal environment within the framework of the Treaty of Rome.

[32] Regulation 3/58 of 25 September 1958, [1958] OJ 30. Regulation 3/58 was the Community's first substantial Regulation. Regulation 1/58 determined the language versions of the Treaty as well as the official languages and institutional working language, see English version Official Journal of the EC 1952–58 published in October, 1972. Regulation 2/58 dealt with the laissez-passer of the European Parliament's members (analogous to a state diplomatic passport); the latter Regulation is not included in Official Journal of the EC 1952–58. See also Y Jorens, 'Overall Concluding Remarks', in Y Jorens (ed) *50 Years of Social Security Coordination—Past, Present, Future* (European Union Publications Office, 2010) 237.

[33] Regulation 4/58 of 3 December 1958, [1958] OJ 30.

[34] S Roberts, 'A Short History of Social Security Coordination', in Y Jorens (ed), *50 Years of Social Security Coordination; Past—Present—Future, Report of the conference celebrating the 50th Anniversary of the European Coordination of Social Security, Prague, 7 & 8 May 2009* (European Commission, DG Employment, 2009) 17.

2.3.3. EU Law—A Breeding Ground for Sovereignty Erosion?

Through the European Economic Community's incorporation of the multilateral ECSC Convention in the growing body of Community law, the international law Convention became a part of a new legal context.[35] The new context—Community and later on Union law—differs from international law in the following ways:

- An independent Union law legislative process; the Commission has the right of initiative, while the Council and the European Parliament legislate jointly.
- The Commission monitors compliance with Union law by ultimately summoning the Member States before the CJEU in the case of an infringement.
- A Regulation is directly applicable and it has to be applied by the national administrations and courts, just like national law.
- The CJEU interprets the law (through infringement procedures and preliminary rulings).
- Other EU law, including EU treaties (primary law) and its general principles can influence the outcome of the interpretation.
- Case law that results from the CJEU is in principle binding not only for the parties involved but for all the legal actors within the EU.
- The duty of sincere cooperation that follows from Article 4.3 TEU additionally strengthens EU legal cooperation so that where there is a conflict of competence, the Member States must disregard their national law.

The ECSC Convention thus underwent a metamorphosis. There was now a completely different set of game rules and the Convention became Community law that the signatory parties 'lost control over'. The Convention ended up in the common (internal) market context with entirely other input values. The Convention had therefore to be reconciled with the idea and terms of the internal market. As is obvious from the comprehensive case law, with around 600 cases in this area,[36] the development has gone much further than it would have, had the Convention stayed in the area of the Coal and Steel Union, parallel with the EC introducing a more limited Regulation with regard to material scope.

However, the question is whether the contracting parties wanted to do differently in 1958. In the negotiations, France wanted to harmonise social security.[37] Moreover, neo-functionalism was a dominant ideology at the time of the Rome Treaty.[38] This school of thought had a snowball effect, growing bigger and bigger

[35] cf F Pennings, ibid,. 117. See also Wyatt who states: 'The principle … is that the national social security systems remain largely intact, but are supplemented by provisions of Community Law designed to compensate for their territorial "shortcomings"'. D Wyatt, 'Social Security Rights of Migrant Workers', [1977] *Common Market Law Review* 414.

[36] cf P Watson, *EU Social and Employment Law*, 2 edn (Oxford, Oxford University Press, 2014) 75.

[37] P Watson, *Social Security Law of the European Communities* (London, Mansell Publishing, 1980) 33 ff.

[38] D Mitrany, one of the leading functionalists, concludes the theory in his classic *A Working Peace System—An Argument for the Functional Development of International Organization* (London, Chatham

and taking everything in its way with it. The masters of the treaty saw no harm in an organic development of the Community, whereby solutions to problems could be applied to more and more new areas, and these would in turn spill over to further areas. This way a common internal market could of necessity grow substantially faster than from lengthy political negotiations that would discuss areas one by one.[39] The snowball effect, as well as independence of the CJEU and its proactive attitude,[40] led the internal market to encompass more than was envisioned in the Treaty, and possibly also to be more far-reaching than what the contracting parties could have predicted.[41]

The question that can be raised is how the post-war states could have solved the economic challenges on their own. Maybe we would have had a Europe where everyone had bilateral agreements with everyone else and it would be at a higher cost than if an agreement had been made jointly—a Europe where, in a worst-case scenario, people would once again begin to distrust one another. The question of such a scenario is imposing itself now. The contracting parties had two world wars fresh in their memories, and thus preferred a joint project to separate parallel tracks of development.

2.4. REGULATION 883/2004

2.4.1. Introduction

The objective of the EU Regulations in the field of social security is relatively simple and straightforward: to coordinate the Member States' social security systems

House, Royal Institute of International Affairs, 1943). For an EU law context see C Barnard, *The Substantive Law of the EU—The Four Freedoms*, 5th edn (Oxford, Oxford University Press, 2016) 15 f and P Craig, 'Integration, Democracy and Legitimacy', in P Craig and G de Búrca (eds), *The Evolution of EU Law*, 2nd edn (Oxford, Oxford University Press, 2011).

[39] cf Monnet's thoughts on cooperation where the economic development would be the carrot: M Burgess, *Federalism and European Union: the Building of Europe, 1950–2000* (Abingdon, Routledge, 2000) 32 ff.

[40] Blank, Hooghe and Marks argue that the Member States are certainly important actors in European cooperation, but they share their powers with independent EU institutions that cannot be in harmony with governmental ministries and authorities that eventually have the executive powers. This complex dynamic on different levels, with independent actors that can fulfil their respective roles in line with the EU Treaty and national constitutions, creates a dynamic EU development that is both difficult to predict and subdue by the Member States: K Blank, L Hooghe and G Marks, 'European Integration from the 1980s: State Centric v. Multi-Level Governance' [1996] *Journal of Common Market Studies* 341–78. Furthermore, even companies and individuals can influence the development by provoking new parameters, and ultimately, through court proceedings. This way the limits are pushed forward little by little. Cf A Stone Sweet and W Sandholtz, 'European Integration and Supranational Governance' [1997] *Journal of European Public Policy* 306, where Blank, Hooghe and Marks conclude that the Member States' governments can influence the integration process but they cannot subdue it entirely.

[41] Which accords with Monnet's far-reaching neo-functionalist thought: M Burgess, *Federalism and European Union: the Building of Europe, 1950–2000* (Abingdon, Routledge, 2000) 35.

without harmonisation. The main idea behind it is to limit territoriality through coordination in such a way that migrating workers do not fall between systems or lose their earned rights.

Regulation 883/2004 is divided into six titles and 11 annexes. The first title (Articles 1–10) contains common provisions that have general application in all the material scopes, as well as aggregation, exportability and non-discrimination. The provisions in Title 2 (Articles 11–16) determine applicable legislation—in other words, which state legislation is applicable for a person who is covered by the Regulation. The material scope covered by the EU's coordination instrument, as well as their specific provisions, can be found in Title 3, which is divided into nine chapters. Titles 4 and 5 contain administrative provisions. Finally, Title 6 contains a number of transitional and final provisions.

Regulation 883/2004 is based on the same principles as the bilateral conventions in the field of social security:

— A person covered by the Regulation will be treated the same way as a citizen of the country where the person is insured (the non-discrimination principle).
— A person covered by the Regulation has the right to acquire/keep earned rights from the competent State, even if he or she is not a resident of the state (the exportability principle).
— People who move to or get a job in another Member State can take into account the rights that they have previously earned (the aggregation principle).
— Those who have earned rights to benefits, on the basis of the periods in other state(s), have the right to receive the part corresponding to the period from the respective Member State (the *pro rata temporis* principle).

From the start, it is important to note that Regulation 883/2004 is based on the person's social security affiliation.[42] In other words, if someone is a Greek national, that does not mean that he or she can turn to the Greek authorities for social security in all situations. He or she needs to turn to the state that the Regulation has determined as competent—the state to which that person belongs. National states and citizenship are thus disconnected from the coordination of social security.

Another point to note is that Regulation 883/2004 is a coordinating Regulation. The Regulation does not harmonise the Member States' social security systems. The systems of the Member States continue to be different. This implies that there will be differences when someone moves from one country to another, and thus from one national social security system to another.

The Member States have never aimed at having "all" the social security encompassed by coordination within the EU. Article 3 lists the following material scope:

a) sickness benefits;
b) maternity and equivalent paternity benefits;

[42] Citizenship has an important role in applicability of the Regulation, since it is mainly applicable for citizens of the Member States, see Art 2, Reg 883/2004.

c) invalidity benefits;
d) old-age benefits;
e) survivors' benefits;
f) benefits in respect of accidents at work and occupational diseases;
g) death grants;
h) unemployment benefits;
i) pre-retirement benefits;
j) family benefits.

These are the social security benefits that the Regulation coordinates when it comes to migrating movements across national borders.[43] If a national benefit does not fall under one of these areas, it will not be covered by the Regulation's framework. In these cases the Member States fully determine the conditions and forms of benefits.[44]

2.4.2. When is Regulation 883/2004 Applicable?

In order for Regulation 883/2004 to be applicable and thereby for a coordination to take place, there are several questions to be answered:

- Has a migratory movement taken place?
- Is the benefit a social security benefit as it is understood by the Regulation?
- Does it fall within the material scope of the Regulation?
- Is the person in question covered by the Regulation?

2.4.2.1. Has a Migratory Movement Taken Place?

Regulation 883/2004 is applicable only in cases when a person has moved between two Member States, Articles 45 and 48 TFEU. This may seem obvious since the Regulation is meant to facilitate free movement within the EU. Within a clearly national situation, there is never a need for coordination of two Member States' social security systems.[45]

Even if it is a matter of migration between two states, it is essential that the movement has taken place within the EU; the EU legal acts are only valid for situations within the EU territory, Article 52 EUT and Article 355 TFEU.

[43] In the negotiations leading to Regulation 883/2004 the Commission wanted to have an open definition of social security, without listing the material scope. Member States were afraid they would lose control over which parts of social security systems are covered, so they opposed the open definition.

[44] However, if a Member State should formulate this legislation as directly discriminatory, the CJEU can apply primary law on free movement of workers.

[45] See the opinion by the Advocate General on the decision from 28 June 2007; Case C-212/06 *Gouvernement de la Communauté française and Gouvernement wallon v Gouvernement flamand* [2008] ECR I-1683, 71–97.

2.4.2.2. *Is the Benefit a Social Security Benefit as it is Understood by the Regulation?*

In order for a benefit to be covered by the coordination rules in Regulation 883/2004, the national benefit needs to be regulated by the national social security system in a Member State. The definition in Article 1(l) states that Regulation 883/2004 covers only social insurances that are nationally regulated. This means that different social insurance solutions built on collective or similar agreements are not covered by the Regulation's coordination rules. The same goes for voluntary insurances or those that are obligatory for a special profession.

Case law shows that the CJEU has been focused on a system built on solidarity (read: an obligatory insurance) that is at a minimum supervised by the state. Furthermore, this system cannot have any commercial interests.[46] If a system does not have these characteristics, it can instead be said to be commercial and as such could be covered by other EU law, primarily competition law.[47]

After establishing that a benefit is de facto statutory, step two is to determine whether the benefit is considered to be a social security benefit covered by the Regulation.

According to Article 9, Regulation 883/2004, the Member States are obliged to enlist all the benefits that are covered by the Regulation's material scope to the Commission, which, after an assessment, then includes these benefits in an annex to the Regulation. If a benefit has been included in the annex, the Member State cannot have the enlisted benefit removed: see *Beerens*[48] and the *Commission v Malta*.[49] However, case law shows that even if a benefit has not been enlisted by a Member State, it can still be considered to be subject to the Regulation's coordination rules. The CJEU examines the aim of a benefit and its prerequisites in detail, so that a benefit can be regarded to be within the material scope despite it not being classified by national legislation as a social security benefit. The Court has been extensive in its rulings in this regard and asserts that the concept of a social security benefit in the Regulation's context should be understood broadly, see *Costa*,[50] *Piscitello*[51] and *Paletta*.[52]

[46] Joined Cases C-159–160/91 *Christian Poucet v Assurances générales de France and Caisse mutuelle régionale du Languedoc-Roussillon and Daniel Pistre and Caisse autonome nationale de compensation de l'assurance vieillesse des artisans (Cancava)* [1993] ECR I-637; Case C-244/94 *Fédération française des sociétés d'assurance, Société Paternelle-Vie, Union des assurances de Paris-Vie and Caisse d'assurance et de prévoyance mutuelle des agriculteurs v Ministère de l'Agriculture et de la Pêche* [1995] ECR I-4013.

[47] cf eg Case C-2018/00 *Cisal di Battistello Venanzio & C Sas v Istituto nazionale per l'assicurazione contro gli infortuni sul lavoro (INAIL)* [2002] ECR I-691 and Case C-350/07 *Kattner Stahlbau GmbH v Maschinenbau- und Metall- Berufsgenossenschaft* [2009] ECR I-1513.

[48] Case 35/77 *Elisabeth Beerens v Rijksdienst voor Arbeidsvoorziening* [1977] ECR 2249.

[49] Case C-12/14 *Commission v Malta*, EU:C:2016:135.

[50] Case 39/74 *Luciana Costa, épouse Mazzier v Belgium* [1974] ECR 1251.

[51] Case 139/82 *Paola Piscitello v Istituto nazionale della previdenza sociale (INPS)* [1983] ECR 1427.

[52] Case C-45/90 *Alberto Paletta et al v Brennet AG* [1992] ECR I-3423.

Another restriction to be taken into account is the notion social assistance. The Regulation does not cover social assistance in accordance with Article 3.5. However, with the development of the welfare state and different political aims, it has become more and more difficult to distinguish between social insurance and social assistance/social aid. The Swedish housing benefit, for example, has the characteristics of both a social insurance, as a benefit for families, and also social assistance, in a way such that the state strives to maintain a good standard of living for its low income residents. For this reason, Sweden has specified to the Commission that, in line with the Regulation's rules, only a part of the housing benefit aimed at families should be seen as a social security benefit in the context of the Regulation.

The CJEU has developed its own criteria over the years, but the main premise is the same: a benefit is considered to be a social security benefit in so far as the receiver is granted the benefit, without discretionary power in separate cases on the basis of personal needs, based on the conditions defined by the law and as long as the benefit falls under the material scope that is explicitly listed in Article 3. This means that social benefits which ensure a person's minimum existence is not within the scope of the Regulation. As an example of borderline cases there are national support programmes for unemployment.[53] See furthermore the case law that developed in recent years, such as *Brey*,[54] *Dano*,[55] *Alimanović*[56] and *García-Nieto*,[57] that points to another direction. See also Chapter 6 for a discussion on this topic.

2.4.2.3. *Within or Outside the Regulation's Material Scope?*

The material scope of the Regulation is comprehensive. Most of the classical social security benefits, such as sickness benefits, child allowance, parental allowance, pension, unemployment benefits, and healthcare, are covered by the Regulation. The systems of the Member States are nonetheless more comprehensive, and if a national benefit does not fall within the Regulation's material scope, this benefit will not be included in the Regulation's framework. Thus, situations can arise where a strict application of the Regulation's material scope results in a person falling between systems, because the Regulation is not applicable. It is legally correct and is a consequence of the European legislator choosing to limit coordination to a certain material scope.

[53] Joined Cases C-22/08 and C-23/08 *Athanasios Vatsouras and Josif Koupatantze v Arbeitsgemeinschaft (ARGE) Nürnberg 900* [2009] ECR I-4585, 45.

[54] Case C-140/12 *Pensionsversicherungsanstalt v Peter Brey*, EU:C:2013:565.

[55] Case C-333/13 *Elisabeta Dano and Florin Dano v Jobcenter Leipzig*, EU:C:2014:2358.

[56] Case C-67/14 *Jobcenter Berlin Neukölln v Nazifa Alimanovic and Others*, EU:C:2015:597.

[57] Case C-299/14 *Vestische Arbeit Jobcenter Kreis Recklinghausen v Jovanna García-Nieto and Others*, EU:C:2016:114.

When referring to CJEU case law for determining a Regulation's material scope, one can distinguish between two groups of case law:

1. Social security benefits which according to the Member States lie outside the Regulation's material scope, which the Commission has questioned in infringement proceedings.
2. Special non-contributory cash benefits (hybrid benefits), which have been or are a part of the annex X to the Regulation. There has been a consensus that these hybrid benefits certainly fall within the Regulation's material scope, however, these should not be exported because they are so tightly linked to the specific living conditions in the Member State. These benefits are therefore exempted, in line with Article 3 paragraph 3, and Article 70 of the Regulation.[58]

As previously mentioned in section 2.1, the social security systems of the Member States are a territorial matter. Even if all the Member States agree that it is important to coordinate the central parts of the social security, this eagerness is less evident when it comes to other parts of a mixed character; where there are purely insurance-based intentions but where strong social ambitions are also asserted. An example is the Austrian supplementary pension for low-income pensioners.[59] This type of support could easily have taken the form of social assistance or, for that matter, tax incentives. However, from a political perspective it was difficult to introduce tax incentives for certain groups, so instead it was more viable to politically show that there is active support for elderly citizens by means of social security.

There are many ways to deal with welfare politics, but they have one thing in common—these arrangements, which have been borrowed from both the social assistance field and social security, are all "consuming"—unlike regular social insurance where at large social contributions stems from the work that contributes to society at large.[60]

[58] These social benefits have often been developed in order to meet specific needs or to protect specific groups. These benefits are on the borderline between classical social insurance and benefits with characteristics of social assistance. The benefits are social security benefits as they provide legally determined rights. However, they also have the appearance of social assistance as they are not dependent on employment-based contributions, but are residence-based benefits whose aim is to provide financial support for the additional costs incurred. These benefits are usually based on the cost situation in the country and built on integration in the country in question that allows the housing requirement. These benefits, when registered by the Commission, do not need to be exported. On the other side, the Member States cannot lay down any requirements of qualified periods for migrating workers who live in the country as the benefits are residence based, Article 70, Regulation 883/2004.

[59] Case C-160/02 *Friedrich Skalka v Sozialversicherungsanstalt der gewerblichen Wirtschaft.* [2004] ECR I-5613.

[60] The European Court of Justice found in Case C-140/12 *Pensionsversicherungsanstalt v Peter Brey*, EU:C:2013:565, that just because a benefit was classified as a non-exportable social security benefit in line with Regulation 883/2004, this did not mean that the same benefit could not be interpreted differently in line with Directive 2004/38, depending on different objectives of legal instruments. See further Ch 6.

When it comes to hybrid benefits, these are an expression of the political will and idea of solidarity that shapes a society. This type of benefit is especially sensitive as being subject to the EU coordination umbrella, since it is primarily directed toward the society itself. Preliminary rulings in Brey[61] and Dano[62] show the balancing act that the CJEU has had to perform.

2.4.2.4. *Within or Outside the Regulation's Personal Scope?*

Article 2 of the Regulation defines that the following persons are a part of the Regulation's personal scope:

1. citizens of a Member State;
2. stateless persons;
3. refugees.

This is on the basis that the persons live in a Member State and are subject to or have been subject to the legislation of one or more Member States.

Additionally, also these persons' family members and descendants are included, regardless of whether they are citizens of a Member State.

The ambit of Regulation 883/2004 therefore extends to many people. The personal scope covers almost all the people living in the Member States.[63] This scope is not focused, like the previous Regulations, Regulations 3/58 and 1408/71, on enabling the free movement of workers, but in a broad sense, Regulation 883/2004 ensures the free movement of the citizens of the Union without explicit requirements on economic activity. Since Regulation 883/2004 covers 'all insured', the focus has moved from workers to covered persons.

The abolition of a restricted personal scope does not, however, imply that it is no longer important "who" the person is. This question has instead been moved lower down the checklist. The definitions of different categories of persons are namely still important, as the scale of coordination is different for different categories. It arises from the Regulation that those who are simply insured in one Member State are only covered by two material scopes in Title III of the Regulation: sickness benefits, maternity and equivalent paternity benefits in Chapter 1, as well as death grants in Chapter 3. It is therefore still of crucial importance whether a person is to be categorised as an insured worker, and thus subject to a majority of the coordination rules, or is to be categorised as an economically non-active union citizen who will be able to receive only a limited coordination of the social security systems. Another closely connected issue is whether the provisions on the applicable legislation in Regulation 883/2004 and 987/2009 can 'open up' residence-based social security systems; see Chapter 6 on this.

[61] Case C-140/12 *Pensionsversicherungsanstalt v Peter Brey*, EU:C:2013:565.

[62] Case C-333/13 *Elisabeta Dano and Florin Dano v Jobcenter Leipzig*, EU:C:2014:2358.

[63] The group of persons not covered are third country residents, who are neither family members of a citizen in a Member State, stateless persons nor refugees.

Categories of Persons

Workers

Generally speaking, since the creation of the European Community, migrating workers have been those whose interests have been most promoted by Union law. In the early years of the Community, the CJEU hammered out an EU legal definition for workers. The CJEU has refined the concept of a worker in relation to the primary law provisions on the free movement of workers in a number of cases from the 1960s onward where the CJEU has extensively interpreted the concept of a worker in its case law.[64]

However, in the context of Regulation 883/2004, the Union notion of a worker has no bearing as Member States are in charge of their social security systems, and the EU system has only a coordinating role. Hence the Member States decide over the access to their systems and, in accordance with this, they have the freedom to 'choose' whom they want to insure and whom they do not want to insure. The Member States insure workers, but it is the national definition for worker and not an EU legal definition that is valid when a migrating person is to be qualified as a worker under the Regulation. See, for example, the CJEU rulings in *Foot-Ball Club D'Andlau*[65] and *Kits van Heijningen*.[66] However, if a Member State tries, in one way or another, to misuse the national definition, the CJEU has found that what is decisive is whether the person in question is covered by the social security insurance for workers, and not whether the person is seen as a worker in the national meaning. See, for example, the reasoning in *Laborero*[67] and *van Poucke*.[68] Thus if a person is covered by a general social insurance, then the person is covered by the personal scope of Regulation 883/2004.

Self-Employed Persons

A group that borders on the classification of workers is that of migrating self-employed persons. This group also forms an important part of the internal market. The CJEU concluded in *de Cicco* that with regard to social security, self-employed persons have the same protection status as workers.[69] Since they pay contributions to the social security system, self-employed persons are considered

[64] cf Case 66/85 *Lawrie-Blum v Land Baden Württemberg* [1986] ECR 2121 and Case 139/85 *RH Kempf v Staatssecretaris van Justitie* [1986] ECR 1741.

[65] Case 8/75 *Caisse primaire d'assurance maladie de Sélestat v Association du Foot-Ball Club d'Andlau* [1975] ECR 739.

[66] Case C-2/89 *Bestuur van de Sociale Verzekeringsbank v GJ Kits van Heijningen* [1990] ECR I-1755.

[67] Case 82/86 *Giancarlo Laborero and Francesca Sabato v Office de sécurité sociale d'outre-mer (OSSOM)* [1987] ECR 3401.

[68] Case C-71/93 *Guido van Poucke v Rijksinstituut voor de Sociale Verzekeringen der Zelfstandigen and Algemene Sociale Kas voor Zelfstandigen* [1994] ECR I-1101.

[69] Case 19/68 *Giovanni de Cicco v Landesversicherungsanstalt Schwaben* [1968] ECR 473.

as workers within the Regulation's understanding. This was confirmed by the Court in *Brack*[70] and *Tessier*.[71]

Since migrating, self-employed persons in these cases worked in a social security system that differentiated between workers and self-employed persons, they could not be considered workers in a broad sense. In these cases, the self-employed were not in a literal meaning covered by the Regulation's coordination. The Council acknowledged this lacuna and with Regulation 1390/81[72] the EU included the self-employed in the coordination of national social security systems. With the Lisbon Treaty, their position has been strengthened, and Article 48 TFEU specifically defines the self-employed as one of two categories that qualify for protection.

Pensioners

An important part of Regulation 883/2004 involves the coordination of pensioners' completed periods in other Member States. Pensioners are covered by the Regulation because they are covered or have been covered by the Member States' legislation in the field of social security.

Students

Students are another large non-working category. This category became a part of the Regulatory system with Regulation 307/99.[73]

All Residents

With Regulation 883/2004, all nationals of the Member States who are or have been subject to the legislation of one or more Member States have been included in the Regulation's scope. However, those who are not economically active citizens of the Union, but are merely residents in the Regulation's terms, are not entitled to the same level of coordination as those who are working. The question of whether the Regulation's residence rule can lead to residence-based social security is an open one; see Chapter 6.

[70] Case 17–76 *MLE Brack, widow of RJ Brack v Insurance Officer* [1976] ECR 1429.

[71] Case 84/77 *Caisse primaire d'assurance maladie d'Eure-et-Loir v Alicia Tessier, née Recq* [1978] ECR 7.

[72] Council Regulation (EEC) No 1390/81 of 12 May 1981 extending to self-employed persons and members of their families Regulation (EEC) No 1408/71 on the application of social security schemes to employed persons and their families moving within the Community [1981] OJ L143.

[73] Council Regulation (EC) No 307/1999 of 8 February, 1999, amending Regulation (EEC) No 1408/71, on the application of social security schemes to employed persons, to self-employed persons and to the members of their families moving within the Community and Regulation (EEC) No 574/72 laying down the procedure for the implemention of Regulation (EEC) No 1408/71 with a view to extend them to cover students [1999] OJ L38.

2.4.3. Principles of the Regulations

As with all EU legislation, Regulation 883/2004 is based on primary law and general principles that are influential throughout the whole Regulation. Unlike previous Regulations, these principles are now to be found in the introductory general chapter.

2.4.3.1. Non-Discrimination

One of the EU cornerstones is that all discrimination on the basis of nationality is forbidden: Article 18 TFEU. This general prohibition is specified in the Regulation's Articles 4 and 5 with regard to the rights and obligations in the context of social security. Both have the same objective—a migrating person cannot end up in a position that is worse than for those living in the country where the person has decided to move to or work. Article 4 states that:

> '... persons to whom this Regulation applies shall enjoy the same benefits and be subject to the same obligations under the legislation of any Member State as the nationals thereof'.[74]

Completed periods and other relevant factors are important for the competent authorities when they decide on the level of the benefit that is to be issued or if a social security benefit is to be granted. Article 5 therefore complements Article 4 in such a way that, even if it is not a question of discrimination, it can pose an obstacle when people cannot claim their completed periods in one Member State in another Member State.

Regulation 883/2004 limits the scope of Article 5 in such a way, however, that the application of the provisions cannot lead to another country becoming competent (transfer of competence) when new circumstances are taken into account: see Recital 11 in the preamble to Regulation 883/2004. Instead, the idea behind the provision is that the country that is initially competent, according to the rules on applicable legislation, will continue to be the competent state. This state, however, needs to take into account the past income, circumstances or events from other Member States.

2.4.3.2. Exportability

One of the main objectives when it comes to cross-border movements in the context of social security, is to ensure that an earned benefit is not paid out merely

[74] This principle of non-discrimination does not require the person in question to live in a Member State in order to be able to claim that non-discrimination is not as such. So it is possible for a person from state A who works in state B to go to live in state C and demand equality of treatment with the citizens of state B. It is also possible that if the national legislation of state B enables the export of pension benefits to, for example, Thailand, a state outside the EU, the same circumstances will be valid for migrating workers from state A when, in their ripe old age, they retreat to a Thai resort, as for citizens from state B.

because the person has moved to another Member State, or that the person lives in another state than the competent state. This is regulated by article 7, Regulation 883/2004.

The Treaty on the Functioning of the European Union has strengthened the exportability principle by Article 48(b) TFEU, making 'constitutional' the notion that there should be a system to ensure that there is payment of benefits to persons resident in the territories of Member States.

Through this formulation there is no theoretical room for the Member States to undermine the principle of exportability in Regulation 883/2004 can be changed by the regular legislative procedure.

2.4.3.3. Aggregation and Pro Rata

If a state requires 40 years of completed periods for an income-based pension, the migrating person will most likely not attain this requirement unless they can receive credit for completed periods from previous states of work. This is why the aggregation principle is important for ensuring free movement of workers across national borders.

The possibility of aggregation is stipulated in Article 6 and it is valid for all the situations included in the Regulation's material scope. In this way the Regulation guarantees that the rights acquired in other Member States are taken into account and they can also be a basis for rights in the competent state.

If the Regulation points out that it is up to the most recent state of work to grant a pension, however, questions arise: should this state pay in full, or should the state where the person in question has worked for the longest period pay, or should the responsibility be shared in some other way? The Regulation foresees that in such circumstances, states are each responsible for their own part, pro rata. This calculation is primarily used in pension benefits, where it can happen that a person has earned pension rights in two or more Member States. The pro rata principle deals with how the completed periods are divided on the basis of the parts a worker can claim from the authorities of the different Member States. A person with completed pension periods from several Member States will have pension calculated in proportion to the total time. Simply put, if a person has worked 40 years in total and 25 of these are spent in state A and 15 in state B, the division of responsibility for payments will be 25/40 and 15/40, respectively. State A will pay out 25/40 of the pension the person would have had, had the person spent his or her whole pension time there, and state B will pay 15/40.

2.4.3.4. Effects of Principles

The principles of the Regulation, non-discrimination, assimilation, aggregation and pro rata, imply that Member States' national social security systems based on territoriality are disregarded in the case of migrating persons who are covered by Regulation 883/2004. A migrating worker can therefore overrule national rules that would otherwise represent an obstacle, such as a requirement of citizenship, residence in the state or long completed periods, in order to be able to receive his or her social security benefits.

2.4.4. Applicable Legislation

2.4.4.1. Introduction

The main issue that bilateral coordination agreements try to solve is determining which state's legislation will be applicable to a person in the case of a cross-border situation. This situation calls for determining the applicable legislation. Through rules on applicable legislation, bilateral agreements aim to avoid both situations where no social security system is applicable and situations where both countries' national systems regard the person in question as insured.

2.4.4.2. Criteria for Determining Applicable Legislation

Determination of the competent Member State under Regulation 883/2004 is not based on a person's citizenship, but on an entirely different set of criteria.

Rules of the Regulation on applicable legislation are exclusive and binding in nature. Persons who, in line with the rules of Regulation 883/2004, are covered by the social security system of one Member State cannot belong in parallel to another Member State's social security system. This is the case regardless of whether or not the person lives in the latter country. Regulation 883/2004 is based, in the same way as bilateral social security agreements, on the principle of *lex loci laboris* for working persons. Article 11.3.a states that an employed person, either as worker or self-employed, is insured in the state where the person works. If a person lives in state A but works in state B, he or she will, according to the Regulation, be subject to the social security regulations of state B. He or she will be insured in state B, even if he or she is a citizen of state A. EU coordination is therefore based on neither residence nor citizenship but considers only where the economic interest of the workers lie.

There are no rules without exceptions, though various migratory movements of economically active require different solutions. The categories listed in the Article 11.3 b–d are special categories which, from the legislative perspective, need to be regulated, where the main rule *lex loci laboris* would otherwise lead to obstruction of the free movement of persons; employed officials remain in their state system of employment when serving abroad, unemployed can be covered by the residence-based system when they receive their payments from the country of residence, in contrast with the fact that their unemployment benefits actually originate from another country, and military personnel working overseas are covered by the social security system of the country of military service.

Furthermore, Regulation 883/2004 also covers all union citizens who are or have been covered by one of the Member State's social security systems. Economically non-active citizens comprise a mixed category. The largest group are pensioners. Other groups include students, but also citizens who, for varying reasons, cannot work or have chosen not to work. This means that economic activity cannot serve as a condition for a person's social insurance affiliation. Instead, the residence principle is used in Article 11.3(e), which determines that:

> '… any other person to whom subparagraphs (a) to (d) do not apply shall be subject to the legislation of the Member State of residence'.

The notion of residence has not been clarified in Regulation 883/2004. For this reason, Regulation 987/2009 complements the term residence in its Article 11. Strictly interpreted, the article is applicable only when the authorities from two Member States cannot agree on whether the residence is in a Member State. The following parameters stem from previous case law of the CJEU:[75]

a) the duration and continuity of presence in the territory of the Member States concerned;
b) the person's situation, including:
   i) the nature and the specific characteristics of any activity pursued, in particular the place where such an activity is habitually pursued, the stability of the activity, and the duration of any work contract;
   ii) his family status and family ties;
   iii) the performance of any non-remunerated activity;
   iv) in the case of students, the source of their income;
   v) his housing situation, and in particular how permanent it is;
   vi) the Member State in which the person is deemed to reside for taxation purposes.

Determining the state legislation through residence will represent a challenge for the Member States with residence-based systems. This is reflected in economically non-active citizens being covered by the social security system solely on the basis of their country of residence. Fears that with Regulation 883/2004, persons will only be covered by the state's social security system through residence without applying the national requirements and qualification periods has led to a clarification through Regulation 988/2009[76] that amends the main Regulation 883/2004. With this Regulation, the legislator has introduced a new Recital 17a into the preamble of Regulation 883/2004 that will take a central place in the interpretation of the social insurance affiliation of those who are economically inactive.

[75] EU Commission's explanatory notes on the key concepts of modernised coordination, http://ec.europa.eu/social/main.jsp?langId=sv&catId=867.

[76] Regulation (EC) No 988/2009 of the European Parliament and of the Council of 16 September 2009 amending Regulation (EC) No 883/2004 on the coordination of social security systems, and determining the content of its Annexes, [2009] OJ L284/43.

This recital should initially be perceived as both the EU and the Member States having it their way:

> 'Once the legislation of a Member State becomes applicable to a person under Title II of this Regulation, the conditions for affiliation and entitlement to benefits should be defined by the legislation of the competent Member State while respecting Community law'.

The Member States have therefore maintained their national qualification conditions even with regard to other union citizens. The other part adds, however, that this right is exercised within the EU legal jurisdiction. See further Chapter 6.

2.5. CONCLUSION

Considering the fact that social security developed within national states, it is natural that territorial restrictions have emerged. By crossing borders, a person risks losing completed periods of benefits, as well as risking of not being included in the 'new' state's social security system. The territorial factor can thus be an obstacle to the movement of workers between states. In order to prevent these potential risks, states have concluded bilateral agreements that neutralise the territorial factors, without diminishing the contracting parties' control over their respective systems.

When one deals with coordination at the EU level, the internal market perspective, Union citizenship, and the Charter of Fundamental Rights have and continue to put national sovereignty in the corner. This sovereignty erosion leads to an area of tension between welfare models of the national states and the EU. This tension challenges common understandings of solidarity in society, in terms of solidarity within the national state or with all the citizens of the Union. This tension is the focus of this monograph and its analysis of the coordination of Member States' social security systems according to Regulation 883/2004.

3

Interpretation Methods as a Factor Promoting Integration

3.1. INTRODUCTION

CHAPTER 3, THROUGH a review of around 200 cases in the field of social security,[1] analyses the legal evolution of the CJEU's textual, systematic and teleological interpretation of Regulation 883/2004.[2]

Due notice is given to the choice of interpretation method as a factor for the promotion of integration.[3] This relationship is confirmed in the review of case law in the field of social security; the CJEU is primarily focused on the impact of the EU law. The consequence of this impact has been the curtailment of Member States' sovereignty/autonomy over their social security systems.

3.2. LEGAL CONTEXT

The Member States have agreed through Regulation 883/2004 on the material and personal scope of coordination, as well as how the coordination of Member States' social security systems will take place. The Member States have thereby agreed on a limited competence for the EU within the field of social security. However, if these input values interact within the internal market, the CJEU has revealed an unpleasant truth about national self-determination in social security in cross-border situations ever since its first decision in *Unger v Bestuur*,[4] where the Court said that the coordination takes place within the context of an internal market.[5] The best of both worlds?

[1] Watson estimates the number of case to be about 500 cases until 2009: P Watson, *EU Social and Employment Law* 2 edn (Oxford, Oxford University Press, 2014) 75. Since 2009 there have been another 100 cases that in one way or another have a bearing on the coordination of social security systems. Cf H Verschueren, 'The EU Social Security Coordination System' in P Syrpis (ed), *The Judiciary, the Legislature and the EU Single Market* (Cambridge, Cambridge University Press, 2012) 182.

[2] Chapter 3 deals with approximately a third of the rulings.

[3] O Due, 'EF-domstolens retspraxis som integrationsfremmende faktor' [1991–92] *Juridisk Tidskrift* 407, 412.

[4] Case 75/63 *MKH Unger, married to R Hoekstra v Bestuur der Bedrijfsvereniging voor Detailhandel en Ambachten te Utrecht* [1964] ECR 177.

[5] ibid, 184 in the English version.

This ambiguity can be seen in the preamble to Regulation 883/2004, which states: 'It is necessary to respect the special characteristics of national social security legislations and to draw up only a system of coordination' (recital 4). Later in the preamble, however, recital 17a states that in case of a conflict of the laws, one should consider not only national law, but the effective EU laws as well: 'Once the legislation of a Member State becomes applicable to a person under Title II of this Regulation, the conditions for affiliation and entitlement to benefits should be defined by the legislation of the competent Member State *while respecting Community law*'.[6] [Emphasis added.]

3.3. INTERPRETATION METHODS AS A FACTOR FOR PROMOTION OF INTEGRATION

The Member States agreed to transfer certain sovereignty to the EU when they take part in the European cooperation. This does not imply that the Member States agreed to give all legislative powers to the EU, or to the CJEU for that matter. Hartley is of the opinion that if the CJEU takes a more proactive, almost legislative role, this is not something that the Member States had initially agreed upon. Hartley is strongly critical and says that there is 'a violation of the rule of law' whenever the CJEU pronounces a preliminary ruling to be in conflict with the EU secondary legislation.[7]

The question that arises is this: If the legislation states A, but the Court decides B, it is clear to everyone that the Court has acted outside of its competence. But what should we think about situations where it is unclear if the law is 'A' or 'a'? Can it be said that the Court in that case has clearly stepped outside of its competence if it rules 'a'?

When deciding on a case, the Court primarily focuses on three interpretation methods:

— A textual (literal) interpretation method.
— A systematic interpretation method.
— A teleological interpretation method.

The textual interpretation method is based on the idea that the legislator's intention is clear from the legal text and it does not require any interpretation.[8] If an EU

[6] Recital 17a was included by Regulation (EC) No 988/2009 of the European Parliament and of the Council of 16 September, 2009; amending Regulation (EC) No 883/2004 on the coordination of social security systems, and determining the content of its Annexes [2009] OJ L284/43. A corresponding formulation does not exist in Regulation 3/58 or Regulation 1408/71, but it is in accordance with the Court's case law. See for example, Case C-228/07 *Jörn Petersen v Landesgeschäftsstelle des Arbeitsmarktservice Niederösterreich* [2008] ECR I-6989 42 and Case C-345/09 *JA van Delft and others v College voor zorgverzekeringen* [2010] ECR I-9879, 84.

[7] T Hartley, *Constitutional Problems of the European Union* (Oxford, Hart, 1999) 43 ff.

[8] cf A Bredimas, *Methods of Interpretation and Community Law* (Amsterdam North Holland, 1978) 15 ff.

secondary legislation is clear and unambiguous, the CJEU will not interpret the rule in a way which contradicts the wording.[9] This is why, for example, the Court applies aggregation rules in the Regulation word for word, when pensions are calculated in cross-border situations; this is a case of textual interpretation.

The textual interpretation method is assumed to respect the fact that the EU does not have independent competence within the field of social security according to the EU Treaty and that Regulation 883/2004 merely coordinates the Member States' social security systems. By adhering to a textual interpretation method, the balance between the pronounced conflicting interests is maintained. In other words, the Member States have certainly agreed to facilitate the free movement of persons, but the Regulation does not lead to the restriction of competence when it comes to their national social security systems.

If the rules cannot be understood through textual interpretation, the CJEU is forced to seek and search for answers in a more comprehensive system.[10] In this context a systematic interpretation method is developed.[11] The systematic interpretation method sets the rules in a larger context, and the CJEU is looking for a system/context.

But what is the context?[12] The challenge for the CJEU in such an interpretation is that the CJEU does not stand on firm ground, as the national constitutional court usually does. A national constitutional court functions in a legal environment which has developed organically for the most part, and there is stability. The CJEU instead functions in a constitutional environment where not only is the balance of the constitution being questioned, but also where vague secondary legislation have to be kept in balance with conflicting interests.[13] Therefore, when the CJEU cannot find an answer in the EU legislation, its interpretation will always be questioned.

The systematic interpretation method is based on a system, and a context.[14] It should be noted that Article 48 TFEU states that the Union needs to support the

[9] cf HG Schermers and DF Walbroek, *Judicial Protection in the European Union*, 6th edn (Haag, Kluwer, 2001) 10 ff.

[10] ibid, 11 f.

[11] ibid, 16 ff; A Bredimas, *Methods of Interpretation and Community Law* (Amsterdam—New York—Oxford, North-Holland, 1978) 17 ff; J Bengoetxea, *The Legal Reasoning of the European Court of Justice* (Oxford, Clarendon, 1993) 240 ff. Cf for a linguistic point of view, M Derlén, *A Castle in the Air: The Complexity of the Multilingual Interpretation of European Community Law* (Alphen aan den Rijn, Kluwer, 2009) 45 ff, as eg illustrated by Case C-103/13 *Snezhana Somova v Glaven direktor na Stolichno upravlenie «Sotsialno osiguryavane»* EU:C:2014:2334 53.

[12] Bengoetxea is of the opinion that the context can be small but also comprehensive: J Bengoetxea, *The Legal Reasoning of the European Court of Justice* (Oxford, Clarendon, 1993) 242.

[13] cf M Dawson, 'The political face of judicial activism: Europe's law-politics imbalance', in M Dawson, B De Witte and E Muir (eds), *Judicial Activism at the European Court* (Cheltenham, Edward Elgar, 2013) 28 ff.

[14] The context can, however, be multi-faceted. See Hartley who acknowledges that even though in Case C-292/89 *The Queen v Immigration Appeal tribunal, ex parte Antonissen* [1991] ECR I-745, the Court judged on the basis of the presumption that the applicable rules have been followed in order to facilitate the free movement of people, it can be the case that this objective was not necessarily the only objective that the Member States had in mind: T Hartley, *Constitutional Problems of the European Union* (Oxford, Hart, 1999) 47.

free movement of workers by adopting such measures in the field of social security as are necessary. But another pronounced objective on the part of the legislator is to ensure that the Member States continue to have authority over their social security systems, where the EU still does not have any competence. It is therefore up to the Court to balance the different aims.[15]

The third interpretation method is the teleological method. The Court interprets the legislation so that it best meets the underlying objective. In this context it is a case of 'effet utile'.[16]

Bredimas defines the teleological method as one that enables the Court either to deviate from the wording that is clearly formulated, but in conflict with the overall objective, or one that fills the holes created by situations that were not foreseen by the legislator.[17]

It is difficult and perhaps not always necessary to categorise the Court's interpretation method when it decides on a case. Different legal interpretation principles are often used alongside each other. For the purpose of this monograph, it suffices to conclude that the constitutional balance changes when textual interpretation is not being used. It is in the shift from the textual to either a systematic or teleological method that a Regulation—initially meant to coordinate the Member States' social security systems—becomes something more than just coordination.

When either of these far-reaching interpretation methods is used, the ever-present constitutional question with regard to the role of the CJEU is raised. Does the Court function as an interpreter, or a self-appointed legislator? The answer to this question depends on the starting point; what is objectionable for one individual can be a logical outcome for someone else, based on the idea EU law supremacy.[18] Syrpis indentifies two extremes: one where case law takes

[15] Weiler states: '[I]t is crucial that the Court demonstrate in its judgements that national sensibilities were fully taken into account. And it must amply explain and reason its decisions if they are not to be not only authoritarian but also authoritative': J Weiler, 'Epilogue: The Judicial Apres-Nice', in G de Búrca and J Weiler, (eds), *The European Court of Justice* (Oxford, Oxford University Press, 2001) 221. Muir, Dawson and de Witte found that the Court has in later years become more unpredictable and also inconsistent. The Court has also shown no understanding for intervening arguments by the Member States. This way there was increasing criticism against the Court activities: E Muir, M Dawson and B de Witte, 'Introduction: the European Court of Justice as a political actor', in M Dawson, B De Witte and E Muir (eds), *Judicial Activism at the European Court* (Cheltenham, Edward Elgar, 2013) 2 ff; see also J Schwarze, 'Balancing EU Integration and National Interests in the Case-Law of the Court of Justice', in *The Court of Justice and the Construction of Europe: Analyses and Perspectives on Sixty Years of Case-Law* (Haag, Asser, 2013) 266 ff.

[16] HG Schermers and DF Walbroek, *Judicial Protection in the European Union* (Haag, Kluwer, 2001) 40. See also P Pescatore, 'The Doctrine of Direct Effect: An Infant Disease of Community Law' [1983] *European Law Review* 155.

[17] A Bredimas, *Methods of Interpretation and Community Law* (Amsterdam—New York—Oxford, North-Holland, 1978) 70.

[18] L Gormley, 'Free movement of goods and EU legislation in the Court of Justice', in P Syrpis (ed), *The Judiciary, the Legislature and the EU Single Market* (Cambridge, Cambridge University Press, 2012) 49.

precedence over legislation, and the other where new legislation keeps circumscribing any case law.[19]

According to the first starting point, the EU Treaties 'guide' in relation to all secondary law. The CJEU relies on primary law for its activities, when interpreting, and does not take secondary law formulations into consideration. The Court can therefore, in accordance with this approach, undermine secondary law that is not in alignment with the overall objective of the internal market. The interpretation method is closest 'to strain[ing] the meaning of legislation so that it most closely corresponds with, and indeed furthers, the Court's conception of the internal market'.[20]

The other extreme starting point is that the internal market should not be solely interpreted by the CJEU. There is instead a political dimension where the governments and parliaments of the Member States, the Commission, the Council, and the European Parliament create legislation based on the principles of primary law. This way the legislation is the applicable law.[21] The Court should therefore show respect to the legislators and restrict itself to the textual interpretation of the secondary law, especially when the legislators agree that there is a certain restriction of free movement. Craig expresses it this way: 'where the Community legislature has given considerable thought to the more particular meaning to be accorded to a right laid down in a Treaty article and expressed this through Community legislation, the Community courts should treat this with respect'.[22]

The current chapter analyses how the CJEU has chosen to observe the different aims in the field of social security, the free movement of persons, and the independent social security systems of the Member States, when it uses either the systematic or the teleological interpretation method.

3.4. STARTING POINT FOR REVIEW OF THE REGULATION

The CJEU has taken a stand over the years in a large number of cases that deal with social security. An analysis of a large share of these decisions has been done to analyse how the internal market has influenced coordination of Member States' social security systems with respect to the characteristics of the Member States.[23]

[19] P Syrpis, 'Theorising the relationship between the judiciary and the legislature in the EU single market', in P Syrpis (ed), *The Judiciary, the Legislature and the EU Single Market* (Cambridge, Cambridge University Press, 2012) 4.

[20] ibid, 5.

[21] Armstrong and Bulmer state that since the Single Act there have been two parallel tracks in the internal market: court-led negative integration and positive integration in the form of a legislative procedure. K Armstrong and S Bulmer, *The Governance of the Single European Market* (Manchester, Manchester University Press, 1998).

[22] Craig, *EU Administrative Law* (Oxford, Oxford University Press, 2006) 520.

[23] The review does not claim to be an outright legal empirical study, using data runs versus carefully selected keywords to arrive at empirically established facts from formulated questions. For an interesting Swedish study see M Derlén and J Lindholm, 'The Court of Justice and the Ankara

What makes this analysis interesting is that the coordination of Member States' social security systems has not been changed. The main idea of free movement of workers has been the same since the Rome Treaty. In other words, there is a development of case law that cannot be explained by having had the primary objective nuanced or changed.[24]

The majority of the decisions by the Court in the field of social security are preliminary rulings. Alter discusses a situation where the Member States have been eager to limit CJEU activism, but where the CJEU's use and understanding of the preliminary rulings in accordance with Article 267 TFEU has significantly restricted the options of the Member States to fully decide over their national legislation.[25]

The analysis categorises the cases into three large groups: one where textual interpretation was applied, one where the CJEU has handled the case in a more systematic context and one where a teleological method was used.

3.5. REGULATION 3/58

As seen in section 2.3, Regulation 3/58 went through a metamorphosis as an international convention negotiated between the Member States of the Coal and Steel Community, being taken over by the European Economic Community as its first substantial Regulation. There were many legal formulations and understandings that thereby came into conflict in this new Community environment. The early case law in the social security field shows, in light of this, an extremely dynamic CJEU. Despite this approach, there were, however, also some preliminary rulings where the Court embraced the textual interpretation method.

Agreement: Exploring the Empirical Approach' [2012] *Europarättslig Tidskrift* 462. No matter how much one might wish otherwise, and notwithstanding method, one can only point to tendencies, not to truths. Spaventa is of the opinion that in the case of a multitude of variables that affect the outcome of proceedings, one must accept that 'it will never be possible to provide an umbrella under which all cases can sit comfortably', E Spaventa, 'The outer limits of the Treaty free movement provisions: Some reflections on the significance of Keck, Remoteness and Deliège', in C Barnard and O Odudu (eds), *The outer limits of European Union Law* (Oxford, Hart, 2009).

[24] cf P Syrpis, 'Theorising the relationship between the judiciary and the legislature in the EU single market', in P Syrpis (ed), *The Judiciary, the Legislature and the EU Single Market* (Cambridge, Cambridge University Press, 2012) 19 ff.

[25] K Alter, *The European Court's Political Power: Selected Essays* (Oxford, Oxford University Press, 2009) 110. Cf on the situation in Sweden when it comes to *ne bis in idem* where the legislator did not change the current legislation, despite the legal development in the CJEU showing the opposite and that the Swedish Supreme Court noted this fact in [2004] NJA 510. Therefore, in the light of the preliminary ruling in Case C-617/10 *Åklagaren v Hans Åkerberg Fransson*, EU:C:2013:105, the legislator was forced to change the Swedish legislation. Cf A Ericsson, 'The Swedish Ne Bis in Idem Saga—Painting a Multi-Layered Picture' [2014] *Europarättslig Tidskrift* 54. However, it should not be forgotten that the national courts steer the CJEU to some degree, through the questions that they pose in preliminary rulings, and that any activism on the part of the CJEU could thereby, at least in theory, be limited. Cf. K Voss, 'But That's Not What I Asked! The Reformulation of Questions Asked in Preliminary Rulings' [2015] *Europarättslig tidskrift* 939.

3.5.1. Textual Interpretation

The preliminary rulings where the CJEU has applied textual interpretation are ones where the CJEU had to decide on how a specific article of Regulation 3/58 was to be applied in certain contexts. In these cases, the Court remained within the framework of the actual article. The Court followed the textual interpretation method in around 30 preliminary rulings that deal with Regulation 3/58. Below is a chronological breakdown of these preliminary rulings, presented in order to create a picture of textual interpretations by the CJEU.

The preliminary rulings in *Kalsbeek*[26] and *Dingemans*[27] from December 1964 raised a question about the supremacy of the Regulation.[28] The question in the cases was whether a recently adopted piece of legislation fell under the framework of the Regulation, even if there was no notification of this new legislation in accordance with the procedures foreseen by the Regulation. The CJEU resolved this question through a purely textual interpretation of the Article 1(b) of Regulation 3/58, which considers that 'die bestehenden und künftigen Gesetze',[29] ie the current law being in force (in Member States) is covered by the Regulation.[30]

The preliminary ruling in *Bertholet*[31] revolves around Article 52 of Regulation 3/58, which is seemingly dependent upon the entry into force of a bilateral agreement or if it is applicble in itself. The Court analyses textually how the Article is constructed, instead of using a context-based reasoning on whether the Regulation and the free movement of workers would be restricted if the application depends on the bilateral agreement's entry into force. The same question was posed in *Heseper Torfwerk*,[32] where the Court chose to follow *Bertholet* verbatim.

The preliminary ruling in *Vaassen* from 1966[33] is a case where a clear interpretation method cannot be pointed out; instead it represents a mixture of textual and

[26] Case 100/63 *G. van der Veen, widow of J. Kalsbeek v Bestuur der Sociale Verzekeringsbank and nine other cases* [1964] ECR 565.

[27] Case 24/64 *AM Dingemans v Bestuur der Sociale Verzekeringsbank* [1964] ECR 647.

[28] The question of the supremacy of the EU law arose in other contexts as well and the CJEU came to the same conclusion in 1978, almost 15 years later, in *Simmenthal*. The CJEU did not, however, refer to *Kalsbeek* and *Dingemans* in this later ruling. Case 243/78 *Simmenthal SpA v Commission* [1980] ECR 593, 17 and 18.

[29] 'Current and future applicable legislation' (my translation).

[30] The CJEU has concluded in addition to this, in a systematic exposition, that if only the legislation that the respective Member State has adopted prior to the Regulation's entry into force was to be covered by the Regulation, the Member States would soon be able to supersede the Regulation with a new legislation in the material scope. See Case 100/63 *Kalsbeek*, first question 2 respective Case 24/64 *Dingemans*, first question p 2 which is a transcript of the reasoning the Court applied in *Kalsbeek*. Cf with current preliminary rulings where the CJEU often strengthens the precedent effect through a teleological interpretation. See, for example, the Court's reasoning in Case C-208/07 *Petra von Chamier-Glisczinski v Deutsche Angestellten-Krankenkasse* [2009] ECR I-6095 56: 'It would be both to go beyond the objective of Regulation No 1408/71 and to exceed the purpose and scope of Article 42 EC to interpret that Regulation as prohibiting a Member State from granting workers and the members of their family broader social protection than that arising from the application of that Regulation.'

[31] Case 31/64 *De Sociale Voorzorg v WH Bertholet* [1965] ECR 81.

[32] Case 33/64 *Betriebskrankenkasse der Heseper Torfwerk GmbH v Egberdina Koster* [1965] ECR 97.

[33] Case 61/65 *Vaassen-Goebbels v Beamtenfonds voor het Mijnbedrijff* [1966] ECR 377.

teleological interpretation with regard to the questions that were the subject of the ruling. From 1967 onwards, with its eight CJEU preliminary rulings,[34] it is possible to start to distinguish between a 'textual case' and a case that requires a larger context, a systematic interpretation, for the Court to be able to adopt a ruling that is in accordance with the legal grounds of the Regulation.

The preliminary ruling in *Guerra*[35] dealt with a definition of the notion of 'authority' in Regulation 3/58. The Court found in the case that the national courts belonged to 'authorities' that could not reject a document written in another official language of the Community. The Court decided this partly through textual interpretation of the applicable Article, and partly by looking back on how the bilateral agreements were applied before Regulation 3/58 came into force. In the preliminary ruling in *Entr'aide médicale*[36] the CJEU concluded, by textual interpretation of Article 52 of Regulation 3/58, that a migrating worker who was involved in a traffic accident while visiting a another Member State as a tourist was covered by the term 'migrating worker', as understood by the Regulation, regardless of the purpose of visit to the Member State.[37] Article 52, according to the Court, was clear on this point. The preliminary ruling in *Brock*[38] deals in detail with the question of how completed periods are acknowledged in accordance with Regulation 3/58; being changed in subsequent Regulations. The Court looks at how the text has changed in a strictly linguistic sense, and based on this evaluation, decides on the case.[39] In the preliminary ruling in *Hakenberg*[40] the CJEU clarified the term *employed* with regard to a French businessman who performed most of

[34] Case 1/67 *Stanislas Ciechelski v Caisse régionale de sécurité sociale du Centre d'Orléans and directeur régional de la sécurité sociale d'Orléans* [1967] ECR 181; Case 2/67 *Auguste de Moor v Caisse de Pension des Employés Privés* [1967] ECR 255; Case 6/67 *Teresa Guerra, widow of Pietro Pace v Institut national d'assurance maladie-invalidité* [1967] ECR 219; Case 9/67 *Kurt Colditz v Caisse d'Assurance Vieillesse des Travailleurs Salariés de Paris* [1967] ECR 229; Case 11/67 *Office National des Pensions pour Ouvriers v Marcel Couture* [1967] ECR 487; Case 14/67 *Landesversicherungsanstalt Rheinland-Pfalz v Joseph Welchner* [1967] ECR 331; Case 18/67 *Argia Cossutta, widow of Giuseppe Pagotto v Office national des pensions pour ouvriers* [1967] ECR 399; Case 19/67 *Soziale Verzekeringsbank v Van Der Vecht* [1967] ECR 445; and Case 22/67 *Caisse Régionale de Sécurité Sociale du Nord-Est v Robert Goffart* [1967] ECR 321.

[35] Case 6/67 *Teresa Guerra, widow of Pietro Pace v Institut national d'assurance maladie-invalidité* [1967] ECR 219.

[36] Case 27/69 *Caisse de maladie des CFL 'Entr'aide médicale' et Société nationale des chemins de fer luxembourgeois v Compagnie belge d'assurances générales sur la vie et contre les accidents* [1969] ECR 405, 3–4.

[37] Unlike *Unger v Bestuur* and *Hessische Knappschaft*, the CJEU chooses not to refer to the articles of the Treaty in order to conclude that a worker is covered per se by the Regulation rules without being a worker who migrates to take up a job. The ruling is therefore in accordance with *Hessische Knappschaft*, but there is no reference to the previously pronounced rulings, nor did the CJEU choose to follow the previous rulings in its argumentation. In *Entr'aide Médicale* the Court pointed instead to the fact that the Regulation itself is sufficiently clear on the issue.

[38] Case 68/69 *Bundesknappschaft v Élisabeth Brock* [1970] ECR 171.

[39] Case 68/69 *Bundesknappschaft v Élisabeth Brock* [1970] ECR 171 5–8.

[40] Case 13/73 *Anciens Etablissements D Angenieux fils aîné and Caisse primaire centrale d'assurance maladie de la région parisienne v Willy Hakenberg* [1973] ECR 935.

his work on the road in Germany. The Court carried out a textual analysis without any digressions from the underlying purpose of the Regulation. The preliminary ruling in *Pennartz*[41] made a stand on how invalidity pension should be calculated in a purely technical sense. Such purely technical preliminary rulings were also to the fore in *Kunz*,[42] *Costa*[43] and *Costers*.[44]

To sum up: the textual preliminary rulings have dealt with articles in Regulation 3/58 that have been in accordance with the objective of supporting the free movement of workers.

3.5.2. Systematic Interpretation in the Context of Primary Law

Already in the first case that came before the Court in the field of social security, *Unger v Bestuur*,[45] the CJEU emphasised the fact that the legal basis, Article 51 (Article 48 TFEU) was to be found in the treaty chapter that dealt with workers under Part 2 of the Treaty—the Foundations of the Community. The Court noted this in its ruling and concluded that:

> The establishment of as complete a freedom of movement for workers as possible, which thus forms a part of the 'foundations' of the Community, therefore constitutes the principal objective of Article 51 and thereby conditions the interpretation of the regulations adopted in implementation of that article.[46]

With this statement, it was clear from the start to the Member States that the CJEU, in cases where the Regulation is not sufficiently clear itself, would read the provisions of the Regulation with the primary law in mind, and not in an isolated way as when interpreting a convention.[47]

[41] Case 268/78 *Jean-Louis Pennartz v Caisse primaire d'assurance maladie des Alpes-Maritimes* [1979] ECR 2411.

[42] Case 35/73 *Ludwig Kunz v Bundesversicherungsanstalt für Angestellte* [1973] ECR 1025. The Court chose in the preliminary ruling to disregard the fact that the subsequent Regulation 1408/71 had expanded social rights when it comes to welfare benefits in the countries of residence, by concluding that Regulation 3/58 does not allow a more generous solution for such a migrating worker.

[43] Case 39/74 *Luciana Costa, épouse Mazzier v Belgium* [1974] ECR 1251.

[44] Case 40/74 *Belgium, Henri Costers and Marie Vounckx v Berufsgenossenschaft der Feinmechanik und Elektrotechnik* [1974] ECR 1323, the preliminary ruling at p 5 points to special difficulties for a migrating worker who lives in a Member State other that the country of work.

[45] Case 75/63 *MKH Unger, married to R Hoekstra v Bestuur der Bedrijfsvereniging voor Detailhandel en Ambachten te Utrecht* [1964] ECR 177. It should be noted that it took six years before the CJEU had to decide its first preliminary ruling in the field of social security. The take-off distance for the national courts was therefore extremely long. Watson found that in 1980, six years after Great Britain had become a member of the Union, UK authorities still had very little knowledge of Regulation 1408/71 and they instead tended to use bilateral agreements which were partially suspended upon EU accession; see P Watson, *Social Security Law of the European Communities* (London, Mansell, 1980) 252.

[46] Case 75/63 *MKH Unger, married to R Hoekstra v Bestuur der Bedrijfsvereniging voor Detailhandel en Ambachten te Utrecht* [1964] ECR 177, fifth clause.

[47] cf F Pennings, 'Coordination of Social Security within the EU context', in A Ortiz, M Olivier and G Vonk (eds), *Social Security and Migrant Workers* (Alphen aan den Rijn, Kluwer, 2014) 117, 118.

In this first preliminary ruling, the CJEU identified a direct connection between primary and secondary law: primary law 'steers' secondary law, regardless of the wording of the secondary law. Secondary law is interpreted against the provisions of primary law, whose objective is to strengthen the free movement of workers.[48] The CJEU decided that this overall objective took over the competing construction of a Regulation merely coordinating and thus allowing that the respective Member State should fully decide who is covered by its own national legislation.

The preliminary ruling in *Nonnenmacher*[49] from June 1964 was the second preliminary ruling in the field of social security. With this ruling, the Court, again, placed Regulation 3/58 in a larger context of primary law: the Rome Treaty and its principle of the free movement of workers. At issue was whether Mrs Nonnenmacher should be considered insured in France or the Netherlands after her husband's death, or whether she would be covered by the social insurance of both countries. The CJEU began by saying that the legal basis for Regulation 3/58 lies in Treaty Article 51.[50] Subsequently, the CJEU set the rules on the applicable legislation in a broader context—the objectives of the primary law—and found that Article 12 of the Regulation was binding when it came to determining the applicable legislation. This binding rule did, however, not exclude parallel payments from other Member States, as long as these were not considered being an obstacle to the free movement of workers within the meaning of the Treaty.

The overriding objective of free movement of workers is facilitated through Article 12 of the Regulation, so that a migrating worker can be sure that he or she is covered by the legislation of the Member State. On the other hand, this guarantee cannot lead to preventing another Member State from adding further social security benefits to a person—for example, through a residence-based system which foresees that all residents are entitled to residence-based benefits. Regulation 3/58 therefore does not have a cancelling effect; thus the Member States cannot use the Regulation to refuse to pay out benefits which, if it was a national case, would be paid out on the basis of the national legislation, by referring to the Regulation that points out another Member State as the competent state.[51]

Part of the preliminary ruling in *Kalsbeek*[52] is based on a systematic interpretation, stating that the Treaty's objective of free movement of workers could

[48] The CJEU, through this ruling, has also indirectly determined that a worker does not need to cross borders with the sole intention of working. Mrs Unger was seen as a worker and had crossed the border in order to visit her parents, but it was enough for activation of the Regulation. This was confirmed in the later preliminary ruling in 44/65, *Hessische Knappschaft v Maison Singer et fils* [1965] ECR 965.

[49] Case 92/63 *M Th Nonnenmacher, widow of HE Moebs v Bestuur der Sociale Verzekeringsbank* [1964] ECR 281.

[50] 'Regulation No 3 was made pursuant to Article 51 of the EEC Treaty…': Case 92/63, *Nonnenmacher* 287.

[51] cf F Pennings, *European Social Security Law* 6 edn (Cambridge - Antwerp - Portland, Intersentia, 2015) 84.

[52] Case 100/63 *G. van der Veen, widow of J. Kalsbeek v Bestuur der Sociale Verzekeringsbank and nine other cases* [1964] ECR 565.

not be achieved if Articles 27 and 28 in Regulation 3/58—on the aggregation of completed pension periods—were interpreted literally and in isolation.

The CJEU continued along the same path, with a broader systematic interpretation in *Hessische Knappschaft*.[53] This case dealt with benefits being paid out on account of a German worker dying during a holiday in France. Regarding the concept of worker, the CJEU found that neither the Treaty nor the Regulation defined a worker *in stricto sensu* as a migrating person that takes on a job position.[54] The Court found that Article 51 of the Treaty did not indicate that its focus is merely workers who would go to another Member State to work. The Court was instead of the opinion that the Treaty of Rome aimed at providing protection for all workers who used their right to free movement, to work, go on holiday, or visit friends or relatives. After finding that Article 51 should be understood broadly, the CJEU found that Regulation 3/58 'certainly corresponds to the objectives of Article 51 of the Treaty'.[55] The objective of the Regulation was therefore not only to promote a move from one Member State to another in order to work. The Regulation was thereby broadened to include all who were considered to be workers and its application was not dependent on the reason for which someone had crossed the national borders. In this way the personal scope was considerably broadened when compared to the joint understanding that the coordination rules are meant only for people crossing borders for work.[56]

In the preliminary rulings that were based on primary law, the CJEU continued to emphasise[57] what was held in *Kaalsbeek*:[58]

> The Regulations in the field of social security have as their basis, their framework and their bounds Articles 48 to 51 of the Treaty, which are aimed at *securing* freedom of movement of workers. [Emphasis added.]

This reasoning is seen again in the only ruling in the field of social security in 1968, *de Cicco*,[59] where the Court included craftsmen in the definition of workers through systematic interpretation. The CJEU continued in 1969, with the *Torrekens*[60]

[53] Case 44/65 *Hessische Knappschaft v Maison Singer et fils* [1965] ECR 965.

[54] cf the reasoning in Case 75/63 *Unger v Bestuur*, which is not as clear when it comes to movement of migrating workers; if movement takes place with the aim to work or for some other reason.

[55] For the first question, Case 44/65 *Hessische Knappschaft v Maison Singer et fils* [1965] ECR 965, 13th clause.

[56] cf also Case 31/64 *De Sociale Voorzorg v WH Bertholet* [1965] ECR 81 which dealt in parts with a person living in Belgium but who travelled through the Netherlands in order to work in another part of Belgium.

[57] See Case 1/67 *Stanislas Ciechelski v Caisse régionale de sécurité sociale du Centre d'Orléans and directeur régional de la sécurité sociale d'Orléans* [1967] ECR 181 2; Case 20/75 *Gaetano d'Amico v Landesversicherungsanstalt Rheinland-Pfalz* [1975] ECR 891 10; and Case 93/81 *Institut national d'assurance maladie-invalidité v Peter Knoeller* [1982] ECR 951 9.

[58] Case 100/63 *G. van der Veen, widow of J. Kalsbeek v Bestuur der Sociale Verzekeringsbank and nine other cases* [1964] ECR 565 1.

[59] Case 19/68 *Giovanni de Cicco v Landesversicherungsanstalt Schwaben* [1968] ECR 473.

[60] Case 28/68 *Caisse Régionale de Sécurité Sociale du Nord de la France v Achille Torrekens* [1969] ECR 125.

and *Duffy*,[61] to place Regulation 3/58 in a larger context in its preliminary rulings. In *Torrekens*, the CJEU's starting point was the objective of the Treaty's Article 51 when interpreting whether a national pension scheme can be within the material scope of the Regulation. In *Duffy*, the situation involved a widow who had a Belgian pension based on her work in Belgium, but also asked for the French widow's pension of her deceased husband who had been working in France. The French authorities interpreted the aggregation rules of the Regulation, Article 11(2) to her disadvantage, and the widow ended up in a position that was worse than if she had been a widow living in France. The CJEU found that such an interpretation of the Regulation was not in accordance with the underlying principle of the free movement of workers.[62]

The pattern with regard to Regulation 3/58[63] during the 1970s is mostly the same; the cases could only be solved by looking at the underlying objectives that arise from Articles 48–51 of the Treaty. A notable preliminary ruling is *Di Bella*,[64] where the framework of the Regulation was found to be insufficiently clear with regard to situations on determining the applicable legislation. The Court concluded in its ruling that this cannot be derived from Regulation 3/58 without taking into account the primary law on the free movement of persons.[65] In the three preliminary rulings of *Heinze*,[66] *Niedersachsen*[67] and *Hamburg*,[68] the CJEU turned to Article 51 to ensure that payments to people with tuberculosis were considered to be part of the material scope of the Regulation, as the scope needs to be understood in a primary law context for migrant workers' best interests. During 1973, the CJEU chose in the preliminary ruling in *Smieja*,[69] to refer to the underlying objective of the Regulation, but strangely enough without direct reference to the Treaty of Rome. In 1973 in *Mancuso*[70] the CJEU repeated the reasoning based on Articles 27 and 28 of Regulation 3/58 that had been used in *Kalsbeek* and stated that these

[61] Case 34/69 *Caisse d'assurance vieillesse des travailleurs salariés de Paris v Jeanne Duffy* [1969] ECR 597.

[62] With this case the first seed was planted for a way forward when it comes to indirect discrimination; see section 4.2.3.

[63] Regulation 1408/71 depended on the adoption of an additional regulation. Regulation (EEC) No 574/72 of the Council of 21 March 1972 fixing the procedure for implementing Regulation (EEC) No 1408/71 on the application of social security schemes to employed persons and their families moving within the Community, [1972] OJ L74/1 was adopted on 21 March 1972. Both Regulations came into force in 1 October 1972. Transition rules made, however, Regulation 3/58 still applicable if the case and the benefits stemmed from before 1972.

[64] Case 3/70 *Caisse de compensation pour allocations familiales des Charbonnages du Couchant de Mons v Francesca Beninato (nee Di Bella), widow of Vicenzo Beninato* [1970] 415.

[65] Case 3/70 *Caisse de compensation pour allocations familiales des Charbonnages du Couchant de Mons v Francesca Beninato (nee Di Bella), widow of Vicenzo Beninato* [1970] 415 10.

[66] Case 14/72 *Helmut Heinze v Landesversicherungsanstalt Rheinprovinz* [1972] ECR 1105.

[67] Case 15/72 *Land Niedersachsen v Landesversicherungsanstalt Hannover* [1972] ECR 1127.

[68] Case 16/72 *Ortskrankenkasse Hamburg v Landesversicherungsanstalt Schleswig-Holstein* [1972] ECR 1141.

[69] Case 51/73 *Bestuur der Sociale Verzekeringsbank v B Smieja* [1973] ECR 1213.

[70] Case 140/73 *Direction régionale de la sécurité sociale de la région parisienne et Caisse d'assurance maladie de Paris v Carmela Mancuso et Caisse nationale d'assurance vieillesse des travailleurs salariés* [1973] ECR 1449.

articles require a broader interpretation than just the textual one. This development continued in 1974, with the preliminary ruling in *Niemann*,[71] where the CJEU continued to put issues in a systematic context. The CJEU found in the preliminary ruling that Article 28 of Regulation 3/58, in cases where its section 3 led to a less beneficial result by aggregation than by application of the national legislation, was not in accordance with the primary law context and it was therefore proclaimed inapplicable in such cases.

3.5.3. Teleological Interpretation

The longer Regulation 3/58 had been in force in the Member States, the greater the impact it had on the national authorities. After a couple of years of the Regulation's existence, more complex issues started to appear, especially because citizens actually started to move freely as well as turning to their former states of affiliation and to request aggregation of completed periods.

Therefore, from 1967 onwards, many preliminary rulings focused on the issue of aggregation and the calculation of completed pension periods from two Member States. If one country had already paid benefits on the basis of its national legislation, should it then use the aggregation rules from Articles 27 and 28 of the Regulation when the benefits from another competent country were brought to the fore? Should this be done even if in some cases it would be to the detriment of the insured?

The overall situation was such that the Articles 27 and 28 turned out to reduce benefits, instead of ensuring that the migrating worker was not negatively affected by a move within the Union. The CJEU dealt with these issues in *Ciechelski*,[72] *de Moor*,[73] *Pace*,[74] *Colditz*,[75] *Goffart*,[76] *Welchner*,[77] *Couture*[78] and *Guissart*.[79] The Court concluded that Articles 27 and 28 of Regulation 3/58 were focused on technicalities of how one should calculate, in the case of parallel benefits. Thus the articles did not focus on the free movement on a more general level. The CJEU chose, therefore, to place the rule of the Regulation in a larger context through a teleological interpretation method, to facilitate the objectives of

[71] Case 191/73 *Rudolf Niemann v Bundesversicherungsanstalt für Angestellte* [1974] ECR 571.

[72] Case 1/67 *Stanislas Ciechelski v Caisse régionale de sécurité sociale du Centre d'Orléans and directeur régional de la sécurité sociale d'Orléans* [1967] ECR 181.

[73] Case 2/67 *Auguste de Moor v Caisse de Pension des Employés Privés* [1967] ECR 255.

[74] Case 6/67 *Teresa Guerra, widow of Pietro Pace v Institut national d'assurance maladie-invalidité* [1967] ECR 219.

[75] Case 9/67 *Kurt Colditz v Caisse d'Assurance Vieillesse des Travailleurs Salariés de Paris* [1967] ECR 229.

[76] Case 22/67 *Caisse Régionale de Sécurité Sociale du Nord-Est v Robert Goffart* [1967] ECR 321.

[77] Case 14/67 *Landesversicherungsanstalt Rheinland-Pfalz v Joseph Welchner* [1967] ECR 331.

[78] Case 11/67 *Office National des Pensions pour Ouvriers v Marcel Couture* [1967] ECR 487.

[79] Case 12/67 *Jules Guissart v Belgium* [1967] ECR 551.

the Rome Treaty and to let these objectives guide the interpretation of Articles 27 and 28 of the Regulation. After the CJEU had determined this perspective, it concluded that a narrow and literal interpretation would mean that the overarching purpose would not be fully effective in the given situations.[80] If the calculation rule of the Regulation for aggregation was used then the Regulation would not be in harmony with the primary law. On the basis of this fact, the CJEU found that the Regulation cannot prevent the application of national legislation—as long as it did not prevent the free movement of workers. The CJEU therefore concluded that Regulation 3/58 could not be used by the national authorities to avoid national obligations, as long as they do not lead to an obstacle in free movement of workers. This ruling was followed by a further 10 preliminary rulings over the years until Regulation 1408/71 became applicable.[81]

3.5.4. Conclusion

Overall, with regard to Regulation 3/58, an unexpectedly small number of preliminary rulings[82] were resolved through textual interpretation.[83] The Court instead relied on systematic interpretation in a majority of the cases, as well as on teleological interpretation with regard to the calculation of pensions in accordance with Articles 27 and 28.

In the light of a large number of cases where the EU has considered a larger context, it can be concluded that Regulation 3/58 was not up to standards when confronted with the principles of the internal market. Paradoxically, instead of promoting the free movement of workers, many rules of the Regulation had a negative influence.

[80] So aggregation should not happen automatically, but one needs to see if the possible outcome would influence free movement of workers.

[81] Case C-32/70 *Union nationale des mutualités socialistes v La Marca Stéphanie* [1970] ECR 987; Case 26/71 *Heinrich Gross v Caisse régionale d'assurance vieillesse des travailleurs salariés de Strasbourg* [1971] ECR 871; Case 27/71 *August Keller v Caisse régionale d'assurance vieillesse des travailleurs salariés de Strasbourg* [1971] ECR 885; Case 28/71 *Eugen Höhn v Caisse régionale d'assurance vieillesse des travailleurs salariés de Strasbourg* [1971] ECR 893; Case 2/72 *Salvatore Murru v Caisse régionale d'assurance maladie de Paris* [1972] ECR 333; Case 140/73 *Direction régionale de la sécurité sociale de la région parisienne and Caisse régionale d'assurance maladie de Paris v Carmela Mancuso and Caisse nationale d'assurance vieillesse des travailleurs salariés* [1973] ECR 1449; Case 20/75 *Gaetano d'Amico v Landesversicherungsanstalt Rheinland-Pfalz* [1975] ECR 891; Case 57/75 *Fernand Plaquevent v Caisse primaire d'assurance maladie du Havre and Directeur régional de la Sécurité sociale de Rouen* [1975] ECR 1581 and Case 75/76 *Silvana Kaucic and Anna Maria Kaucic v Institut national d'assurances maladie invalidité* [1977] ECR 495.

[82] Only one of the cases is an infringement case, Case 150/79 *Commission v Belgium* [1980] ECR 2621, where both Regulation 3/58 and Regulation 1408/71 were applicable.

[83] Around 30 out of 81 cases. Aside from those already described in section 3.5.1, noteworthy are Case 73/72 *Hubert Bentzinger v Steinbruchs-Berufsgenossenschaft* [1973] ECR 283; Case 82/72 *CJ Walder v Bestuur der Sociale Verzekeringsbank* [1973] ECR 599; Case 130/73 *Magdalena Vandeweghe and others v Berufsgenossenschaft für die chemische Industrie* [1973] ECR 1329; Case 32/76 *Alfonsa Saieva v Caisse de compensation des allocations familiales de l'industrie charbonnière des bassins de Charleroi et de la Basse-Sambre* [1976] ECR 1523 and Case 275/81 *GF Koks v Raad van Arbeid* [1982] ECR 3013.

3.6. REGULATION 1408/71

3.6.1. Introduction

There is a consensus that Regulation 3/58 was not a high-quality piece of legislation.[84] Discussions on changing Regulation 3/58 had been ongoing since 1963, one year before the Court had even made its first preliminary ruling, in *Unger v Bestuur*.[85] The rulings prior to the new Regulation 1408/71, which made extensive use of systematic interpretation, as seen in section 3.5.2, are indicative of this, since the CJEU could not rely on the Regulation itself.

With regard to Regulation 1408/71, the majority of the preliminary rulings revolve around reading and understanding the specific rules of the Regulation or how the calculations are to be performed in cross-border situations and thus focus on a textual interpretation. However, the Court still applies systematic and teleological interpretation methods when the Regulation does not sufficiently solve the issues.

As most of the rulings are extensive and space here is limited, only a selection is presented to illustrate the legal situation.

3.6.2. Textual Interpretation

When the Court first started applying Regulation 1408/71, it is notable that the Court used the textual interpretation method for the first five years.

The first preliminary ruling based on Regulation 1408/71, *Callemeyn*,[86] dealt with Belgian social security benefits to the disabled covered by Article 4.1 of the Regulation and its definition of benefits for the disabled. The Court compared Article 4.1.b, which deals with 'invalidity benefits, including those intended for the maintenance or improvement of earning capacity', under the formulation of Article 1 t of the Regulation. The Court found that this comparison lead to a broad understanding of the notion of a social security benefit. Therefore, the Court concluded through textual interpretation, that this benefit was covered by the material scope of the Regulation.

The preliminary rulings from 1975 and 1976, *Galati*,[87] *Borella*,[88] and *Aulich*,[89] all deal with questions of how to apply the rules of calculation. The preliminary

[84] The Member States wanted better protection for the migrating workers than what Regulation 3/58 could offer, and the administrative procedures turned out not to function so well. Cf Watson, *Social Security Law of the European Communities* (London, Mansell, 1980) 53; Roberts, 'A Short History of Social Security Coordination', in Y Jorens (ed), *50 Years of Social Security Coordination; Past—Present—Future, Report of the conference celebrating the 50th Anniversary of the European Coordination of Social Security*, Prague, 7 & 8 May 2009 (European Commission, 2009) 18.

[85] Case 75/63 *MKH Unger, married to R Hoekstra v Bestuur der Bedrijfsvereniging voor Detailhandel en Ambachten te Utrecht* [1964] ECR 177.

[86] Case 187/73 *Odette Callemeyn v Belgium* [1974] ECR 553.

[87] Case 33/75 *Benito Galati v Landesversicherungsanstalt Schwaben* [1975] ECR 1323.

[88] Case 49/75 *Camilla Borella v Landesversicherungsanstalt Schwaben* [1975] ECR 1461.

[89] Case 103/75 *Walter Th Aulich v Bundesversicherungsanstalt für Angestellte* [1976] ECR 697.

ruling in *Foot-Ball Club d'Andlau*[90] from 1975 is perhaps the first ruling that is more on the point of principle, where the Court used textual interpretation. The matter involved determining the legislation applicable to German musicians, taking into account that they played a couple of times a year in Belgium at events organised by the Belgian d'Andlau football club. The rule of applicable legislation in Regulation 1408/71 is clear and points in this context to Germany. The CJEU found no reason to waive this rule and explained only in passing that the objective of the rule is to prevent the application of several national legislations in parallel.[91] The Court did, however, not go into further detail but simply concluded that the Regulation is clear on that point.

At the end of 1976, there was the preliminary ruling in *Mouthaan*,[92] which dealt with issues on unemployment. This ruling is different from the previous cases as it makes a referral to the clarifications in the preamble. In *di Paolo*[93] from the beginning of 1977, the Court also adopted a narrow view or model of explanation, in which the contents of the Articles are explained through the rules of the Regulation.

After the first five years with Regulation 1408/7 in place, more complex situations emerged that called for a systematic interpretation in the 1980s in a rather comprehensive way.[94] However, the approach is still that if the Court can rule only on the basis of the Regulation itself, it does so.[95] Examples for this include *Menzies*,[96] *Browning*[97] and *Vermaut*,[98] all of which deal in different aspects with how to calculate specific social security benefits.

[90] Case 8/75 *Caisse primaire d'assurance maladie de Sélestat v Association du Foot-Ball Club d'Andlau* [1975] ECR 739.

[91] ibid 7.

[92] Case 39/76 *Bestuur der Bedrijfsvereniging voor de Metaalnijverheid v LJ Mouthaan* [1976] ECR 1901.

[93] Case 76/76 *Silvana di Paolo v Office National de l'Emploi* [1977] ECR 315.

[94] See Case 67/79 *Waldemar Fellinger v Bundesanstalt für Arbeit, Nürnberg* [1980] ECR 535; Case 79/81, Case 104/80 *Kurt Beeck v Bundesanstalt für Arbeit* [1981] ECR 503; Case 116/80 *Rijksdienst voor Werknemerspensioenen v Giorgio Celestre et al* [1981] ECR 1737 (on the lattter two cases, see H Knorpel, 'Social Security Cases in the Court of Justice of the European Communities' [1981] *CMLR* 97, 110 ff); Case 242/83 *Caisse de compensation pour allocations familiales du bâtiment, de l'industrie et du commerce du Hainaut v Salvatore Patteri* [1984] ECR 3171 (see esp the Court's conclusion at p 9 that the objective of Art 51 of the EEC Treaty [Art 48 TFEU] is essential for interpretation of the Regulations that the Council has adopted within the area of social security for migrating workers); Case 284/84 *LA Spruyt v Bestuur van de Sociale Verzekeringsbank, te Amsterdam* [1986] ECR 685; Case 43/86 *Bestuur van de Sociale Verzekeringsbank v JA de Rijke and LAC de Rijke-Van Gent* [1987] ECR 3611; Case 58/87 *Josef Rebmann v Bundesversicherungsanstalt für Angestellte* [1988] ECR 3467 (cf JG Monroe, 'A Review of the Case Law of the Court of Justice on Migrant Workers and Social Security July 1987 to July 1989' [1990] *CMLR* 547, 563 ff; Case 368/87 *Lieselotte Hartmann Troiani v Landesversicherungsanstalt Rheinprovinz* [1989] ECR 1333.

[95] cf Knorpel, who is of the view that 1982 had been 'notable rather for amplifying and developing received doctrines and resolving minor points of interpretation than for any major innovations or departures of principle': H Knorpel, 'Social Security Cases in the Court of Justice of the European Communities, 1982' [1984] *CMLR* 241.

[96] Case 793/79 *Alastair Menzies v Bundesversicherungsanstalt für Angestellte* [1980] ECR 2085.

[97] Case 22/81 *R v Social Security Commissioner, ex parte Norman Ivor Browning* [1981] ECR 3357.

[98] Case 55/81 *Georges Vermaut v Office national des pensions pour travailleurs salariés* [1982] ECR 649.

The preliminary ruling in *Brusse*[99] from 1984 deals with the exemption rule of the determination of the applicable law in Article 17 of Regulation 1408/71, which allows the authorities of the relevant Member States to agree to make an exception in the rules that outline the competent state.[100] The reason for this possible exception is that the framework of the Regulation could be oppressive in a particular case, but it could also be for purely practical reasons.[101] The case dealt with the question whether Article 17 could be used retroactively to make an exception for Brusse with regard to the British social security system, as he had simultaneously been paying contributions to the Dutch system. The Court concluded that there is nothing in Article 17 that prevents it from being used retroactively. The Court came to a classic conclusion: if nothing prevents it, it can be done.[102] The Court chose to look at the system purely textually; it examined how the provisions in the Regulation function with one another before adding that the exception rule in Article 17 is meant to address situations that are difficult for the worker in accordance with Articles 13–16. The Court could have argued that the option of retroactivity could be seen from the perspective of the primary law, because if there is no such last resort, many potential workers will think twice before deciding to change countries. However, no such teleological reasoning was used.

Even during the 1990s, textual interpretation was still prevalent; answers were 'self-evident', even though argumentation could have been stronger and in a broader context.

The question of how to regard a subsidiary occupation (two lessons, two times a week) which after retirement was regarded as a major occupation was brought to the fore in *Kits van Heijningen*.[103] The CJEU found that the definition of employment in Regulation 1408/71 did not stipulate any requirements regarding the work itself and completely disregarded the fact that the Dutch legislation did not take into account the hours worked, but only whether or not the person had worked on the first day of the month when the request for benefits was submitted. The Court could have claimed that it is important to interpret the concept of worker in the light of free movement of workers from the perspective of primary law, as in *Unger v Bestuur*.[104] However, the ruling is in line with *Merluzzi*,[105] where a similar issue depended solely on the Regulation. By disregarding certain inconvenient facts in the preliminary rulings, the Court has resolved these

[99] Case 101/83 *Raad van Arbeid v PB Brusse* [1984] ECR 2223.

[100] Art 17 is now Art 16 in Regulation 883/2004.

[101] What facilitates the ruling is the condition that the insured, together with his or her employer, must request the exception. This active choice indicates that the insured has evaluated the situation and is aware of advantages and disadvantages that this request entails from the perspective of social insurance. Furthermore, Art 17 can only be used if doing so is to the advantage of the insured.

[102] Case 101/83 *Raad van Arbeid v PB Brusse* [1984] ECR 2223, 20.

[103] Case C-2/89 *Bestuur van de Sociale Verzekeringsbank v GJ Kits van Heijningen* [1990] ECR I-1755.

[104] Case 75/63 *MKH Unger, married to R Hoekstra v Bestuur der Bedrijfsvereniging voor Detailhandel en Ambachten te Utrecht* [1964] ECR 177.

[105] Case 80/71 *Adalgisa Merluzzi v Caisse Primaire Centrale d'Assurance Maladie de la Région Parisienne* [1972] ECR 175.

atypical situations purely textually, and in this way it respected the competence of the Member States.[106]

The preliminary ruling in *van Poucke*[107] from 1994 dealt with the rules on determining the applicable legislation in Regulation 1408/71. Van Poucke was employed as a military doctor in Belgium, but he also had a private practice in the Netherlands. The Belgian authorities requested contributions paid by van Poucke to the social insurance scheme for self-employed persons in Belgium for the work he performed in the Netherlands. The crux of the matter was whether van Poucke could be covered by the Regulation at all, as he was employed as a civil servant in Belgium.[108] The Court found that van Poucke was covered by the personal scope of the Regulation as a self-employed person in the Netherlands and, as a consequence of the Regulation, he needed to pay social contributions for his activity in the Netherlands to Belgium, as Belgium was the competent state.[109] The preliminary ruling is a textbook example of syllogism, where the decision to pay the social contributions stems from the premise that if he was covered by the personal scope, Belgium was the competent state, and it is up to the competent state to decide on the collection of social contributions.

It can be observed that in the mid-1990s the CJEU again turned to systematic interpretation.[110] Then, from the latter part of the 1990s and onward, the Court went back to textual interpretation. The *Plum*,[111] *Fitzwilliam*[112] and *Banks*[113]

[106] cf Case C-121/92 *Staatssecretaris van Financiën v A Zinnecker* [1993] ECR I-5023, where a self-employed person worked in Germany and the Netherlands, but neither state considered him insured because he worked too little. The situation was such that Zinnecker was not covered by the Regulation. A situation arose which was certainly questionable, but correct in a legal sense through textual interpretation. Here, the CJEU once again disregarded national qualifications in its preliminary ruling and concluded that Zinnecker, according to the Regulation, should be covered by the Dutch legislation, based on the Dutch formulation in the annex to Regulation 3/58, which left a pretty open interpretation of who is considered self-employed in the context of the Regulation. The only problem, which the CJEU did not pay attention to, was that the annex could not be made applicable because Zinnecker could not invoke the Regulation!

[107] Case C-71/93 *Guido van Poucke v Rijksinstituut voor de Sociale Verzekeringen der Zelfstandigen and Algemene Sociale Kas voor Zelfstandigen* [1994] ECR I-1101.

[108] Civil servants are not covered by the Regulation's personal scope, Art 2(3).

[109] cf with regard to the payment of social contributions, Case 8/75 *Caisse primaire d'assurance maladie de Sélestat v Association du Foot-Ball Club d'Andlau* [1975] ECR 739.

[110] Se eg Case C-98/94 *Christel Schmidt v Rijksdienst voor Pensioenen* [1995] ECR I-2559; Case C-227/94 *E Olivieri-Coenen v Bestuur van de Nieuwe Algemene Bedrijfsvereniging* [1995] ECR I-3301; Case C-482/93 *E Klaus v Bestuur van de Nieuwe Algemene Bedrijfsvereniging* [1995] ECR I-3551; Case C-443/93 *Ioannis Vougioukas v Idryma Koinonikon Asfalisseon (IKA)* [1995] ECR I-4033; Case C-308/93 *Bestuur van de Sociale Verzekeringsbank v JM Cabanis-Issarte* [1996] ECR I-2097; Case C-245/94 *Ingrid Hoever and Iris Zachow v Land Nordrhein-Westfalen* [1996] ECR I-4895; Case C-340/94 *EJM de Jaeck v Staatssecretaris van Financiën* [1997] ECR I-461; Case C-88/95 *Bernardina Martínez Losada, Manuel Fernández Balado and José Paredes v Instituto Nacional de Empleo (INEM) and Instituto Nacional de la Seguridad Social (INSS)* [1997] ECR I-869; Case C-266/95 *Pascual Merino García v Bundesanstalt für Arbeit* [1997] ECR I-3279.

[111] Case C-404/98 *Josef Plum and Allgemeine Ortskrankenkasse Rheinland, Regionaldirektion Köln* [1998] ECR I-9379.

[112] Case C-202/97 *Fitzwilliam Executive Search Ltd v Bestuur van het Landelijk instituut sociale verzekeringen* [2000] ECR I-883.

[113] Case C-178/97 *Barry Banks m.fl. and Théâtre royal de la Monnaie* [2000] ECR I-2005.

cases, all dealing with sensitive political issues of posting workers, shows a Court that balances the Treaty with the Regulation. These three cases were about posting workers from one Member State to another, where the CJEU used a narrow reasoning based on the preliminary ruling from 1970, in *Manpower*.[114] This approach by the Court was later confirmed in 2006 in *Herbosch Kiere*.[115] The CJEU found in the cases that a certificate required by the Regulation (Form E101, now A1) from the posting state assumes that the competent authorities have correctly assessed that the posted workers should be covered by the social security system of the Member State where the posting company is established, and that this form is binding for the Member State where the worker has been posted.[116]

In the first decade of the 2000s, textual interpretation was used predominantly for cases dealing with calculations and situations that included neither discrimination nor hindering effects.[117]

Verschueren is of the opinion that the CJEU has returned to a more textual interpretation in recent years, where the rules of the Regulation are applied even though another outcome could have been expected.[118] The rulings that confirm this trend are *von Chamier-Glisczinski*,[119] *Commission v Spain*[120] and *van Delft*,[121] from 2009 and 2010. In all three cases the Court chose not to turn to primary law, but instead to limit itself to the Regulation's wordings.[122] The preliminary ruling in

[114] Case 35/70 *Manpower* [1970] ECR 1251.

[115] Case C-2/05 *Rijksdienst voor Sociale Zekerheid v Herbosch Kiere NV* [2006] ECR I-1079.

[116] The Court chose in this case not to touch the other side of the posting; the frequent use of 'cheap labour' sent from Member States with lower social contributions. But looking into this out of a purely textual perspective, this drawback does not affect in any way the freedom of movement of workers.

[117] eg Case C-471/99 *Alfredo Martínez Domínguez, Joaquín Benítez Urbano, Agapito Mateos Cruz and Carmen Calvo Fernández v Bundesanstalt für Arbeit, Kindergeldkasse (BAK)* [2002] ECR I-7835; Case C-373/02 *Sakir Öztürk v Pensionsversicherungsanstalt der Arbeiter* [2004] ECR I-3605; Case C-372/02 *Roberto Adanez-Vega v Bundesanstalt für Arbeit* [2004] ECR I-10761; Case C-153/03 *Caisse nationale des prestations familiales v Ursula Schwarz, née Weide* [2005] ECR I-6017; Case C-154/05 *JJ Kersbergen-Lap, D Dams-Schipper v Raad van Bestuur van het Uitvoeringsinstituut Werknemersverzekeringen* [2006] ECR I-6249; Case C-265/05 *José Perez Naranjo v Caisse régionale d'assurance maladie Nord-Picardie* [2007] ECR I-347.

[118] H Verschueren, 'The EU social security co-ordination system: A close interplay between the EU legislature and judiciary', in P Syrpis (ed), *The Judiciary, the Legislature and the EU Single Market* (Cambridge, Cambridge University Press, 2012) 199.

[119] Case C-208/07 *Petra von Chamier-Glisczinski v Deutsche Angestellten-Krankenkasse* [2009] ECR I-6095.

[120] Case C-211/08 *European Commission v Spain* [2010] ECR I-5267.

[121] Case C-345/09 *JA van Delft and others v College voor zorgverzekeringen* [2010] ECR I-9879.

[122] Verschueren asserts that the outcome of *Commission v Spain* was particularly unexpected, as all preliminary rulings with regard to cross-border health care up to that point had acknowledged the competences of Member States to shape their own health systems but in an overall assessment a limitation to the free movement of services could not be accepted. What Verschueren does not take into consideration is that the situation in *Commission v Spain* is different from previous case law in the field of health care. In the case of tourists requiring medical care, health care is not the main objective of the visit to another Member State. In such cases, the need for health care arises suddenly, as a result of a traffic accident or deterioration of a person's health. In the cross-border health care cases, the health care was the primary focus, and because it is seen as a service, it cannot be restricted in line with Art 49 TFEU, cf Case C-211/08 *European Commission v Spain* [2010] ECR I-5267 61. With this in mind the CJEU is not being more cautious.

Fassbender-Firman[123] from 2014 confirms this tendency—the CJEU concluded that the current Articles of Regulation 1408/71 do not give reason for an extensive understanding, in the light of a textual and a subsequent systematic interpretation. The Court emphasised that the Regulation has its limitations and that these should be respected:

> It is a requirement of the principles of legal certainty and of transparency that migrant workers and their family members should have the benefit of a clear precise legal situation enabling them to ascertain not only the full extent of their rights but also, as the case may be, the limitations of those rights.[124]

From 2009 to 2016, some 50 rulings were handed down which show a mixed picture, but a general tendency of the Court has been to restrain its judicial creativity. This is partly a result of using textual interpretation, and partly because of a narrow systematic interpretation, see further section 3.6.3.

Systematic interpretation dominates in the preliminary rulings from the 2010s, while textual interpretation appears in cases that deal with more obvious questions.[125] In the preliminary ruling in *Casteels*[126] the Court had the possibility of widening the Regulation to collective agreements, as the question raised was on possible direct effects of Article 48 TFEU. Instead, without further discussion, the CJEU determined that Article 48 TFEU does not have a direct effect. In the infringement case of *Commission v Germany*, there was no doubt that the German social security benefit for the disabled could not be exempted from export.[127] Another preliminary ruling with textual interpretation was *Format*,[128] which dealt with legal framework for issuing Form E101 to posted Polish construction workers. The preliminary rulings in *Lachheb & Lachheb*[129] and *Hliddal & Bornand*[130] revolved around the material scope with regard to different types of national parental benefits, and here textual interpretation was used to determine the Regulation's material scope. For similar textual reasonings on the subject of the material scope of the Regulation, see also the later preliminary rulings of *Würker*[131]

[123] Case C-4/13 *Agentur für Arbeit Krefeld—Familienkasse v Susanne Fassbender-Firman* EU:C:2014:2344.

[124] ibid 44.

[125] cf the joined cases *X v Inspecteur van Rijksbelastingdienst* (C-72/14) and *TA van Dijk v Staatssecretaris van Financiën* (C-197/14), EU:C:2015:564 45.

[126] Case 379/09 *Maurits Casteels v British Airways plc* [2011] ECR I-1379.

[127] Case C-206/10 *European Commission v Federal Republic of Germany*, EU:C:2011:283.

[128] Case C-115/11 *Format Urządzenia i Montaże Przemysłowe sp. z o.o. v Zakład Ubezpieczeń Społecznych* EU:C:2012:606.

[129] Case C-177/12 *Caisse nationale des prestations familiales v Salim Lachheb et Nadia Lachheb* EU:C:2013:689.

[130] Case 216/12 *Caisse nationale des prestations familiales v Fjola Hliddal* (C-216/12) and *Pierre-Louis Bornand* (C-217/12) EU:C:2013:568. Cf AP van der Mei, 'Overview of Recent Cases before the Court of Justice of the European Union (July–September 2013)' [2014] *European Journal of Social Security* 73, 82 ff.

[131] Case 32/13 *Petra Würker v Familienkasse Nürnberg* EU:C:2014:107. Cf AP van der Mei, 'Overview of Recent Cases before the Court of Justice of the European Union (July–September 2013)' [2014] *European Journal of Social Security* 371, 373 ff.

and *Wiering*.[132] The same reasoning is applied by the CJEU in *Bouman*,[133] where the Court proclaimed that the contents and scope of the term 'optional insurance' should be determined with regard to both the wording and its context.[134]

3.6.3. Systematic Interpretation in the Context of Primary Law

As noted, the CJEU interpreted Regulation 1408/71 textually for almost five years from it coming into force. This shows that the legislator had succeeded in upgrading the coordination with Regulation 1408/71, in accordance with the monograph's thesis that the Court uses systematic interpretation only when the Regulation textually does not support the free movement of workers.

The legislator had meant with the inclusion of an exemption in Article 46(3) to solve the problems arising from Regulation 3/58 with regard to the calculation of pensions according to Articles 27 and 28.[135] However, when Article 46(3) was introduced, it turned out that it gave rise to so many serious obstacles to the aggregation of insurance periods that the Court decided to disregard the Article in the preliminary ruling in *Petroni*.[136] The Court found in the preliminary ruling that it was no longer possible to continue interpreting the rules in the light of free movement of workers, as it did with preliminary rulings based on Regulation 3/58. To continue with this case-by-case interpretation was no longer an option, as there were too many unfavourable results of combining the current articles on calculations. The Court therefore declared that Article 46(3) should be disregarded in cases where it restricts the free movement of workers.[137] Instead the CJEU held that the calculations should lead to the best possible outcome—on the basis of calculation based on either the Regulation or national law.[138]

It is striking how often the Court uses the expression 'in the light of' when it applies systematic interpretation to the state of affairs at hand. When the Court uses this expression, it signals a systematic interpretation where the Regulation is

[132] Case 347/12 *Caisse nationale des prestations familiales v Ulrike Wiering and Markus Wiering*, EU:C:2014:300. See AP van der Mei, 'Overview of Recent Cases before the Court of Justice of the European Union (July–September 2013)' [2014] *European Journal of Social Security* 371 ff.

[133] Case C-114/13 *Theodora Hendrika Bouman v Rijksdienst voor Pensioenen* EU:C:2015:81.

[134] ibid 31.

[135] See above section 3.5.3.

[136] Case 24/75 *Teresa and Silvana Petroni v Office national des pensions pour travailleurs salariés (ONPTS), Bruxelles—Belgien* [1975] ECR 1149.

[137] Case 24/75 *Teresa and Silvana Petroni v Office national des pensions pour travailleurs salariés (ONPTS), Bruxelles—Belgien* [1975] ECR 1149 21. Cf Case 19/76 *Pietro Triches v Caisse de compensation pour allocations familiales de la région liégeoise* [1976] ECR 1243 152.

[138] The ruling led to a positive integration in the form of a change in Art 46(3); Council Regulation (EEC) No 1248/92 of 30 April 1992 amending Regulation (EEC) No 1408/71 on the application of social security schemes to employed persons, to self-employed persons and to members of their families moving within the Community and Regulation (EEC) No 574/72 laying down the procedure for implementing Regulation (EEC) No 1408/71, [1992] OJ L136/7.

part of the wider primary law setting; the Regulation is therefore sufficient, even if the Court stretches it to its extreme limits in certain preliminary rulings.[139]

In the *Pierik I* and *Pierik II* cases from 1978, the ambivalent attitude of the CJEU towards using concrete connections between primary law and the Regulation was obvious.[140] Pierik dealt with a health care service that Mrs Pierik had received in another Member State, but which the competent state refused to compensate as there was no prior permission given by the competent Member State as foreseen by Regulation 1408/71.[141] The Court used instead a systematic interpretation in *Pierik II,*[142] where it finds that Article 22 in the Regulation is:

> Within the context of the general objectives of the Treaty ... one of the measures intended to permit a worker who is a national of one of the Member States of the Community ... to receive benefits in kind provided in any other Member State.

This way the Court established a rule in the wider context of the internal market, regardless of whether the crossing of borders happened with the aim to work.[143] However, the Court does not explain in detail which general objectives of the Treaty enable a worker to go abroad for health care.[144]

In the preliminary ruling in *Belbouab*[145] from 1978, the CJEU chose to partly waive the questions posed by the national courts and to interpret the Regulation in a systemic context. The case involved a French citizen who became an Algerian citizen during his time working in Germany. The question of the German court was whether this person's working periods in France, with the aggregation of the periods from Germany in accordance with Regulation 1408/71, was count for nothing because by the time the benefits were calculated, he was no longer within the personal scope of the Regulation. Article 2 of Regulation 1408/71 requires that a person who is covered as a worker or has been covered by the legislation of one of several Member States, should also be a citizen of a Member State.

[139] eg Case C-406/93 *André Reichling v Institut national d'assurance maladie-invalidité* [1994] ECR I-4061, 21; Case C-481/93 *R Moscato v Bestuur van de Nieuwe Algemene Bedrijfsvereniging* [1995] ECR I-3525, 27; Case C-482/93 *E Klaus v Bestuur van de Nieuwe Algemene Bedrijfsvereniging* [1995] ECR I-3551, 21; Case C-251/94 *Eduardo Lafuente Nieto v Instituto Nacional de la Seguridad Social (INSS) and Tesorería General de la Seguridad Social (TGSS)* [1996] ECR I-4187, 33 and 38; and Case C-244/97 *Rijksdienst voor Pensioenen v Gerdina Lustig* [1998] ECR I-8701, 30.

[140] cf also Case 51/73 *Bestuur der Sociale Verzekeringsbank v B Smieja* [1973] ECR 1213.

[141] The *Pierik* case was 20 years before the ground-breaking cases of *Kohll* and *Decker*, where the Court chose to look at health care as services and goods, respectively. See section 5.3.2.

[142] Case 117/77 *Bestuur van het Algemeen Ziekenfonds Drenthe-Platteland v G Pierik* [1978] ECR I-825.

[143] Cf Case 75/63 *MKH Unger, married to R Hoekstra v Bestuur der Bedrijfsvereniging voor Detailhandel en Ambachten te Utrecht* [1964] ECR 177 and Case 44/65 *Hessische Knappschaft v Maison Singer et fils* [1965] ECR 965.

[144] The Court clarified the limitations of health care at the same time as health care became accessible abroad, Case 182/78 *Bestuur van het Algemeen Ziekenfonds Drenthe-Platteland v G Pierik* [1979] ECR 1977.

[145] Case 10/78 *Tayeb Belbouab v Bundesknappschaft* [1978] ECR 1915.

This requirement of citizenship is the crux of the matter—when should a person be a citizen according to the Regulation? Is it when the person works or when the person asks for benefits? The CJEU referred in paragraph 7 of the preliminary ruling to the principle of legitimate expectations. This goes hand in hand with the requirement of citizenship, which refers only to the working period. The CJEU clarifies that this principle stems from Article 94.2 of the Regulation, which acknowledges and protects legitimate expectations when they have been acquired by a citizen in a Member State. The interpretation is far-reaching, but the Court chose to draw the conclusion from the rules of the Regulation, and not to decide the case on the general principle of legitimate expectations.

The preliminary ruling in *van Roosmalen*[146] dealt with the issue of whether an unpaid priest could be seen as self-employed, thus be covered by the rules of the Regulation on export of the Dutch invalidity benefits to his country of residence, which was Belgium. The issue was resolved by the CJEU's reference to the objective of Article 51 of the primary law Regulation, which is 'to contribute towards the establishment of the greatest possible freedom of movement for migrant workers'.[147] With this objective in mind, the Court decided that the unpaid priest should be seen as self-employed as understood by Regulation 1408/71. The Court could have stopped here in its ruling, but instead chose to strengthen it by adding that this free movement 'is one of the foundations of the Community'. The Court had not only used the primary law principle of free movement of workers in *van Roosmalen*, but also expressed that it is in a cornerstone of the Community.

A relevant question is whether the Regulation can limit a Member State to apply its own national legislation. This issue has been topical, primarily in the cases that dealt with the rules on determining the applicable legislation, where the view of the Member States—that the Regulation has a cancelling effect—was questioned by the CJEU in the preliminary rulings in *Bosmann*,[148] *von Chamier-Glisczinski*[149] and *Hudzinski*.[150]

[146] Case 300/84 *AJM van Roosmalen v Bestuur van de Bedrijfsvereniging voor de Gezondheid, Geestelijke en Maatschappelijke Belangen* [1986] ECR 3097.

[147] Case 300/84 *AJM van Roosmalen v Bestuur van de Bedrijfsvereniging voor de Gezondheid, Geestelijke en Maatschappelijke Belangen* [1986] ECR 3097.

[148] Case C-352/06 *Brigitte Bosmann v Bundesagentur für Arbeit–Familienkasse Aachen* [2008] ECR I-3827.

[149] Case C-208/07 *Petra von Chamier-Glisczinski v Deutsche Angestellten-Krankenkasse* [2009] ECR I-6095.

[150] Joined Cases C-611/10 and C-612/10 *Waldemar Hudzinski v Agentur für Arbeit Wesel–Familienkasse* (C-611/10) and *Jaroslaw Wawrzyniak v Agentur für Arbeit Mönchengladbach–Familienkasse* (C-612/10) EU:C:2012:339. In *Bosmann* the Court found that it is possible with parallel national benefits as long as these benefits are not paid on the basis of requested contributions or if there is a request for insurance. The CJEU has additionally clarified this approach with rulings in *von Chamier-Glisczinski* and *Hudzinski*, by emphasising that the principle of the Treaty on free movement is not meant to limit/cancel the national social security system of a state. Therefore, the rules of the Regulation on applicable legislation exist only to prevent cumulative risks that can create an impediment to free movement of persons.

This matter had already been dealt with in 1980, in *Jordens-Vosters*,[151] which revolved around the issue whether a complementing compensation by the Netherlands for health care could be issued to a person who was covered by Dutch insurance but living in Belgium. Article 19 of Regulation 1408/71 on sickness benefits regulates the situation where a person lives in a country (B) that is not the competent country (A). The health care is provided, according to the Regulation, by the national system of country B, but country A pays for it. In *Jordens-Vosters* the situation was that the Dutch legislation on invalidity could pay for parts that were outside the national Belgian care. It was 'extra care' in a purely national Dutch context. Could the same generous application be applied in cross-border situations and be added to the Belgian health care despite the Regulation stating that the health care to be given was the Belgian? The CJEU found that understanding the Regulation as restricting the Dutch national law to be applied, in cases when the insured would receive less benefits than if the person had obtained care only under the national legislation, would mean that this is incompatible with both the objective of the Regulation and the purpose of the scope of application of Article 51.[152] Furthermore, the Court maintained that Article 19 of the Regulation was created with the purpose of avoiding collision—namely to avoid the issuance of double benefits. When the Dutch legislation allowed further benefits than those foreseen in the rule of collision, they were not in conflict with Article 19.[153]

Jordens-Vosters differs from *Bosmann* and the subsequent preliminary rulings because in those cases it was a question of determining the applicable legislation. *Jordens-Vosters* dealt instead with the material scope—the question involved Belgian health care that should be given in accordance with the Regulation, thereby removing the possibility to allow the Netherlands' compensation for extra health care, which resulted from purely textual interpretation of Article 19.

The *Jordens-Vosters* and *Bosmann* cases are two sides of the same coin: can the rules of coordination be seen as absolute and lead to restricting the Member States issuing additional social security benefits that would have been issued on the basis of the national legislation? These cases deal with national benefits that are not in collision with the competent/designated Member State's systems: hence their issuance do not lead to a restriction to the free movement of persons. In other words, a person should always get the best of both worlds—except in cases that deal with a genuine collision, which would restrict the free movement of persons.

[151] Case 69/79 *W Jordens-Vosters v Bestuur van de Bedrijfsvereniging voor de Leder- en Lederwerkende Industrie* [1980] ECR 75.

[152] cf the Court's reasoning for aggregation of periods in Case 24/75, where Petroni summarised the legal situation.

[153] Art 19 is slightly odd in this context. It does not designate a competent country, but determines the level of health care or, even more so, a type of health care that should be issued in the country of residence at the expense of the competent state. If the insured person does not live in the competent state, there are two options to choose from: the country of residence provides health care on its own terms or the country of residence provides health care that is given in the competent state. The latter option is not realistic because the country of residence cannot change its health care system to fit health care in accordance with the patient's affiliation.

A similar situation occurred with regard to aggregation and eligibility for orphan benefits. In the four preliminary rulings of *Rossi*,[154] *Laterza*,[155] *Gravina*,[156] and *D'Amario*,[157] the CJEU developed an exception, or put differently, a clarification of Article 78 of the Regulation, to the single state rule. The Court held that in a case where an orphan's benefits from a former competent state would have been higher, the single state rule does not apply, and hence the former Member State has to pay the difference between the two states' benefits. Again sticking to the single state rule situation would have been against the whole underlying objective of the Regulation—to ensure the free movement of workers. It is important to note in this case that the CJEU does not choose to disregard the secondary law, but aims to interpret the Regulation in such a way that Article 78 will not be applied in these exceptions.[158]

In its preliminary ruling in *Salgado Alonso*[159] from 2005 the CJEU found that national legislation can have a hindering effect when migrating workers encounter difficulties in fulfilling national rules. This case indicates the illusory freedom of the Member States when they shape their national social security systems. The Court determined that the Member States are free to shape their own systems as long as they respect EU law, before continuing with a detailed analysis of whether the Spanish legislation could be found to have a hindering effect.[160] The same reasoning was used in the *Allard* case,[161] where the CJEU concluded that the current social contributions need to be paid by everyone who is covered by Belgian social security in a neutral way and that migrating self-employed people shall not be affected more than other categories.

The preliminary ruling in *van Pommeren-Bourgondiën*[162] illustrates a situation where the national legislation prompted a discriminatory treatment. AJ van Pommeren-Bourgondiën lived in Belgium but had worked all her life in the Netherlands. In 1996, she became unwell and from 1997 she received an invalidity benefit. After an amendment of the Dutch legislation, she was informed that from 1 January 2000, when the amendment would take place, she would be covered by the social security of the Netherlands for the employed, but that she would no longer be fully covered by the Dutch system as she did not reside in the Netherlands.

[154] Case 100/78 *Claudino Rossi v Caisse de compensation pour allocations familiales des régions de Charleroi et de Namur* [1979] ECR 831.

[155] Case 733/79 *Caisse de compensation des allocations familiales des régions de Charleroi et de Namur v Cosimo Laterza* [1980] ECR 1915.

[156] Case 807/79 *Giacomo Gravina and others v Landesversicherungsanstalt Schwaben* [1980] ECR 2205.

[157] Case 320/82 *Benito D'Amario v Landesversicherungsanstalt Schwaben* [1983] ECR 3811.

[158] For a critical analysis of *D'Amario* see H Knorpel, 'Social Security Cases in the Court of Justice of the European Communities 1983' [1985] *CMLR* 43, 58 ff.

[159] Case C-306/03 *Cristalina Salgado Alonso v Instituto Nacional de la Seguridad Social (INSS) and Tesorería General de la Seguridad Social (TGSS)* [2005] ECR I-705.

[160] cf recital 17 a, Regulation 883/2004.

[161] Case C-249/04 *José Allard v Institut national d'assurances sociales pour travailleurs indépendants (INASTI)* [2005] ECR 4535.

[162] Case C-227/03 *AJ van Pommeren-Bourgondiën v Raad van bestuur van de Sociale verzekeringsbank* [2005] ECR I-6101.

The Court emphasised in its ruling that even if the Member States retain their competence to shape their own social security systems, they have to respect EU law when exercising these competences, and this should be the case particularly with regard to the free movement of workers.[163] The Court held that the requirement on residence set by the Dutch legislation, under which a person is only covered by parts of the compulsory social security benefits when not residing in the Netherlands, was in accordance with Article 45 TFEU if the conditions of joining an optional supplementary insurance were not less favourable than the conditions of the compulsory social security system enjoyed by the people living in the country. It turned out, however, that according to new legislation in the Netherlands, people living abroad no longer had the right, even optionally, to be fully covered by the Dutch system. The Court therefore held that those living abroad were treated in a less beneficial way than people living in the Netherlands. The Netherlands had therefore disregarded the underlying objective of the Regulation.

In the Finnish preliminary ruling in *Nikula*[164] the CJEU again acknowledged the rights of states to decide on their social security systems.

In the same way, the CJEU has 'sweetened the bitter pill' in the controversial health care cases. In the first preliminary ruling in *Kohll*,[165] the Court emphasised, before opening Pandora's Box, that the Community law does not limit the competence of the Member States when it comes to shaping their social security systems.[166]

A certain restraint on the part of the Court is noticeable regarding the preliminary rulings of the 2010s having systematic elements. In *Bartlett*,[167] the CJEU found by applying a narrow systematic approach that the British Disability Living Allowance, paid to persons with disabilities, in order to strengthen the mobility of people with disabilities, was correctly enlisted as a hybrid benefit, and therefore exempt from export.[168] This preliminary ruling is one of the few where the questioned benefit had not been dismissed from the exemptions set out in Annex IIa.[169]

[163] cf Case C-135/99 *Ursula Elsen v Bundesversicherungsanstalt für Angestellte* [2000] ECR I-10409.

[164] Case C-50/05 *Maija Terttu Inkeri Nikula* [2006] ECR I-7029. The Court emphasised that in calculating the Finnish health care contributions, those who had used the right to free movement and had worked in another country should not end up in a less favourable position from those who 'stayed at home'. Mrs Nikula received two national pensions, and by taking the Swedish pension (for which she had paid contributions) in consideration for the Finnish social security contribution, she paid more contributions than Finnish pensioners. If Mrs Nikula could prove that the Swedish contributions had already been paid, the Finnish authorities could not, in line with EU law, calculate the contribution being paid by including the Swedish pension.

[165] Case C-158/96 *Raymond Kohll v Union des caisses de maladie* [1998] ECR I-1931.

[166] ibid, 17.

[167] Case 537/09 *Ralph James Bartlett et al v Secretary of State for Work and Pensions* [2011] ECR I-3417.

[168] ibid 27.

[169] cf Case C-299/05 *Commission of the European Communities v European Parliament and Council of the European Union* [2007] ECR I-8695, where the Swedish disability allowance and health care benefits were seen as sickness benefits instead of being regarded as modern solutions for disability.

The preliminary ruling in *Partena*[170] saw the CJEU introducing a common EU legal definition of the notion of 'location' (where activities take place). The Court emphasised that the national legislation determines who is to be regarded as employed or self-employed. With regard to the term 'location', pointing to which Member State is competent, the CJEU, however, found that:

> If that concept was also a matter for the legislation of the Member States, it could be subject to contradictory definitions or interpretations by the Member States in question and could lead, for any given person, to the cumulative application of different legislation to the same activity. That overlapping could result in that person having to pay a double social insurance contribution for a single income and would thus penalise a person who had exercised his right to freedom of movement as enshrined in the EU law, which would be in clear contradiction to the objectives of Regulation No 1408/71.[171]

The Court was therefore of the opinion that, in the light of the free movement of persons that the Regulation promotes, the term 'location' cannot, irrespective the Regulation being based on coordination, be left to be determined by the Member States.

The outcome of the preliminary ruling in *Wencel*[172] consisted of a textual interpretation of the rules on applicable legislation, where the Court found that Poland could not withdraw a pension retroactively, unless the rules were neutral and did not influence the migrating workers to a greater degree than those who are insured 'at home'. The Court underlined however, added that Article 45 TFEU restricted the Polish rules, making it less appealing to move across borders.

In the same manner, in *Mulders*[173] the CJEU strengthened its reasoning that the sickness periods taken into account when calculating a pension should be seen in the context of free movement of workers. The CJEU relies also on the underlying objective of Regulation 1408/71 and its special provisions on health insurance of pensioners in *van der Helder* and *Farrington*.[174]

In *Saleminik*[175] and *Bakker*,[176] the Court made a very sophisticated systematic interpretation when it concluded that the residence requirement under Dutch legislation was not in line with the rules of Regulation 1408/71 on determining the applicable legislation. Both preliminary rulings were made in the light of the free movement of workers. The same approach was taken in *Mertens*,[177] where

170 Case C-137/11 *Partena ASBL v Les Tartes de Chaumont-Gistoux SA*, EU:C:2012:593.

171 ibid, 54.

172 Case C-589/10 *Janina Wencel v Zakład Ubezpieczeń Społecznych w Białymstoku*, EU:C:2013:303.

173 Case C-548/11, *Edgard Mulders v Rijksdienst voor Pensioenen*, EU:C:2013:249.

174 Case C-321/12 *F van der Helder and D Farrington v College voor zorgverzekeringen*, EU:C:2013:648. See AP van der Mei, 'Overview of Recent Cases before the Court of Justice of the European Union' (July–September 2013) *European Journal of Social Security* 73. 85 ff.

175 Case C-347/10 *A Salemink v Raad van bestuur van het Uitvoeringsinstituut werknemersverzekeringen*, EU:C:2012:17.

176 Case C-106/11 *MJ Bakker v Minister van Financiën*, EU:C:2012:328.

177 Case C-655/15 *HJ Mertens v Raad van bestuur van het Uitvoeringsinstituut werknemersverzekeringen*, EU:C:2015:62.

the CJEU found that the Regulation articles for determining the competent state in the event of unemployment were not in line with the general aim to have the unemployed covered by the state offering the best conditions for obtaining a new job. The underlying objective with determining the applicable legislation was also emphasized in *De Ruyter*.[178] In subsequent preliminary rulings, such as *Fischer-Lintjens*[179] and *ONEm*,[180] the Court interpreted systematically within the framework of the Regulation, concluding that its current rules were in agreement with the Regulation's overall objective.

The cases that stick out in 2010, in terms of far-reaching systematic interpretations and which strengthen the free movement of workers, are *da Silva Martins*,[181] *García*[182] and *Hudzinski*.[183]

In *da Silva Martins* the Court decided upon whether there is an option to be entitled to a benefit from a previous country of employment, even in the case the country of residence is the competent state. The reasoning of the Court is not concise, but concludes that since the contributions had been paid to the German insurance system, and da Silva Martins would be deprived of a benefit for which there was no risk of doubling, such limitation would be prohibitive to the free movement of workers.[184]

The preliminary ruling in *García* can be considered as explicit, since the entitled persons chose not to apply for certain benefits from the competent state (Spain) so that there would still be an option to be entitled to benefits from the previous competent state (Germany) in accordance with the rules of the Regulation.[185] The Court held in the preliminary ruling that while an extensive understanding of the Spanish and German benefits would bring an end to this type of fraud, this was not possible, as it would be regarded as an obstacle to the free movement of workers.[186]

The preliminary ruling in *Evans*[187] from January 2015 is another example of the cautious attitude of the CJEU,[188] where a systematic interpretation is

[178] Case C-623/13 *Ministre de l'Économie et des Finances v Gérard de Ruyter*, EU:C:2015:123, 33 ff.

[179] Case C-543/13 *Raad van bestuur van de Sociale verzekeringsbank v E Fischer-Lintjens*, EU:C:2015:359, 41 & 42.

[180] Case C-248/15 *Office national de l'emploi (ONEm) v M and M v Office national de l'emploi (ONEm) and Caisse auxiliaire de paiement des allocations de chômage (CAPAC)*, EU:C:2016:220 31.

[181] Case C-388/09 *Joao Filipe da Silva Martins v Bank Betriebskrankenkasse-Pflegekasse* [2011] ECR I-5737.

[182] Case C-225/10 *Juan Pérez Garcia and others v Familienkasse Nürnberg* [2011] ECR I-10111.

[183] Joined Cases C-611/10 and C-612/10 *Waldemar Hudzinski v Agentur für Arbeit Wesel–Familienkasse* (C-611/10) and *Jaroslaw Wawrzyniak v Agentur für Arbeit Mönchengladbach–Familienkasse* (C-612/10), EU:C:2012:339.

[184] cf M Cousins, 'Overview of Recent Cases before the European Court of Human Rights and the European Court of Justice (April 2011–June2011)' [2011] *European Journal of Social Security*, 371, 380 ff.

[185] Case C-225/10 *Juan Pérez Garcia and others v Familienkasse Nürnberg* [2011] ECR I-10111, 47.

[186] ibid, 51–53.

[187] Case C-179/13 *Raad van bestuur van de Sociale verzekeringsbank v LF Evans*, EU:C:2015:12.

[188] cf H Verschueren, 'The EU social security co-ordination system: A close interplay between the EU legislature and judiciary', in P Syrpis (ed), *The Judiciary, the Legislature and the EU Single Market* (Cambridge, Cambridge University Press, 2012) 199.

complemented with a narrow textual interpretation—leading in the end to the conclusion that the competence of the Member States is not restricted with regard to the detailed conditions for joining a Member State's social security system.

Finally, it can be concluded, in short, that the ruling in *Hudzinski* confirms *Bosmann*[189] and *von Chamier-Glisczinski*,[190] through a systematic interpretation method. The Court found in *Hudzinski* that it is fully possible to receive benefits from two Member States simultaneously, regardless of the single state rule. This is possible as long as the objective of the Regulation—to strengthen free movement of workers—is not restricted.[191] Here, the Court adopted an extensive systematic interpretation by stating that the opposite was actually true when the German legislation supported free movement. The preliminary ruling in *Franzen* from spring 2015 can be seen as a consolidation of the case law in this field, by confirming that the country of residence can issue residence-based social security benefits, regardless of another state being the competent one, since the objective of the Regulation would not be restricted in the given situation.[192]

Overall, it can be concluded that just as was the case with Regulation 3/58, the Court has used a systematic interpretation method for the rules of the Regulation when the textual method does not suffice to promote the objective of the Article 48 TFEU.

3.6.4. Teleological Interpretation

The preliminary ruling in *van Munster*[193] from 1994 clearly illustrates the teleological interpretation method used by the Court.[194] The pattern visible in this case, as well as in those before and after it, points to the fact that the complexity of the Regulation forces the CJEU to turn to a teleological interpretation based on the general principles of free movement of workers in order to reach a solution that goes beyond the legal framework of the Regulation.

In *van Munster* the issue at stake was the payment of pension benefits to Mr van Munster from both the Netherlands and Belgium, in accordance with the payments based on years of employment (the pro rata principle). The Dutch law

[189] Case C-352/06 *Brigitte Bosmann v Bundesagentur für Arbeit–Familienkasse Aachen* [2008] ECR I-3827.

[190] Case C-208/07 *Petra von Chamier-Glisczinski v Deutsche Angestellten-Krankenkasse* [2009] ECR I-6095.

[191] Joined Cases C-611/10 and C-612/10 *Waldemar Hudzinski v Agentur für Arbeit Wesel–Familienkasse* (C-611/10) and *Jaroslaw Wawrzyniak v Agentur für Arbeit Mönchengladbach–Familienkasse* (C-612/10), EU:C:2012:339 57.

[192] Case C-382/13 *CE Franzen and Others v Raad van bestuur van de Sociale verzekeringsbank*, EU:C:2015:261. The first question of whether the number of hours worked would affect the ruling on the applicable legislation is also based on a clear systematic interpretation, ibid, 39–53.

[193] Case C-165/91 *Simon JM van Munster v Rijksdienst voor Pensioenen* [1994] ECR I-4661.

[194] cf M Moore, 'Freedom of Movement and Migrant Workers' Social Security: an Overview of the Court's Jurisprudence 1992–1997' [1998] *CMLR* 409, 410 ff.

provided for pensions[195] whereby everyone had the right to an individual pension. This system also included two levels of pension payments, depending on whether the previously employed pensioner's spouse was also retired. If the spouse was working, the individual pension was paid out on the basis of the previous income of the person who retired. If the pensioner's spouse did not work, but was still not of retirement age, there was an addition for the household equal to that person's coming pension.[196] This addition was withdrawn when the other spouse retired as well and started to receive a pension. However, the total amount of pension for a household was kept at the same level as when the working family member retired. Thus there was a generous advance on the part of the Netherlands. The Belgian national pension system, on the other hand, differentiated between pensions calculated on the basis of a household and individual pensions. When calculating the level of payment, the Belgian pension was higher if it was household-based.

In *van Munster*, the spouse received an addition to the pension from the Netherlands, since the wife did not work but had still not reached the age of retirement. When she reached the retirement age, this addition ended as she received an individual pension. As noted above, the Dutch system was designed to ensure that the sum of the spouses' pension was unchanged. When the Belgian authorities learned that Mrs van Munster received an individual pension, they reduced, according to Belgian law, the Belgian pension of Mr van Munster to the level of an individual pension, irrespective of the fact that the total pension sum in the Netherlands remained the same.

Observed separately, both national systems seem logical. In this case, textual interpretation of the national rules as well as the Regulation led to a loss of pension, which would not have happened had Mr van Munster worked in only one Member State throughout his working life.

The CJEU found that the Belgian legislation was neutral—it did not differentiate between Belgian citizens and citizens of other Member States.[197] The CJEU however, placed this issue in a larger EU legal context and concluded that:

> it is not, however, in dispute that the aim of Articles 48 and 51 of the treaty would not be met if, through exercising their right to freedom of movement, migrant workers were to lose social security advantages guaranteed to them by the laws of a Member State. Such a consequence might discourage Community workers from exercising their right to freedom of movement and would therefore constitute an obstacle to that freedom.[198]

[195] The change in pension calculations by the Netherlands followed the directive on gender neutral legislation with regard to social security, Council Directive 79/7/EEC of 19 December [1978] on the progressive implementation of the principle of equal treatment for men and women in matters of social security, [1979] OJ L6.

[196] The background of this system was that the household should be in the same economic situation before the spouse is retired, as after the spouse retires.

[197] Case C-165/91 *Simon JM van Munster v Rijksdienst voor Pensioenen* [1994] ECR I-4661 19.

[198] ibid, 27.

Thus the Court concluded that the Belgian law was not the problem, but instead the interaction with the Dutch legislation.

The Regulation did not foresee an exception in cases where a textual application of the aggregation of pensions would lead to loss of income for a migrating worker. Furthermore, the national legislation was not discriminating per se. On the other hand, the outcome was not desirable with regard to the free movement of workers. The Court concluded that regardless of the fact that there is no discrimination, an obstacle still exists in the coordination of the two national legal systems.[199] The CJEU therefore ruled that the Belgian court needed to solve the national case so that the court: 'as far as it is possible, prevent[s] its interpretation from being such as to discourage a migrant worker from actually exercising his right to freedom of movement.'[200]

There was a similar approach in the preliminary ruling *Vougioukas,*[201] decided in the Grand Chamber.[202] A Greek doctor, Vougioukas, worked in public service for Greece, but had also worked in Germany. The Regulation was not applicable because Vougioukas was a civil servant. Civil servants were (at that time) excluded from the personal scope of the Regulation and therefore could not apply its rules for aggregation of completed periods. Under national law, Greece aggregated periods during which public doctors worked in private practice in Greece. The corresponding periods abroad, however, were not observed under Greek law. The Court acknowledged the hindering effect that the Greek legislation could have on migrating workers. The Court therefore held that the free movement of workers was hindered by the Greek legislation and Vougioukas should be able to aggregate his German completed periods in the same way civil servants in Greece had their private Greek practice periods aggregated. The end result was as if the Regulation had been applied. Verschueren asserts that the outcome of *Vougioukas* indicates that the Court chooses to regard the rules of the Regulation as:

> not so much the ceiling they were intended to be, but merely a floor to be supplemented by additional rights that the CJEU derives directly from the Treaty.[203]

[199] See also section 4.2.4.

[200] Case C-165/91 *Simon JM van Munster v Rijksdienst voor Pensioenen* [1994] ECR I-4661 35; Case C-262/97 *Rijksdienst voor Pensioenen v Robert Engelbrecht* [2000] ECR I-7321, is a direct continuation of *van Munster,* since it deals with the same issues again by the same Belgian court. What prompted the new preliminary ruling was the fact that national legislation prevented national authorities from disregarding a national law. The CJEU once again emphasised that the hindering effects that arose in the *van Munster* case were not allowed by EU law and also by the obligation of sincere co-operation and the need to disregard national legislation preventing national authorities from following the preliminary ruling in *van Munster.*

[201] Case C-443/93 *Ioannis Vougioukas v Idryma Koinonikon Asfalisseon (IKA)* [1995] ECR I-4033, see also section 5.2.2.

[202] R White, *EC Social Security Law* (Harlow, Longman, 1999) 32 ff; F Pennings, *European Social Security Law* 6 edn (Cambridge - Antwerp - Portland, Intersentia, 2015) 18 ff. See also M Moore, 'Freedom of Movement and Migrant Worker's Social Security: an Overview of the Court's Jurisprudence 1992–1997', [1998], *CMLR* 413 ff.

[203] H Verschueren, 'The EU social security co-ordination system: A close interplay between the EU legislature and judiciary', in P Syrpis (ed), *The Judiciary, the Legislature and the EU Single Market* (Cambridge, Cambridge University Press, 2012) 196.

Verschueren states that it is particularly worrisome that the legislator had explicitly exempted certain groups from the personal scope of the Regulation. However, this was not taken into account by the CJEU in *Vougioukas,* when it chose to apply the Treaty instead of the excluding personal scope of the Regulation.[204] Verschueren's indignation illustrates the tension that is created between a coordination instrument and the internal market's legal landscape. The logic of the internal market seems to be that no obstacles are allowed, even if secondary legislation has restricted the personal scope.[205]

The preliminary ruling in *Nemec*[206] is another illustration of how the Court applied a teleological interpretation method when Regulation 1408/71 did not suffice. *Nemec* deals with the calculation of a level of invalidity pension, where the Regulation 1408/71 was not to the migrating worker's benefit.

Nemec, working and residing in Belgium, had been exposed to asbestos in his previous work in France and received compensation for the related occupational injury. The French authorities calculated the compensation for injury at work, according to Regulation 1408/71, on the basis of Nemec's average salary during his last working years in France. However, Nemec had also worked in Belgium in the previous 10 years and he was of the opinion that his more recent (and higher) Belgian salary should constitute the basis for calculation of the level of the French benefit. The dilemma for the Court was that according to Article 58.1 of the Regulation, the basis for calculation was the salary earned in the territory of the former competent state (France). Had Nemec continued to work in France, his French salary would have been the basis for the calculation of his rights. The fact that Nemec used his right of free movement and started working in Belgium led to his compensation level being based on his last income in France, which was from 10 years earlier. The situation could, therefore, be considered a hindrance for Nemec.[207] The CJEU declared that the obligation not to discriminate against migrant workers meant that the benefits should be the same as if Nemec had not exercised his right to free movement.[208] Article 58.1 of the Regulation was

[204] ibid, 197 ff.

[205] cf J-P Lhernould, 'Coordination in the Context of Internal Market Rules or How to Resolve the Midlife Crisis', in Y Jorens (ed), *50 Years of Social Security Coordination: Past—Present—Future* (Luxembourg, European Commission, 2010) 129, 139 ff.

[206] Case C-205/05 *Fabien Nemec v Caisse régionale d'assurance maladie du Nord-Est* [2006] ECR I-10745.

[207] cf Case C-137/04 *Amy Rockler v Försäkringskassan* [2006] ECR I-1441; Case C-185/04 *Ulf Öberg v Försäkringskassan* [2006] ECR I-1453 and Case C-212/06 *Gouvernement de la Communauté française and Gouvernement wallon v Gouvernement flamand* [2008] ECR I-1683.

[208] Case C-205/05 *Fabien Nemec v Caisse régionale d'assurance maladie du Nord-Est* [2006] ECR I-10745, 41. Cf the Court's reasoning when it comes to calculating invalidity and old age pensions in Case C-406/93 *André Reichling v Institut national d'assurance maladie-invalidité* [1994] ECR I-4061; Case C-251/94 *Eduardo Lafuente Nieto v Instituto Nacional de la Seguridad Social (INSS) and Tesorería General de la Seguridad Social (TGSS)* [1996] ECR I-4187; Joined Cases C-31/96–C-33/96 *Antonio Naranjo Arjona v INSS, Francisco Vicente Mateos v INSS and TGSS and INSS v Laura García Lázaro* [1997] ECR I-5501; and Case C-153/97 *Aristóteles Grajera Rodríguez v INSS and TGSS* [1998] ECR I-8645.

applicable, but since it would not be in accordance with the aim of free movement of workers to take Nemec's 10-year-old French salary into account when calculating the level of the benefit, the Court held that Nemec's level of salary should instead be considered as the one he would have had, had he continued to work in France. This teleological interpretation completely alters Article 58.1.[209]

As a last illustration, the preliminary ruling in *Leyman*[210] reveals another gap in the coordination which is a result of differing national legislations.[211] *Leyman* dealt with different approaches by Belgium and Luxembourg on how a person would receive invalidity pension. Under the Belgian system, a person needed to be considered incapable of work for a year, receiving sickness benefits. When the incapacity was determined to be permanent, the person was transferred to the system of invalidity insurance and started to receive invalidity pension. The system in Luxembourg, on the other hand, had no equivalent transitional period and therefore an entitled person would receive invalidity pension from day one.

In light of the above, Leyman, who was entitled to both states' invalidity schemes, was to receive her first Belgian invalidity benefit after one year, and thus being able to aggregate both states' invalidity benefits in accordance with Regulation 1408/71 after one year of the Belgian transitional period. If she had been covered by only the Belgian social security system, she would not have fallen between the systems, because she could simply request sickness benefits during the transitional period.

Regulation 1408/71 governed aggregation of invalidity periods, but could not compensate for Leyman's loss of income in accordance with the Member States' competence to shape their own systems. The Court held, irrespective of this fact, that the consequences of the Belgian legislation were not in line with Article 39 EC (Article 45 TFEU) and decided, just as it had in *van Munster*, that the Belgian authorities needed to disregard the legislation in order to promote the free movement of workers.[212]

In the 2010s, there have so far been five preliminary rulings with teleological interpretation.[213] The first two were *Bergström*[214] and *Dumont de Chassart*[215] in which the Court held that the aggregation of completed periods does not

[209] cf Verschueren who is of the opinion that the CJEU acts as legislator in *Nemec*, since it regards Art 58.1 as *contra legem* to its wording. Paradoxically, according to Verschueren, instead of acknowledging the rule, the Court creates new law. H Verschueren, 'The EU social security co-ordination system: A close interplay between the EU legislature and judiciary', in P Syrpis (ed), *The Judiciary, the Legislature and the EU Single Market* (Cambridge, Cambridge University Press, 2012) 190.

[210] Case C-3/08 *Ketty Leyman v Institut national d'assurance maladie-invalidité (INAMI)* [2009] ECR I-9085.

[211] cf Case C-228/07 *Jörn Petersen v Landesgeschäftsstelle des Arbeitsmarktservice Niederösterreich* [2008] ECR I-6989.

[212] Case C-3/08 *Ketty Leyman v Institut national d'assurance maladie-invalidité (INAMI)* [2009] ECR I-9085, 49.

[213] Apart from those analysed see also Case C-523/13 *Walter Larcher v Deutsche Rentenversicherung Bayern Süd*, EU:C:2014:2458; Case C-266/13 *L Kik v Staatssecretaris van Financiën*, EU:C:2015:188.

[214] Case C-257/10 *Försäkringskassan v Elisabeth Bergström* [2011] ECR I-13227.

[215] Case C-619/11 *Patricia Dumont de Chassart v Office national d'allocations familiales pour travailleurs salariés (ONAFTS)*, EU:C:2013:92.

depend on periods in two Member States; instead it is sufficient to use periods from the Member State from which the person has migrated.[216] The reasoning by the Court is initially based on a strict literal interpretation of the Regulation, amplified by a teleological intrepretation that creates a new notion of aggregation where an aggregation may exist—even in cases where there is nothing to aggregate.[217]

In the third preliminary ruling in *Gardella*,[218] recalling its ruling in *Vougioukas*, the Court confirmed that even though a public servant is not covered by the Regulation, that does not mean that this person cannot aggregate completed insurance periods.[219]

Just as it did when interpreting Regulation 3/58, the CJEU has made use of a teleological interpretation method when neither a textual nor a systematic approach sufficed. By the teleological interpretation method the Court disregards parts of the Regulation that seem to give rise to hindrances with regard to the free movement of workers. Through the teleological method, the CJEU thus strengthens the impact of EU law, regardless of Member States' desire to have a limited coordination of their social security systems.

3.6.5. Conclusion

The CJEU has generally taken a more textual stance to Regulation 1408/71, with *Petroni*[220] being a significant exception where the calculation of pension benefits in accordance with Article 46(3) was not considered to be applicable in situations that would limit free movement. This textual interpretation tendency lasted until the mid-1990s, when the Court broke new ground by introducing the non-discrimination principle in the field of social security[221] and far-reaching preliminary rulings on cross-border health care.[222] However, textual interpretation continues to dominate, in spite of these developments from the 2000s.

[216] The equal treatment of facts from another Member State by the Court is further developed in section 4.3 below.

[217] See also section 4.3.

[218] Case 233/12 *Simone Gardella v Istituto nazionale della previdenza sociale (INPS)*, EU:C:2013:449.

[219] cf *Amy Rockler v Försäkringskassan* [2006] ECR I-1441 and Case C-185/04 *Ulf Öberg v Försäkringskassan* [2006] ECR I-1453; see section 5.2.1. See also AP van der Mei, 'Overview of Recent Cases before the Court of Justice of the European Union' [July–September 2013] *European Journal of Social Security* 73, 79 ff.

[220] Case 24/75 *Teresa and Silvana Petroni v Office national des pensions pour travailleurs salariés (ONPTS), Bruxelles—Belgien* [1975] ECR 1149.

[221] See also section 4.2.

[222] See also section 5.3.

3.7. REGULATION 883/2004

Regulation 883/2004 has been in force since 1 May 2010. Between then and the end of 2016, 10 preliminary rulings have been given.

By comparison with Regulation 3/58, there was a delay of over five years before the CJEU passed a ruling, in 1964—*Unger v Bestuur*.[223] In the case of the Regulation 1408/71, the CJEU passed a ruling three years after the Regulation had entered in force (in *Callemeyn*),[224] and there were five preliminary rulings the following year.

Both Regulation 3/58 and Regulation 1408/71 were marked with far-reaching preliminary rulings at a relatively early point. In the case of Regulation 883/2004, the preliminary ruling in *Brey*[225] can be considered its *Unger v Bestuur* or *Petroni*. This preliminary ruling is presented in detail in Chapter 6 below. Here it suffices to say that *Brey* is not only one of the most important, but also one of the most complex preliminary rulings recently given by the CJEU in the field of social security. The ruling has bearing on both the relationship between the national social security systems and Regulation 883/2004, as well as with regard to the relationship between the Regulation and Directive2004/38,[226] which can have an impact on the long term sustainability of national social security systems.

What characterises all three ground breaking preliminary rulings is that they take a broader approach. Both *Unger v Bestuur* and *Petroni* are based on the free movement of workers in a broad systematic context. Similarly, in *Brey*, the Court tried to place the Austrian social benefit and its eligibility requirement in two, parallel legal contexts.[227]

On the basis of a mere 10 preliminary rulings, it is difficult to conclude that the CJEU has taken a decisive step in a textual or a more systematic direction. It is, however, to be noted that the CJEU did not question the new rules that had been introduced in the field of unemployment. Namely, the Court established in *Jeltes*[228] that the legislator wanted to change the unemployment rules, by introducing new formulations into Article 65.2. The Court found that the new rule could certainly be seen as hindering some cross-border migrants who were unemployed and who could no longer receive compensation from their previous states. With

[223] Case 75/63 *MKH Unger, married to R Hoekstra v Bestuur der Bedrijfsvereniging voor Detailhandel en Ambachten te Utrecht* [1964] ECR 177.

[224] Case 187/73 *Odette Callemeyn v Belgium* [1974] ECR 553.

[225] Case C-140/12 *Pensionsversicherungsanstalt v Peter Brey*, EU:C:2013:565.

[226] Directive 2004/38/EC of the European Parliament and of the Council of 29 April 2004 on the right of citizens of the Union and their family members to move and reside freely within the territory of the Member States amending Regulation (EEC) No 1612/68 and repealing Directives 64/221/EEC, 68/360/EEC, 72/194/EEC, 73/148/EEC, 75/34/EEC, 75/35/EEC, 90/364/EEC, 90/365/EEC and 93/96/EEC, OJ [2004] L 158.

[227] cf AP van der Mei, 'Overview of Recent Cases before the Court of Justice of the European Union' [July–September 2013] *European Journal of Social Security* 73; 75 f.

[228] Case C-443/11 *FP Jeltes and others v Raad van bestuur van het Uitvoeringsinstituut werknemersverzekeringen*, EU:C:2013:224.

a textual interpretation of the current Article 65.2, as well as a rare reference to the Regulation's preparatory work,[229] the Court, however, found that the de facto aim of Regulation 883/2004 was to change the coordination of the unemployment benefits.

The preliminary ruling in *I v Health Service Executive*[230] shows that the CJEU takes into account what people personally consider to be their place of residence. The circumstances were however very specific for the Irish citizen I, who fell ill during a stay in Germany with a life-threatening illness that left him tied to the healthcare provided by Germany. Even though I spent 11 years in Germany, he was still seen as a resident of Ireland, by the Court, since, among other reasons, he did not consider himself to be a resident of Germany.[231]

The preliminary ruling in *I* was on Article 11.3.e, determining the applicable legislation on basis of residence.[232] The preliminary ruling in *Ministerstvo práce a sociálních věcí v B*,[233] in contrast, ruled, in a systematic direction, that the term *residence* with regard to workers in Regulation 883/04 has not undergone a significant change in relation to the same term in Regulation 1408/71, and the fact that Czech citizen B—who worked in France and thereby was covered by French social security in accordance with the rules of the Regulation—owned a registered residence in Czech Republic did not influence the ruling on insurance affiliation.[234]

The fifth ruling, *Dano*,[235] decided by the Grand Chamber, confirms *Brey* in finding that hybrid benefits are within the jurisdiction of Directive 2004/38 and therefore can be made subject to a right of residence. The Court referred in these parts to its reasoning in *Brey*. The same goes for *Alimanović*[236] and *García-Nieto*[237] which also deal with the relation between Regulation 883/2004 and Directive 2004/38.

[229] The CJEU has on a few occasions referred to preparatory work, such as in Case 6/60 *Jean E Humblet v Belgium* [1960] ECR 1125, with reference to negotiations between the Member States. The CJEU found that one could not draw any conclusions what the parties intended with specific wording in the minutes to the current legislative act. A relatively new reference appeared in Case C-583/11 *P Inuit Tapiriit Kanatami and others v European Parliament and EU Council*, EU:C:2013:625, where the CJEU refers to preparatory works in order to determine that the change in the TFEU in the right of action has given both legal and physical persons option to, under less strict conditions, seek annulment of acts with general applicability, with the exception of legislative acts. See also Case C-443/11 *FP Jeltes and others v Raad van bestuur van het Uitvoeringsinstituut werknemersverzekeringen*, EU:C:2013:224, 33–34.

[230] Case C-255/13 *I v Health Service Executive*, EU:C:2014:1291.

[231] ibid 56.

[232] cf M Cousins, 'Habitual Residence: Factor (Legal) Fiction?—Commentary on the Case of I v Health Service Executive at the European Court of Justice' [2014] *European Journal of Social Security* 385 who argues that the CJEU's argumentation shows a preliminary ruling where a person, to an almost undue extent, is placed at the centre.

[233] Case C-394/13 *Ministerstvo práce a sociálních věcí v B*, EU:C:2014:2199. See also AP van der Mei, 'Overview of Recent Cases before the Court of Justice of the European Union' [January—September 2014] *European Journal of Social Security* 371, 376 ff.

[234] Case C-394/13 *Ministerstvo práce a sociálních věcí v B*, EU:C:2014:2199, 35.

[235] Case C-333/13 *Elisabeta Dano and Florin Dano v Jobcenter Leipzig*, EU:C:2014:2358.

[236] Case C-67/14 *Jobcenter Berlin Neukölln v Nazifa Alimanovic and Others*, EU:C:2015:597.

[237] Case C-299/14 *Vestische Arbeit Jobcenter Kreis Recklinghausen v Jovanna García-Nieto and Others*, EU:C:2016:114.

Trapkowski[238] dealt with the issue of which parent is entitled to parental benefits, and is based on a textual interpretation, where the Court found that the framework of the Regulation does not make any difference between parents; both have the right to claim benefits, and it is for the national authorities to decide on the rights to the benefits.

In the preliminary ruling of *Knauer* the Court found that the broadest systematic interpretation was to be used on how to understand the assimilation of facts, Article 5, Regulation 883/2004: 'in determining the scope of a provision of EU law … its wording, context and objectives must all be taken into account.'[239]

The tenth preliminary ruling, *Commission v Malta*,[240] underlines that the Regulation is a coordination Regulation, where each Member State reports the social security benefits it considers to be covered by this coordination to the Commission. Thus it is not up to the other Member States to question social security benefits that are not on the list of benefits covered by the Regulation. Here, the Court determines through textual interpretation, supported by the principle of sincere cooperation, that a state independently has to report and enlist the social security benefits to be covered by the coordination.

It can be seen as symptomatic, but the fact that six of the 10 preliminary rulings focus on the notion of residence indicates the impact of Union citizenship; it also indicates a possible increase in individualisation of the concept of residence in the context of social security, as seen in *I v Health Service Executive*.

3.8. CONCLUSION

Chapter 3 has analysed how the CJEU's interpretation methods has had an impact on the coordination of the social security system under Regulation 3/58, Regulation 1408/71 and Regulation 883/2004.

The conclusion is that when it comes to national social security systems, sovereignty erosion has increased in relation to the internal market and that this erosion continues, notwithstanding the interpretation method.

A first limitation of the Member States' independent decision-making already occured when the original six Member States agreed upon an EU legal coordination of the national social security systems. In situations where the Regulation insufficiently promoted the free movement for workers, the Court has used a systematic or teleological interpretation method and in that way strengthened the Regulation's impact. These preliminary rulings, in turn, have led the EU legislator to consolidate the Regulation so that it is in line with the case law and the current

[238] Case C-378/14 *Bundesagentur für Arbeit—Familienkasse Sachsen v Tomislaw Trapkowski*, EU:C:2015:720.

[239] Case C-453/14 *Vorarlberger Gebietskrankenkasse and Alfred Knauer v Landeshauptmann von Vorarlberg and Rudolf Mathis*, EU:C:2016:37, 27.

[240] Case C-12/14 *Commission v Malta*, EU:C:2016:135.

standing of the EU law. This means that sovereignty is continuously eroding, now through positive integration, over time.

The internal market and Article 48 TFEU have served as starting points for the analysis of whether the CJEU interpretation methods can be seen as a factor of integration. It is, however, important to note that Article 48 TFEU focuses on the free movement for workers, not on a coordination of the national social security systems; the European Parliament and the Council are to

> adopt such measures in the field of social security as are necessary to *provide freedom of movement for workers* [emphasis added]; to this end, they shall make arrangements to secure for employed and self-employed migrant workers and their dependants:
>
> (a) aggregation, for the purpose of acquiring and retaining the right to benefit and of calculating the amount of benefit, of all periods taken into account under the laws of the several countries;
> (b) payment of benefits to persons resident in the territories of Member States.

Nevertheless, Member States have strived to achieve a balance between the free movement of workers and states' desire to maintain the independence of their national social security systems. For this reason, Regulation 883/2004 emphasises in its recitals:

> (1) [T]he rules for the *coordination* of national social security systems fall within the framework of the free movement of persons
>
> …
>
> (4) [I]t is necessary to respect the special characteristics of national social security legislation and to only *draw up* a system of *coordination*. [Emphasis added.]

As the majority of the rulings analysed refer to Regulation 3/58 and Regulation 1408/71, it is important to note that in 1958 the Member States still had not experienced the full impact of EU law. This is why it is not surprising that Regulation 3/58 tried to balance the aim of promoting the free movement of workers and the independence of the national social security systems. In the recitals to the preamble, Regulation 3/58, recital 4, notes the importance of having a coordination that would secure the completed periods of migrating workers.

By the time Regulation 1408/71 was adopted, the EU legal environment had changed and the Member States had become more aware of the inherent dynamics of EU law. This is why Regulation 1408/71 speaks in its preamble about taking into account the differences between the States when coordination is developed in order to facilitate the free movement of workers:

> (2) Whereas the existing provisions for coordination can, as a whole, be developed, improved and to some extent simplified at the same time, *taking into account the considerable differences existing* between national social security legislations. [Emphasis added.]

Both Regulation 1408/71 and Regulation 883/2004 emphasise that the Member States still are in charge of their systems and that the Regulation only coordinates systems within the internal market. It has, furthermore, been confirmed, in case law as well, that the Member States have the competence to shape their own national social security systems.[241]

There is no doubt that there is an obvious conflict between the far-reaching free movement of workers and a more limited coordination. The primary law focuses on enabling a free movement of workers; the secondary law emphasises the respect for the national systems, parallel to this objective, referring to the fact of the Regulation being limited to the coordination of the Member States' social security systems.

The paradox is that the Member States are aware that the free movement of workers is essential for the internal market. At the same time, the Member States wish to retain their national social security systems untouched. For this reason, the Member States have underlined this ambiguous relation in the first revision of Regulation 883/2004, in connection with the enactment of Regulation 987/2009.

The new Recital 17a talks about a balance between these two opposite interests:

> 17 a) Once the legislation of a Member State becomes applicable to a person under Title II of this Regulation, the conditions for affiliation and entitlement to benefits should be defined by the legislation of the competent Member State while respecting Community law.[242]

The monograph's analysis of more than 300 cases in the field of social security, the majority of which are preliminary rulings, shows that the CJEU has acted dynamically when interpreting the original Regulation 3/58. As shown, the Court has based its rulings in a majority of the cases on primary law. This stands in strong contrast to *Watson*, who is of the opinion that the CJEU only became proactive in the preliminary rulings that dealt with cross-border healthcare in *Kohll* and *Decker*.[243] *Rasmussen* is of the understanding that the CJEU was biding its time after its rulings *van Gend en Loos* in 1963 and *Costa v ENEL* in 1964, before becoming active again when the legislative processes within the European Economic Community ground to a halt.[244] In the light of the rulings by the CJEU with regard to Regulation 3/58, one can, however, observe a pro-active Court ever since its first ruling in the social security field back in 1963.

The general picture from 1972 onwards, when Regulation 1408/71 became applicable, shows almost the opposite tendencies. Textual interpretation initially

[241] See eg Case 238/82 *Duphar BV and others v Netherlands* [1984] ECR 523, 16 and Case C-70/95 *Sodemare SA, Anni Azzurri Holding SpA and Anni Azzurri Rezzato Srl v Regione Lombardia* [1997] ECR I-3395, 27; Case C-158/96 *Raymond Kohll v Union des caisses de maladie* [1998] ECR I-1931, 19; Case C-282/11 *Concepción Salgado González v Instituto Nacional de la Seguridad Social (INSS) and Tesorería General de la Seguridad Social (TGSS)*, EU:C:2013:86 35; Case C-179/13 *Raad van bestuur van de Sociale verzekeringsbank v LF Evans*, EU:C:2015:12 33; and Case C-515/14 *Commission v Cyprus*, EU:C:2016:30, 38.

[242] Regulation (EC) No 988/2009 of the European Parliament and of the Council of 16 September 2009 amending Regulation (EC) No 883/2004 on the coordination of social security systems, and determining the content of its Annexes, [2009] OJ L 284/43.

[243] P Watson, *EU Social and Employment Law* 2nd edn (Oxford, Oxford University Press, 2009) 72.

[244] H Rasmussen, *European Court of Justice* (Copenhagen, GadJura, 1998) 23 and 55.

dominated, only to shift in a more systematic direction five years later, and was then replaced in the second half of the 1990s by a new textual interpretation period. The rulings from the new century are mainly built on systematic reasoning, as the issues before the Court are not especially obvious.

Depending on the perspective, there are two tendencies: one where the Court, in a quantitative way, has been more proactive when interpreting Regulation 3/58 than Regulation 1408/71, and another perspective where the EU seems to have been more inconsistent with interpreting Regulation 1408/71.

When analysing these tendencies, one has to keep in mind two things. First, Regulation 1408/71 was a significantly more precise legislative product from the beginning taking into consideration the specific EU legal environment. While Regulation 3/58 was initially a legislative product created between states, Regulation 1408/71 was instead a 'real' product of EU law. Regulation 1408/71 also incorporated the case law of Regulation 3/58, thus consolidating the sovereignty erosion that had already taken place. As Regulation 1408/71 was updated in accordance with the objective set out in Article 48 TFEU, there was therefore no imminent need for the CJEU to read the Regulation 'in the light of' the primary law.

Secondly, one can be tricked into thinking that this textual interpretation implies that the CJEU respected the Member States' desire to maintain their sovereignty over their social security systems. This would indeed be the case if the coordination and Regulation 1408/71 had been static. What needs to be taken into account is the fact that Regulation 1408/71 has continuously been amended. It was amended more than 30 times, with case law consolidated and changes in national legislations observed, and that in itself implies a type of consolidated sovereignty erosion over the years. When the CJEU interpreted the consolidated Regulation 1408/71 it did so by a textual interpretation, but a textual interpretation that has very little in common with Regulation 3/58 and its original idea of coordination.[245]

Irrespective of this, a general picture of how the CJEU has acted in the field of social security still emerges.[246] The monograph's analysis shows that the CJEU relies on the wording of the Regulation as long as it supports the free movement of workers. The textual interpretation is thus limited to cases where the interpretation of the legal framework already follows the objective of Article 48 TFEU on implementing free movement for workers. In other words, as long as the rules of

[245] Regulation 1408/71 came to be amended on an average of once a year until it was replaced by Regulation 883/2004: H Verschueren, 'The EU social security co-ordination system: A close interplay between the EU legislature and judiciary', in P Syrpis (ed), *The Judiciary, the Legislature and the EU Single Market* (Cambridge, Cambridge University Press, 2012) 178. See also Roberts, 'A Short History of Social Security Coordination', in Y Jorens (ed), *50 Years of Social Security Coordination; Past—Present—Future*, Report of the conference celebrating the 50th Anniversary of the European Coordination of Social Security, Prague, 7 & 8 May 2009 (European Commission, 2009) 24.

[246] cf N Nic Shuibhne, *The Coherence of EU Free Movement Law* (Oxford, Oxford University Press, 2013) 9.

the Regulation are not contradictory and are in accordance with the overall objective, there is no reason to disregard the secondary law.

The analysis has also shown that, where it finds the Regulation's framework to be vague or insufficient to promote the freedom of workers, the CJEU turns to the overall primary law objective, instead of respecting the more limited coordination mechanisms.[247]

When the Regulation is placed in a broader context from the perspective of the CJEU, it looks like 'the beginning of the end' for an absolute autonomy of the Member States over their social security systems. As social security forms a crucial part of a national state, the Member States have naturally been interested in keeping their autonomy when it comes to their social security systems. This can be observed in the Member States' interventions before the CJEU over the years.[248] Most of these interventions from the Member States are based on the view that one cannot or rather should not broaden or interpret a preliminary ruling outside the Regulation and by doing that avoiding the primary law effect, as shown in the chapter.[249]

Finally, the analysis in Chapter 3 shows that a teleological interpretation method has been applied by the CJEU when unexpected circumstances arise, irrespective of the national rules at stake being neutral. When that is the case, the Court fills this gap by finding that the outcome of the national rule makes free movement of workers more difficult.

In conclusion, a framework can be said to exist in the field of social security where, since *Unger v Bestuur*, the CJEU has consequently given free movement of workers first priority. The Court has not, according to the analysis, taken into

[247] The CJEU is certainly bound by the construction of the preliminary ruling, since it needs to answer the questions posed by the national courts. The Court has, however, often preferred to reformulate a question and eventually seek further clarifications from the national court, rather than to reject the request: M Broberg and N Fenger, *Preliminary References to the European Court of Justice* (Oxford, Oxford University Press, 2010) 403 ff. See for example reformulations of the House of Lords seven principal issues and 22 questions in Case C-372/04 *The Queen, on the application of Yvonne Watts v Bedford Primary Care Trust and Secretary of State for Health* [2006] ECR I-4325. The Court reformulated these questions and narrowed them down to four more general questions.

[248] A German statement in Case 14/67 *Landesversicherungsanstalt Rheinland-Pfalz v Joseph Welchner* [1967] ECR 331, on the question of understanding how certain German periods are calculated for pensions from two Member States is indicative. The German Government said in its intervention that: 'The German Government, *on whose initiative the system was amended*, was aware of the problem and when it gave its approval to Regulation No. 3 and to Regulation No. 130/63 it was with the intention that the system *should not* be extended to the "substitute" periods.' [Emphasis added.] In other words, Germany tried to explain to the CJEU that the changes made in the Regulation are to be followed, since the Member States agreed on them. Also notable is the statement by the Italian Government in Case 112/76 *Renato Manzoni v Fonds national de retraite des ouvriers mineurs* [1977] ECR 1647, 1651: 'since the Community rules do not establish a common social security system, the rules for co-ordinating the various schemes do not apply when the right to specific benefits is acquired on the basis of a single national legislation'. Here the argument by Italy was that, in certain cases, the Regulation was not to be applied, even though the case was in the material scope of the Regulation.

[249] See for example the argumentation by the Member States with regard to cross-border healthcare, see also section 5.3.

consideration in any significant way the second underlying objective: the respect for independent national social security systems.

Social security systems are built on collective solidarity. This solidarity is now challenged by an individual perspective, where the internal market looks after the best interests of migrating workers.[250]

The remaining question is whether the CJEU has gone too far in its integration aspirations; has it crossed the line and acted as a legislator, with free movement of workers given priority status? *Wiklund* observes how a Europeanisation of the law has led to a new balance between lawyers and politicians, where the judges of the CJEU are on the border between the two.[251] *Bengoetxea* emphasises, on his side, the special role of the Treaty and asserts that the Court acts within its jurisdiction. Bengoetxea is of the opinion that the objective of the Treaty was and is to support integration and the completion of the internal market.[252] The Treaties are strongly objective-oriented, with objectives that the CJEU needs to fulfil in its judicial activities. *Rasmussen* is of a diametrically opposite opinion, stating that there is no legal ground for the CJEU to act as a 'legislator'. According to Rasmussen, the Treaty was never meant to allow the Court to lead the political and legal development, and points to the crisis of confidence that is created when rulings by the Court become political.[253]

Since the Member States have legally limited the competence of the Court, in order to respect the Member States' independent social security systems, one could state that every ruling where the Regulation is placed in the context of the internal market is a political ruling. On the other hand, according to Article 48 TFEU, Regulation 883/2004 has been enacted to ensure free movement of workers. How should the Court, which is bound by the Treaty in its interpretation, act so that these opposing interests are both respected? Is there a margin for the Court or does it have to be either/or? *Bengoetxea*, *MacCormick* and *Moral Soriano* propose here a view that the borderline between law and politics is not so sharp in the case of the EU law. Opposite to the persistent criticism, Wiklund and Rasmussen, they

[250] In Chs 6 and 7 it can be observed how Union citizenship and the EU Charter of Fundamental Rights challenge the national security systems from other perspectives.

[251] O Wiklund, 'Taking the World View of the European Judge Seriously—some reflections on the role of ideology in adjudication', in O Wiklund (ed), *Judicial Discretion in European Perspective* (Stockholm, Norstedts, 2003) 31. See also Weatherill, who is of the opinion that the Court should not act as a legislator in situations related to the internal market. S Weatherill, 'Supply of and Demand for Internal Market Regulation: Strategies, Preferences and Interpretation', in N Nic Shuibhne (ed), *Regulating the Internal Market* (Cheltenham, Edward Elgar, 2006) 38.

[252] J Bengoetxea, 'The Scope for Discretion, Coherence and Citizenship', in O Wiklund (ed), *Judicial Discretion in European Perspective* (Stockholm, Norstedts, 2003) 49. See also T Koopmans, 'Methods of Interpretation', in Wiklund, ibid 81. Koopmans is of the opinion that there is an interaction within the EU law between the specific secondary law rules and the overarching objectives. He takes *Unger v Bestuur* as an example of a preliminary ruling where the interpretation and objective goes hand in hand and where the Court relied on the objective in order to reach a decision that would be in accordance with the law.

[253] H Rasmussen, *European Court of Justice* (Copenhagen, GadJura, 1998) 24.

are of the opinion that EU law is more an area where law and politics overlap. The issue is therefore not to decide what law is and what should be seen as politics, but to take a stand on how to act in the area where law and politics intertwine.[254] Bengoetxea, MacCormick and Moral Soriano are therefore of the opinion that it is not productive to criticise the Court when it seemingly goes beyond textual interpretation. Instead, the questions should be 'whether and by what considerations its decisions are justified, or at the very least, rationally justifiable'.[255]

If this idea is accepted, it can be concluded that the Court has mainly ruled in the field of social security in favour of the internal market, since the Regulation is meant to ensure the free movement of workers. When the Court interprets the Regulation textually, the Regulation is in line with the free movement of workers.

When the Court leads the legislator to take a more integrated direction, it is a case of complex interaction. In theory, the balance will be reinstated; the legislator creates law while the Court rules. However, there is a dynamic process where the Court finds itself in a grey area, and forces the legislator to act, unless the Court takes on a judicial activism that challenges politics. What came first, the chicken or the egg?

We are back again at the starting point and we need to discern the legislator's intentions with regard to the free movement of workers and how it is supported by Article 48 TFEU. The wording of Article 45 TFEU talks about how the free movement of workers needs to be secured. This creates a legal framework of competence for the CJEU (and its judicial activities), where the Court is bound by its mandate, in accordance with Article 19.1 TEU—to ensure that in the interpretation and application of the Treaties the law is observed.[256]

The situation, however, is that the Member States have not given the Court carte blanche in the field of social security, so the Court has still to respect the independence of the national systems. In line with this, one can observe that lately there have been preliminary rulings that respect the wording of the Regulation, even though the Court could have applied a systematic approach.[257]

If there is no clarity on how the Regulation is to be applied in different cross-border situations, then the free movement of persons is hampered at an initial

[254] J Bengoetxea, N MacCormick and L Moral Soriano, 'Integration and Integrity in the Legal Reasoning of the European Court of Justice', in C de Búrca and J Weiler (eds), *The European Court of Justice* (Oxford, Oxford University Press, 2001) 43.

[255] ibid, 44.

[256] Nic Shuibhne concludes that when the original treaty versions are observed, it is obvious that the language in them makes a difference between the (assumed) law and the right. These versions indicate a larger room for manouevre for the Court than what can be found in the Regulations and secondary law. Nic Shuibhne concludes that 'when the Court is "ensuring that the law is observed", it is also empowered to determine what that law actually is'. N Nic Shuibhne, N., *The Coherence of EU Free Movement Law* (Oxford, Oxford University Press, 2013) 2.

[257] cf H Verschueren, 'The EU social security co-ordination system: A close interplay between the EU legislature and judiciary', in P Syrpis (ed), *The Judiciary, the Legislature and the EU Single Market* (Cambridge, Cambridge University Press, 2012) 199 f.

stage, when a migrating person hesitates to move because the competent authorities are not sure whether the Regulation or the primary law has precedence. For this very reason, the authorities from the Member States need to keep themselves on their toes when it comes to systematic and teleological interpretations. It is not enough to apply the Regulation; a broader EU law analysis is required, with a special focus on the internal market. When an outcome can seem deterrent or repellent, the Member States need to apply the EU law so that no 'damage' is done.[258]

It goes without saying that the competent authorities have difficulties in setting aside national legislation and rely on the EU obligation of sincere cooperation in situations where the law is uncertain. The correct application of the EU law is therefore passed on to the national courts and ultimately to the CJEU. This leads to a continued court-driven development where the CJEU takes the lead and not the Regulation.

[258] cf Spaventa: 'the binary approach adopted by the CJEU to expand the rights of individuals without challenging the legality of Community secondary legislation'. E Spaventa, 'The Impact of Articles 12, 18, 39 and 43 of the EC Treaty on the Coordination of Social Security Systems', in Y Jorens (ed), *50 Years of Social Security Coordination: Past—Present—Future* (Luxembourg, European Commission, 2010) 113. See also E Spaventa, 'The Constitutional Impact of Union Citizenship', in U Neergaard, R Nielsen and L Roseberry (eds), *The Role of Courts in Developing a European Social Model: Theoretical and Methodological Perspectives* (Copenhagen, DJØF, 2010) 155 ff.

4

From Equal Treatment to Market Access

4.1. THE PRINCIPLE OF NON-DISCRIMINATION

4.1.1. Introduction

THE PRINCIPLE OF non-discrimination is based on the idea, simply put, that similar situations should be handled the same way, irrespective of nationality.[1] This principle has been developed over the years by the CJEU, and four main tracks can be observed:

1. direct discrimination;
2. indirect discrimination;
3. the market access model;
4. the exit model.

When assessing a situation of potential direct or indirect discrimination, a comparison is made between two groups of persons (between Member States' citizens and migrating workers) in a given setting. Thereafter, it is possible to see if there is any difference in the outcome with regard to the two groups of persons. When it comes to market access, there is no need for such causality assessment. It suffices if a rule *itself* can adversely affect free movement of persons. The market access model also means that constitutional balances are more easily put at the fore, as exceptions to a market access are possible if the Member States provide acceptable and objective reasons for its national legislation. This is especially provocative in light of the fact that the Member States' social security systems are only coordinated, and the Member States still 'own' their systems. The exit model finally has the reverse perspective where the competent state's legislation hinders or discourages its citizens to move freely.

This chapter is divided into three sections. Section 4.2 analyses how Regulation 883/2004 refers to the principle of non-discrimination in its various forms. It is followed by section 4.3, which deals with the equal treatment of facts—a special

[1] See Case C-127/07 *Société Arcelor Atlantique et Lorraine, et al. v Premier ministre, Ministre de l'Écologie et du Développement durable, and Ministre de l'Économie, des Finances et de l'Industrie* [2008] ECR I-9895, 23 and case law referred to therein. See also T Tridimas, *The General Principles of EU Law*, 2nd edn (Oxford, Oxford University Press, 2006) 61 ff.

aspect in equal treatment that is of great importance for cross-border movements in the context of social security.

4.2. APPLICATION OF THE PRINCIPLE OF NON-DISCRIMINATION IN THE FIELD OF SOCIAL SECURITY

4.2.1. Introduction

Coordination can paradoxically be more difficult to implement than harmonisation. Coordination should avoid becoming a harmonisation and at the same time, it should function smoothly in combination with the Member States' changes in their respective social security systems. Naturally, there are areas of tension.

The CJEU has underlined over the years that the Member States have unrestricted competence to shape their own national social security systems.[2] This freedom, however, does not mean that the EU law cannot influence these systems; the Member States' systems need to function within the EU legal context.[3] Regulation 883/2004 aims to strengthen the free movement of persons, and the principle of non-discrimination in its various forms is of essential importance for the Regulation in this aim.[4]

This section of Chapter 4 analyses when (in which situations) and how the CJEU has developed the principle of non-discrimination in the field of social security. The question *when* is answered by comparing when the respective equal treatment approaches were introduced and when they started to be observed in the field of social security. The question *how* is answered through a more thorough analysis of the current case law.

It is important to observe that Regulation 883/2004 and its predecessors are based on the principle of non-discrimination; a migrating worker should enjoy social security benefits of the competent state in the same way as the competent states' citizens. Equal treatment is ensured by two principles on which the Regulation is built: aggregation and exportability.

This section is divided into four sub-sections and the analysis follows the chronological development of non-discrimination by the CJEU: direct discrimination, indirect discrimination, the market access model and the exit model.

[2] cf Case 238/82 *Duphar BV and others v Netherlands* [1984] ECR 523; Case C-70/95 *Sodemare SA, Anni Azzurri Holding SpA and Anni Azzurri Rezzato Srl v Regione Lombardia* [1997] ECR I-3395, 27; and Case C-158/96 *Raymond Kohll v Union des caisses de maladie* [1998] ECR I-1931, 19.

[3] Case C-158/96 *Raymond Kohll v Union des caisses de maladie* [1998] ECR I-1931, 19.

[4] cf P Watson, *Social Security Law of the European Communities* (London, Mansell, 1980) 35 ff; D Sindbjerg Martinsen, 'Social Security Regulation in the EU: The De-Territorialization of Welfare?' in G de Búrca (ed), *EU Law and the Welfare State—In Search of Solidarity* (Oxford, Oxford University Press, 2005).

4.2.2. Direct Discrimination

Direct discrimination is when two groups of people are treated differently. The difficulties in determining whether there is a direct discrimination lie in assessing whether the compared situations are truly equal.[5]

In the field of social security, unequal treatment can result from requirements of nationality or residence. Furthermore, it can appear in connection with aggregation of previous completed periods from other Member States and eligibility requirements in the new competent Member State.

The objective of the Regulation is to neutralise the national social security systems that are based on nationality and/or residence in cross-border situations. For this reason, it is not especially remarkable that the first preliminary ruling dealing with direct discrimination was only delivered 15 years after Regulation 3/58 was enacted. This fact can be taken as confirmation that the coordination functioned well and that the competent authorities relied on the Regulation and acknowledged migrating workers' social security benefits irrespective of whether the national legislation required residence.

Furthermore, over the years, the Member States' legislation has adjusted to the EU law requirements for equal treatment. According to the analysis of the case law below, there are few rulings that deal with direct discrimination. Adjustment to the principle of non-discrimination has taken place either through the inclusion of a paragraph in social security legislation on the fact that EU law 'could limit the applicability of national rules',[6] or by national laws being nationality-neutral.

The first preliminary ruling that dealt with discrimination in the field of social security was *Smieja*,[7] which dealt with a Dutch pension regulation. In order to qualify for a pension, a person needed to be either a Dutch citizen or a resident of the country. This legislation was a classic example of a territorial social insurance within a Member State, which the Regulation aims to bring down in cross-border movements within the Union. The CJEU had no difficulty in concluding that the principle of non-discrimination in the Regulation (Article 8 at the time, in Regulation 3/58) aimed to remove unequal treatment based on nationality, and that basing refusal to pay out benefits on the fact that Smieja was not a Dutch citizen was not viable. The Court stated that:

> This provision is designed to ensure for workers covered by the regulations equality in the area of social security without distinction as to nationality, by prohibiting any discrimination in such matters arising from the national legislation of Member States.[8]

[5] cf the Court's reasoning in Joined Cases C-502/01 and C-31/02 *Silke Gaumain-Cerri v Kaufmännische Krankenkasse–Pflegekasse and Maria Barth v Landesversicherungsanstalt Rheinprovinz* [2004] ECR I-6483, 35.

[6] cf the Swedish Social Security Act, Socialförsäkringsbalk (2010:110), 2 kap., 5 §.

[7] Case 51/73 *Bestuur der Sociale Verzekeringsbank v B Smieja* [1973] ECR 1213.

[8] Case 51/73 *Bestuur der Sociale Verzekeringsbank v B Smieja* [1973] ECR 1213 11.

The preliminary ruling in *Fiege*[9] from the same year dealt with the acknowledgment of completed periods in the colony of French Algeria, which in the meantime had become an independent state. French law acknowledged these completed periods for French citizens, but not for citizens of other Member States, and thereby direct discrimination was a fact. The CJEU found that such periods should be acknowledged for all other Member States' citizens in the context of the Regulation. The CJEU chose to reinforce its ruling by stating that in addition to the Regulation, the primary law principle of non-discrimination was also applicable in the situation.[10] This additional argument was not decisive, but a way for the CJEU to underline the importance of equal treatment with regard to the coordination of social security systems.

Direct discrimination is mainly apparent in legislation that makes a clear distinction between a Member State's own citizens and those who have migrated from other Member States. For example, in the infringement case from 1980, *Commission v Belgium*,[11] the issue was the calculation of an index; according to national legislation, this calculation could only be done if a person was a Belgian national or a resident of Belgium. Furthermore, in *Camera*[12] the CJEU annulled a Belgian legislation that required residence for payment of early retirement pension.

The preliminary ruling in *van Pommeren-Bourgondiën*[13] illustrates how amendments in national legislation can give rise to discrimination. The Dutch court in *van Pommeren-Bourgondiën* wanted clarification of whether EU law allowed amendments of national legislation, according to which a person who had been employed in the country could be fully insured if still residing in the Netherlands, but would no longer be fully insured if he or she moved to another Member State.[14] The Court observed in its preliminary ruling that according to new Dutch legislation, a person living abroad would no longer be covered by certain family benefits, which created a difference between those who lived in the Netherlands and those who lived in another Member State; therefore, there was a case of direct discrimination.[15]

[9] Case 110/73 *G Fiege v Caisse régionale d'assurance maladie de Strasbourg* [1973] ECR 1001.

[10] Case C-110/73 *G Fiege v Caisse régionale d'assurance maladie de Strasbourg* [1973] ECR 1001 14.

[11] Case 150/79 *Commission v Belgium* [1980] ECR 2621.

[12] Case 92/81 *Antonia Camera, married Caracciolo, v Institut national d'assurance maladie-invalidité and Union nationale des mutualités socialistes* [1982] ECR 2213.

[13] Case C-227/03 *AJ van Pommeren-Bourgondiën v Raad van bestuur van de Sociale verzekeringsbank* [2005] ECR I-6101.

[14] However, there was an option when moving to another Member State to sign up for an additional insurance and thus continue to be covered.

[15] cf Joined Cases C-502/01 and C-31/02 *Silke Gaumain-Cerri v Kaufmännische Krankenkasse–Pflegekasse and Maria Barth v Landesversicherungsanstalt Rheinprovinz* [2004] ECR I-6483 35 where the Court found that both EU citizenship and the Regulation precluded unequal treatment in a comparable situation.

Another situation where the principle of non-discrimination arises is when the Regulation itself, despite its objective, is directly discriminatory. The coordination has led in certain situations to results that turned out to be more deterrent than if a person had relied solely on the national legislation. In order not to set aside the rules of the Regulation or annul them, the CJEU has, in such cases, chosen to interpret the current articles of the Regulation 'in the light of' the objective of the Treaty. For example, in *Mancuso*,[16] where the Member States and the Commission had to consider complex calculation rules of Articles 27 and 28 of Regulation 3/58 with regard to aggregation of pension periods, the CJEU found that:

> A different interpretation would lead to a discrimination at the expense of the migrant worker by giving him, in the same legal circumstances, smaller rights than those accorded to the worker who completes the whole of his occupational career in a single Member State.

The CJEU's preliminary rulings with regard to direct discrimination are few, and most of these are neutralised through Article 4, Regulation 883/2004 in itself, as it is directly applicable in the Member States.

Indirect discrimination is a more disguised form of unequal treatment, and determining a causality is more complex. For this reason, it took some time after the CJEU passed its first ruling with regard to the free movement of people in *Smieja* for indirect discrimination to enter the coordination of social security.

4.2.3. Indirect Discrimination

Parallel to obvious and open (direct) discrimination by the national legislation, there can be less obvious discriminatory effects that do not make a distinction between groups of people in an open way, but which make life more difficult for citizens of other Member States who are crossing borders than for the citizens of the competent Member State.

EU law is focused on impact rather than wordings and therefore it has developed a multifaceted principle of non-discrimination.[17] This understanding of the principle of non-discrimination digs into the competence of national legislation in a more comprehensive way than direct discrimination. In direct discrimination, it is usually obvious protectionist measures that are in question, while in indirect discrimination it is more an issue of territorial limitations of a welfare state that follows from the inherent structures of the social security systems.

[16] Case 140/73 *Direction régionale de la sécurité sociale de la région parisienne and Caisse d'assurance maladie de Paris v Carmela Mancuso and Caisse nationale d'assurance vieillesse des travailleurs salariés* [1973] ECR 1449 16.

[17] AP van der Mei, *Free Movement of Persons within the European Community—Cross Border Access to Public Benefits* (Oxford, Hart, 2003) 75, and G Davies, *Nationality Discrimination in the European Internal Market* (Haag, Kluwer, 2003) 28 ff.

In the preliminary ruling in *Kenny*[18] from 1978, the CJEU declared for the first time that an indirect discrimination is not in line with the Regulation:

> if the conditions for loss or suspension of the right were defined in such a way that they would in fact more easily be satisfied by nationals of other Member States than by those of the State of the competent institution.[19]

If *Kenny* is put in the time-line of the general development of free movement of persons, it can be observed the first indirect discrimination case was introduced by the CJEU in 1974, with *Sotgiu*.[20] Four years later, the CJEU transferred these assessment grounds to the national court in *Kenny*. In this way the assessment grounds were expanded for the cases of unequal treatment at hand; the national court had to assess whether the British legislation would put British citizens before Kenny.

A year after *Kenny*, the CJEU dealt with another potential indirect discrimination in *Toia*.[21] The backstory was that France had introduced a benefit that was a national premium for less affluent mothers who had many children.[22] This French support, according to the law, was meant for French mothers with French children. An Italian citizen, Toia, was residing in France and applied for the benefit, even though not all of her children were French citizens. The competent French authority took into consideration the Regulation's principle of non-discrimination and allowed Toia to request the benefit, even though she was an Italian citizen. However, the benefit was not granted in full, as not all substantive conditions were fulfilled: only two of her six children were French citizens. There was no direct discrimination because Toia was allowed to request the benefit. There was, however, a discriminatory effect when compared to French mothers because, in accordance with French law, the children's nationality follows that of their parents. The CJEU said that there was no direct discrimination, but concluded that the rules on equal treatment:

> prohibit not only patent discrimination, based on the nationality of the beneficiaries of the social security schemes, but also all disguised forms of discrimination which, by the application of other distinguishing criteria, lead in fact to the same result.[23]

The conclusion of the Court in *Toia*—that even indirect discrimination is prohibited in accordance with the Regulation—has far-reaching effects for national social security systems, as a welfare state can have other aims than just paying for loss of income in the case of sickness, pregnancy or retirement. A welfare state might wish to promote childbearing, or to encourage people to work beyond their retirement age, or it can aim to adopt rules of control (of fraud) in order to restrict

[18] Case 1/78 *Patrick Christopher Kenny v Insurance Officer* [1978] ECR 1489.

[19] ibid, 17.

[20] Case 152/73 *Giovanni Maria Sotgiu v Deutsche Bundespost* [1974] ECR 153.

[21] Case 237/78 *Caisse régionale d'assurance maladie de Lille (CRAM) v Diamante Toia, gift Palermo* [1979] ECR 2645.

[22] ibid, 3.

[23] ibid, 12.

benefits to the state territory.[24] These aspirations can fall under the broader context that constitutes indirect discrimination.

The preliminary ruling in *Roviello*[25] confirms the CJEU's stance that indirect discrimination can arise in cross-border situations covered by the Regulation. The Court held in *Roviello* that the Court on several occasions had struck not only at open (direct), but also at disguised (indirect) discrimination.[26] With this in mind, the CJEU found that even if the German national legislation was neutral, it was easier for German craftsmen to qualify for the highest category of a pension benefit than for migratory workers, as qualifications/certificates of vocational competence from other Member States were judged differently. This calculation was found by the CJEU to be indirectly discriminatory. This understanding of indirect discrimination is also being withheld by the CJEU in the preliminary rulings in *Paraschi*,[27] *Duchon*,[28] *Celozzi*,[29] and *Klöppel*,[30] all of which confirm that the Regulation's principle of non-discrimination addresses both direct and indirect discrimination. See also *de Ruyter*, where the Court concluded that if a person covered by one Member State system of social security in accordance with the Regulation's rules on applicable legislation irrespective of this fact was required to fund the host state's social security system, this would amount to indirect discrimination.[31]

As indirect discrimination concerns the outcome rather than open distinction between people, the principle can be applied in more and also unforeseen situations;[32] it exposes national social security systems aims, rather than discriminatory legislation. The CJEU's delay in introducing indirect discrimination into the field of social security indicates that the Court was aware that this introduction would de facto expose and lead to a new balance of the Member States' competence in the field of social security as there is a shift to whether the Member States can justify their national legislations rather than the coordination respecting the Member States' autonomy.

[24] For the latter see Case C-406/04 *Gérald De Cuyper v Office national de l'emploi* [2006] ECR I-6947. The CJEU approved the Belgian request for residence in Belgium because controls of whether a person is actually unemployed need to be done without prior notice. If a person resides abroad, such control is not possible.

[25] Case 20/85 *Mario Roviello v Landesversicherungsanstalt Schwaben* [1988] ECR 2805.

[26] ibid, 14.

[27] Case 349/87 *Elissavet Paraschi v Landesversicherungsanstalt Württemberg* [1991] ECR I-4501, 16.

[28] Case C-290/00 *Johann Franz Duchon v Pensionsversicherungsanstalt der Angestellten* [2002] ECR I-3567, 38.

[29] Case C-332/05 *Aldo Celozzi v Innungskrankenkasse Baden-Württemberg* [2007] ECR I-563, 13 and 23.

[30] Case C-507/06 *Malina Klöppel v Tiroler Gebietskrankenkasse* [2008] ECR I-943.

[31] Case C-623/13 *Ministre de l'Économie et des Finances v Gérard de Ruyter*, EU:C:2015:123, 39.

[32] cf Case C-237/94 *O'Flynn v Adjudication Office* [1996] ECR I-2617.

4.2.4. The Market Access Model

The articles of the Treaty that deal with the free movement of workers do not have an equivalent to market access as is the case with regard to the free movement of goods, Article 34 TFEU. The EU was therefore cautious and relatively late in applying the market access model on the free movement of workers—it was introduced only in *Säger*[33] in 1991.[34]

As seen in section 4.2.2, the CJEU has not applied direct discrimination to a significant extent in the field of social security. This is because equal treatment constitutes the linchpin of coordination under Regulation 883/2004 and its predecessors. Most situations involving direct discrimination have been resolved merely by applying the Regulation. Indirect discrimination, however, is more far-reaching and it took time before the CJEU held that indirect discrimination constitutes a part of the Regulation's principle of non-discrimination. In light of this, it could have been expected that the market access model would, just as the case with regard to indirect discrimination, develop the principle from *Säger* onwards until it gradually became a part of the principle of non-discrimination in the field of social security as well. Thus it is somewhat surprising that even though the market access model has far-reaching influence on national competences, the coordination of social security systems is based on this principle ever since Regulation 3/58 in the form of the aggregation principle.[35]

The Regulation is based on the fact that there are differences between national social security systems, and that these differences *themselves* give rise to effects that restrict the free movement of persons. The coordination by the Regulation therefore aims to bridge these hindering effects by prescribing that the aggregation of earned periods from different Member States has to take place in cases where national legislation leads to a loss or to a risk of losing earned rights, which as a result can make it less appealing to take employment in another Member State.

The Court concluded in *Cabanis-Issarte,*[36] that the Regulation contains provisions that are meant to prevent workers from losing social security benefits to which they would have been entitled had they stayed in their last country of work. The case law from the 1990s, such as *Masgio,*[37] *Drake,*[38] and *Paraschi,*[39] confirms

[33] Case C-76/90 *Manfred Säger v Dennemeyer & Co Ltd* [1991] ECR I-4221. See also C Barnard, *The Substantive Law of the EU—The Four Freedoms* (Oxford, Oxford University Press, 2016) 225 ff.

[34] Other preliminary rulings that observed the market model are, among others, Case C-19/92 *Dieter Kraus v Land Baden-Württemberg* [1993] ECR I-1663; Case C-224/98 *Marie-Nathalie D'Hoop v Office national de l'emploi* [2002] ECR I-6191.

[35] Art 6, Regulation 883/2004.

[36] Case C-308/93 *Bestuur van de Sociale Verzekeringsbank v JM Cabanis-Issarte* [1996] ECR I-2097, 40.

[37] Case C-10/90 *Maria Masgio v Bundesknappschaft* [1991] ECR I-1119, 17.

[38] Case C-12/93 *Bestuur van de Nieuwe Algemene Bedrijfsvereniging v VA Drake* [1994] ECR I-4337, 22.

[39] Case C-349/87 *Elissavet Paraschi v Landesversicherungsanstalt Württemberg* [1991] ECR I-4501, 22.

Lepore & Scamuffa,[40] which determined that previously completed periods are to be respected, even in situations where there is no direct or indirect discrimination.

The preliminary ruling in *Moscato* illustrates the legal position in a nutshell by finding that:

> The rule on the aggregation of insurance, residence or employment periods, laid down by Article 51(a) of the Treaty and as implemented, in particular, by Article 38(1) of Regulation No. 1408/71 in relation to invalidity insurance, constitutes one of the basic principles of coordination governing the Community of social security schemes in the Member States, its purpose being to ensure that the exercise of the right, conferred by the Treaty, to the freedom of movement does not have the effect of depriving a worker of social security advantages to which he would have been entitled if he had spent his working life in only one of the Member State. Such a consequence might in practice discourage Community workers from exercising their right to freedom of movement and would therefore constitute an obstacle to that freedom.[41]

There are striking similarities to the market access model, since it aims to remove rules or actions, irrespective of whether they are discriminatory or not, that prevent market access or access to another Member State's labour market. The principle of the Regulation—aggregation of completed periods—is based on the same idea; if a migrating worker has completed periods that are at risk of being lost, or periods in one Member State which can be deemed invalid when that person moves to another Member State, it is unappealing to work in another Member State. This risk of losing completed periods is not based on a discriminatory situation, but it is a result of the Member States' independent systems functioning side-by-side in cross-border settings.

The market access model has, however, been applied in situations where despite the Regulation, a hindering effect on the free movement of workers has occurred.

The preliminary ruling in *van Munster*[42] illustrates this situation in a striking way. In *van Munster* the issue was the payment of pensions to Mr van Munster by both the Netherlands and Belgium, in accordance with the Regulation's rules for payments based on years of employment. The level of pension contributions was calculated, in accordance with the coordination principle of the Regulation, by using national rules. Considered separately, these national systems seemed completely logical, but when they were to be combined in the context of the Regulation, there was a loss of income for Mr van Munster which would not have happened had he worked in one Member State all his life. The Regulation had no solution for this problem. The Court had no choice but to apply the market access

[40] Joined Cases C-45/92 and C-46/92 *Vito Canio Lepore and Nicolantonio Scamuffa v Office national des pensions* [1993] ECR I-6497.

[41] Case C-481/93 *R Moscato v Bestuur van de Nieuwe Algemene Bedrijfsvereniging* [1995] ECR I-3525, 28.

[42] Case C-165/91 *Simon JM van Munster v Rijksdienst voor Pensioenen* [1994] ECR I-4661. See also section 3.6.4 for specific circumstances of the matter.

model that would not punish Mr van Munster for having exercised his right to work in another Member State.[43]

Leyman[44] is another example of the market access model being applied by the CJEU. As in *van Munster*, the CJEU concluded that the situation Leyman faced 'places that worker at a disadvantage in relation to those who are in the same situation of definitive incapacity to work but who have not exercised their right of freedom of movement'.[45] This disadvantage, according to the Court, was 'hardly compatible' with the free movement of workers, so the authorities needed to disregard this legal framework in light of the EU law principle of cooperation in good faith.[46]

The two above-mentioned preliminary rulings deal with situations where national legislations negatively affected the free movement of people. However, the rules of the Regulation itself can also create this kind of hindrance. In *Pinna I*[47] the rules of the Regulation with regard to determining the applicable legislation created a hindrance for more generous French national rules. With regard to this fact, the CJEU declared that:

> Nevertheless, the achievement of the objective of securing free movement for workers within the Community, as provided for by Articles 48 to 51 of the Treaty [45–48 TFEU], is facilitated if the conditions of employment, including social security rules, are as similar as possible in the various Member States. That objective will, however, be imperilled and made more difficult to realize if unnecessary differences in the social security rules are introduced by the Community Law. It follows that the Community rules on social security introduced pursuant to Article 51 of the Treaty must refrain from adding to the disparities which already stem from the absence of harmonization of national legislation.[48]

In light of this, the Court found that the rules of the Regulation created an obstacle to a sound market access, as the level of family benefits exported according to the Regulation to another Member State turned out lower than the same level of family benefits paid in the respective country.

To summarise, it can be concluded that Regulation 883/2004 ensures access to the social security system of the new competent Member State through the principle of aggregation. The Regulation's principle of exportability works the same way when it neutralises residence requirements for payment of social security benefits.

[43] In order to reach the Regulation's objective in this case, the Court stated that national authorities had to respect the loyalty obligation emanating from the Treaty and cooperate to find a solution that relied on the primary law Art 48 32, Case C-165/91 *Simon JM van Munster v Rijksdienst voor Pensioenen* [1994] ECR I-4661. See also Case 249/85 *Albako Margarinefabrik Maria von der Linde GmbH & Co. KG v Bundesanstalt für landwirtschaftliche Marktordnung* [1987] ECR 2345 13 ff that determined the loyalty obligation of the Member States and their authorities.

[44] Case C-3/08 *Ketty Leyman v Institut national d'assurance maladie-invalidité (INAMI)* [2009] ECR I-9085.

[45] ibid, 46.

[46] ibid, 48–49.

[47] Case 41/84 *Pietro Pinna v Caisse d'allocations familiales de la Savoie* [1986] ECR 1.

[48] Case 41/84 *Pietro Pinna v Caisse d'allocations familiales de la Savoie* [1986] ECR 1 21.

As seen above, the CJEU has used the market access model when the Regulation's rules were applicable, but their correct application would influence the free movement of people. In these situations the CJEU has held that with regard to the EU law principle of sincere cooperation, the competent authorities need to deviate from national legislation.

4.2.5. The Exit Model

Cases where a citizen wishes to go to another Member State to exercise the right to free movement, but would be worse off, or risks being worse off when compared to people who stayed, can be regarded as hindered from an exit. This is a situation quite opposite to the market access model that focuses on how national legislation deal with migrating workers moving to another Member State; here, market access is already obstructed upon departure. However, just as with regard to the market access model, Regulation 883/2004 neutralises national legislation that would obstruct departure from a Member State. The aggregation principle of Regulation 883/2004 prescribes that all of the departing person's completed period must be taken into account.[49] Furthermore, also the Regulation's exportability principle can play an active role as benefits will be paid out irrespective of a national law restricting payments abroad.

Just as with the market access model, the situations of the exit model, in the context of social security, are to be found where the Regulation is either not applicable or its framework did not foresee a hindering outcome in a cross-border situation.

An example of the latter is found in the preliminary ruling in *Nikula*.[50] The CJEU underlined in its decision that the Member States maintain an autonomous right to decide upon their systems regarding social security contributions. However, the Court concluded that when doing so, Member States needs to take into account that those who have exercised their right to freely move and work in another Member State shall not end up in a position that is worse than if they had stayed at home.

The Court has also applied the exit model in situations where only primary law has been applicable, such as in *Vougioukas*,[51] *Öberg*[52] and *Rockler*,[53] where the CJEU repeated its findings in *Masgio*:[54] the provisions that prohibit or deter someone from leaving their home country and exercising their right to free

[49] R White, *EC Social Security Law* (Harlow, Longman, 1999) 65 ff.
[50] Case C-50/05 *Maija Terttu Inkeri Nikula* [2006] ECR I-7029.
[51] Case C-443/93 *Ioannis Vougioukas v Idryma Koinonikon Asfalisseon (IKA)* [1995] ECR I-4033.
[52] Case C-185/04 *Ulf Öberg v Försäkringskassan* [2006] ECR I-1453.
[53] Case C-137/04 *Amy Rockler v Försäkringskassan* [2006] ECR I-1441.
[54] Case C-10/90 *Maria Masgio v Bundesknappschaft* [1991] ECR I-1119.

movement are seen as hindering, even if these provisions are applied irrespective of nationality.[55]

The exit model thus has a bearing in situations that are not covered by the Regulation's personal or material scope, and which in some way give rise to a shadow effect. This effect appears regardless of the Member States having independent competence; the internal market influences national social security systems, no matter whether the situation is covered by Regulation 883/2004 or not.

4.2.6. Objective Justifications and the Problems with Proportionality

Member States' national welfare models are based on an idea of national solidarity. The EU aims, on the other hand, to support free movement from the perspective of integration, to guarantee migrating workers access to the social security system in the Member State of employment. Regulation 883/2004 tries to bridge these two opposing interests by dismantling the territorial scope of the national social security systems using the principle of non-discrimination.

As seen in section 4.2.4, market access is the model that leads to the biggest effects on national social security systems, as there is not necessarily a causality between the obstructive rule and the outcome. There is a general tendency toward rulings based on the market access principle.[56] This tendency is criticised by both Davies[57] and Barnard.[58] The latter finds that the balance of interests has shifted, from attention to whether a national law hinders free movement, to the situation in which Member States are exposed, to 'opportunistic challenges to a whole variety of national laws never intended to interfere with free movement'.[59]

One of few examples when the CJEU found that a hindering restriction has been deemed proportionate is the preliminary ruling in *Geven*,[60] where the CJEU found that the German rules were indirectly discriminatory, as the law entailed a residence requirement in order to be eligible for a German childcare allowance.[61] The Court found, however, that the German objective with the childcare allowance, which was to support childbearing in Germany, was objectively justifiable.[62]

[55] ibid, 17 and 18.

[56] C Barnard, 'Derogations, Justifications and the Four Freedoms: Is State Interest Really Protected?', in C Barnard and O Odudu (eds), *The Outer Limits of European Union Law* (Oxford, Hart, 2009) 285 and 289.

[57] G Davies, *Nationality Discrimination in the European Internal Market* (Haag, Kluwer, 2003) ch 7, 'Discrimination is Better than Market Access'.

[58] C Barnard, *The Substantive Law of the EU—The Four Freedoms* (Oxford, Oxford University Press, 2016) 228 ff.

[59] ibid 220.

[60] Case C-213/05 *Wendy Geven v Land Nordrhein-Westfalen* [2007] ECR I-6347.

[61] The referring national court had in its request for a preliminary ruling raised a question based on Regulation 1612/68, not Regulation 1408/71. Therefore, the question on whether the rules of Regulation 1408/71 were applicable was not brought to the fore.

[62] It is interesting how the same objective justification ground was rejected by the CJEU in Case C-237/78 *Caisse régionale d'assurance maladie de Lille (CRAM) v Diamante Toia, gift Palermo* [1979] ECR 2645.

The Court further concluded that the German residence requirement was proportionate as it enabled, through an exception rule, that frontier workers, under certain circumstances, could also receive the benefit.

The preliminary ruling in *De Cuyper*[63] shows that the CJEU agrees that it is justifiable that there are effective means of control of social security benefits. The CJEU approved the Belgian requirement of residence in Belgium with regard to unemployment benefits, since it is not possible for Belgium to carry out fraud controls in other Member States. The Member States have further been successful in asserting planning needs in *Smits & Peerbooms*[64] and the need for maintaining a financial balance in *Habelt.*[65]

Nevertheless, national issues such as distribution of welfare and family policy are naturally directed inward and do not take into consideration cross-border situations. Such national eligibility requirements are thus at risk of being seen as indirectly discriminating or as an obstacle to market access. Dougan talks about how the Court, every time it goes beyond the Regulation, curtails the sovereignty of political authorities.[66] Furthermore, national eligibility requirements often do not show flexibility; instead they are categorical for reasons of legal certainty. Thus even if national considerations are accepted as objectively acceptable reasons, it is difficult for them to cope with the subsequent assessment of proportionality, since the internal market aspect is not what the national legislator had in mind.

4.3. EQUAL TREATMENT OF FACTS

4.3.1. Introduction

Equal treatment can be ensured in various ways. It does not necessarily involve national legislations making a distinction; it can also be authorities not taking into account facts or events from another Member State in accordance with national legislation.

The CJEU found in *Roviello,*[67] *Kauer,*[68] *Paraschi,*[69] and *Duchon*[70] that when national legislation does not take into account circumstances in another state, this may be against the principle of non-discrimination.

[63] Case C-406/04 *Gérald De Cuyper v Office national de l'emploi* [2006] ECR I-6947.

[64] Case C-157/99 *BPM Smits, married Geraets v Stichting Ziekenfonds VGZ and HTM Peerbooms v Stichting CZ Groep Zorgverzekeringen* [2001] ECR I-5473.

[65] Joined Cases C-396/05, C-419/05 and C-450/05 *Doris Habelt* (C-396/05), *Martha Möser* (C-419/05) and *Peter Wachter* (C-450/05) *v Deutsche Rentenversicherung Bund* [2007] ECR I-11895.

[66] M Dougan, 'Expanding the Frontiers of EU Citizenship by Dismantling the Territorial Boundaries of the National Welfare States', in C Barnard and O Odudu (eds), *The Outer Limits of European Union Law* (Oxford, Hart, 2009) 149 ff.

[67] Case 20/85 *Mario Roviello v Landesversicherungsanstalt Schwaben* [1988] ECR 2805.

[68] Case C-28/00 *Liselotte Kauer v Pensionsversicherungsanstalt der Angestellten* [2002] ECR 1343.

[69] Case C-349/87 *Elissavet Paraschi v Landesversicherungsanstalt Württemberg* [1991] ECR I-4501.

[70] Case C-290/00 *Johann Franz Duchon v Pensionsversicherungsanstalt der Angestellten* [2002] ECR I-3567.

Regulation 883/2004 codified this case law by introducing a new article. Article 5 of the Regulation adds on to the general equal treatment principle in Article 4, by stating that the Member States should take into account equivalent benefits acquired under the legislation of another Member State, as well as taking account of like facts or events occurring in any Member State as though they had taken place in its own territory.

Article 5 can be understood in different ways. Does it deal with merely a codification of current case law, or can its wording also lead to an expansion of the material scope of the Regulation so that Article 5 changes national legislation in the sense of a matter?[71]

If a person applies to have completed periods from another Member State acknowledged, according to Article 5 a, it needs to be a case of 'equivalent benefits'. If it is a question of essentially different benefits, equal treatment is not possible. *Knauer* is the first preliminary ruling that deals with how to understand the term 'equivalent benefits'.[72] The CJEU held in that case that a purely textual reading of Article 5 does not clarify this. Furthermore, the CJEU stated that the fact that the two benefits are covered by the Regulation is not enough for them to be considered as 'equivalent benefits'. The Court emphasised instead that what needs to be determined is the objective of those social security benefits.[73] In light of this precondition, the CJEU found that the two old-age benefits in *Knauer* had the same overall objective—to secure the same standard of living as before the retirement. By this overall objective the CJEU could treat the two pensions as 'equivalent benefits'. The CJEU chose in *Knauer* not to rest upon the differences in the construction of the benefits. Instead, the Court placed the focus on the overall objective of the social security benefits. In this sense one can trace a possible future expansion of the material scope of Article 5, where the Member States will no longer be able to hide behind technicalities with regard to their social security benefits.

4.3.2. Case C-257/10 *Swedish National Social Insurance Office v Elisabeth Bergström*

Can the income earned in another Member State form a basis for calculation of national benefits, even when there is no income to aggregate with from the (new) competent state? The *Bergström* case[74] illustrates this intricate issue.

[71] Rennuy is of the opinion that the provisions go further than just codifying: N Rennuy, 'Assimilation, Territoriality and Reverse Discrimination: a Shift in European Social Security Law?' [2011] *European Journal of Social Law* 289, 293.

[72] Case C-453/14 *Vorarlberger Gebietskrankenkasse and Alfred Knauer v Landeshauptmann von Vorarlberg and Rudolf Mathis*, EU:C:2016:37.

[73] Case C-453/14 *Vorarlberger Gebietskrankenkasse and Alfred Knauer v Landeshauptmann von Vorarlberg and Rudolf Mathis*, EU:C:2016:37, 34.

[74] Case C-257/10 *Försäkringskassan v Elisabeth Bergström* [2011] ECR I-13227.

This preliminary ruling dealt with a Swedish citizen, Elisabeth Bergström, who had worked in Switzerland since 1994. She had a daughter in 2002 and the family decided to move back to Sweden some time afterwards. Elisabeth Bergström did not take a job in Sweden as she stayed at home with her daughter. She applied for Swedish parental benefit based on the income that she had in Switzerland, invoking the bilateral agreement between Switzerland and the EU, according to which this situation is covered by Regulation 1408/71.[75]

The Swedish National Social Insurance Office (*Försäkringskassan*) rejected Elisabeth Bergström's request for parental benefit based on the income she had earned in Switzerland. She was instead granted the basic parental benefit on the basis of residence in Sweden. The *Försäkringskassan* held in its decision that the rules of the Regulation were applicable to the case; however, in light of EU law and national law, in order to receive parental benefit above the basic level, at least one last working day must have been carried out in Sweden; unless a person has worked in Sweden, there is no Swedish period to be aggregated with the Swiss period.

Article 72 of Regulation 1408/71, regulating the aggregation of the employment periods with regard to family benefits, seems to support the *Försäkringskassan*'s understanding:

> Where the legislation of one Member State makes acquisition of the right to benefits conditional upon the completion of periods of employment, the competent institution of that State shall take into account, to the extent necessary, periods of employment completed in the territory of any other Member State, as if they had been completed under its own legislation.

En route the *Bergström* case passing through the Swedish Administrative Courts, the CJEU decided its preliminary rulings *Rockler*[76] and *Öberg*,[77] where the CJEU found that the rules of primary law dealing with free movement can be applied to Swedish family benefits. In light of these preliminary rulings, the Swedish Supreme Administrative Court requested a preliminary ruling by the CJEU with regard to two questions:

1. Under European Union law, in particular [the Agreement] and Article 72 of [Regulation No 1408/71], can a qualification period for family benefit in the form of income-related benefit for childcare be completed in its entirety through employment and insurance in Switzerland?
2. Under European Union law, in particular [the Agreement] and Articles 3(1) and 72 of Regulation No 1408/71, is income earned in Switzerland to be equated with domestic income in the determination of entitlement to family benefit in the form of income-related benefit for childcare?'

[75] Agreement between the European Community and its Member States, of the one part, and the Swiss Confederation, of the other, on the free movement of persons [2002] OJ L114/6.

[76] Case C-137/04 *Amy Rockler v Försäkringskassan* [2006] ECR I-1441.

[77] Case C-185/04 *Ulf Öberg v Försäkringskassan* [2006] ECR I-1453.

The question was, in essence, whether a person with only Swiss periods of employment was eligible for Swedish parental benefit on a higher income-related level—a question of 'aggregation' without aggregation—and in addition if the level of parental allowance could be determined on the basis of the Swiss income.

The CJEU first concluded that Elisabeth Bergström was to be regarded as a migrating worker when she returned to Sweden and applied for family benefits. The CJEU added that, in accordance with the Regulation and the EU-Switzerland Agreement, a person does not need to work in Sweden to still be regarded as a migrating worker according to the Regulation.[78]

The CJEU concluded by textual interpretation that neither the rules of the Regulation nor the rules of the EU-Switzerland Agreement require a person to have one period aggregated with another period.[79] This interpretation was set in a systematic setting by the Court emphasising that the rules on aggregation needs to be understood in the EU legal context, as the objective of the Regulation, based on Articles 45 and 48 TFEU, is to:

> secure the aggregation for migrant workers and their dependants, for the purposes of acquiring and retaining the right to benefit and of calculating the amount of benefit, of 'all periods' taken into account under the laws of the several countries.[80]

The Court concluded that the aim of the EU-Switzerland Agreement is to ensure free movement of workers between the signatories. Furthermore, the principle of non-discrimination in Article 8a in the Agreement ensures that migrating workers will be treated equally with those who have not exercised their right to free movement.[81]

In light of the above, it was not possible, according to the CJEU, for the Swedish National Insurance Office to request that an insurance period should have been completed in Sweden, in order to have the Swiss periods taken into account for the process of aggregation.[82]

4.3.2.1. *The Preliminary Ruling's Incidental Value*

One may question whether a preliminary ruling on the EU-Switzerland Agreement can have a general binding effect on EU law.

A preliminary ruling is certainly binding for the national court that turns to the CJEU. However, preliminary rulings can have the general effect of a precedent, so

[78] Case C-257/10 *Försäkringskassan v Elisabeth Bergström* [2011] ECR I-13227, 26–28 and 33.

[79] ibid, 41.

[80] ibid, 42.

[81] ibid, 43.

[82] The CJEU also had to decide whether the Swiss salary could constitute a basis for the level of payments of parental allowance. In this respect, the CJEU relied on relevant articles dealing with calculation in combination with the objective-led interpretation, as the rules assume that there is an income in Sweden to which the Swiss income can be compared. The Court found that income based on sickness benefits should be based on the corresponding Swedish salary. Therefore, the Court did not take Bergström's Swiss income as the basis.

that in principle, all national courts need to take into consideration the case law that follows the preliminary rulings by the CJEU. It is up to national courts to turn to the CJEU with a question of interpretation, if they are not sure whether the preliminary ruling is relevant to a case they need to resolve.[83]

When it comes to *Bergström*, the fact is that the CJEU resolved the preliminary ruling on the basis of both Regulation 1408/71 and the EU-Switzerland Agreement. The ruling is universally valid, because the Agreement rests on facilitating the free movement of workers between the signatory parties. Furthermore, article 16.1 of the EU-Switzerland Agreement stipulates that the rights and obligations from Regulation 1408/71 have a corresponding effect in the relations between Switzerland and the EU Member States. *Bergström* was, in line with this, confirmed some years later by the CJEU preliminary ruling in *Dumont de Chassart*,[84] where it was once again held that aggregation of insurance periods does not depend on completed periods in two Member States, but suffices with completed periods from the Member State from which the person has migrated.[85]

4.3.2.2. What is Aggregation, Actually?

Purely semantically, the word 'aggregation' means that one needs to have one thing to be added (aggregated) with another thing. The Oxford Dictionary explains the term aggregate as 'the formation of a number of things into a cluster'. If a person has only completed periods from one Member State or a signatory state, then purely semantically, that person can hardly aggregate these periods with nothing. Taking into account the different language versions of the Member States, there is no indication of any ambiguous translations of the wording in Article 72. Different translations speak more of a need to have one thing to aggregate with in order for aggregation to take place.[86]

EU law, however, differs from semantics. Can it be required in an EU law context that there is 1+1=aggregation, or is it enough to have 1+0 for aggregation to happen? Watson is of the opinion that: 'Aggregation … means the adding together of insurance periods paid in different countries.'[87] Pennings confirms this by saying that: 'the periods completed in a foreign country and those completed under the regulation of the state where benefits are claimed are aggregated'.[88]

[83] cf M Broberg and N Fenger, *Preliminary References to the European Court of Justice* (Oxford, Oxford University Press, 2010).

[84] Case C-619/11 *Patricia Dumont de Chassart v Office national d'allocations familiales pour travailleurs salariés (ONAFTS)*, EU:C:2013:92.

[85] ibid, 50.

[86] cf *totalisation* (Fr), aggregation (En), *Zurücklegung* (De).

[87] P Watson, *Social Security Law of the European Communities* (London, Mansell Publishing, 1980) 17.

[88] F Pennings, *European Social Security Law* 6th edn (Cambridge - Antwerp - Portland, Intersentia, 2015) 10.

So how can an aggregation then take place? Coordination of the social security systems in the EU stems from bilateral conventions developed in Europe in the early 1900s. These conventions included, as an important part, rules on aggregation of insurance periods. The ILO Convention from 1935 on migrating workers' maintenance of pension rights, which is no longer in force, can serve as an example of how aggregation is defined.

Article 2

1. The insurance periods spent by persons who have been affiliated to insurance institutions of two or more Members, shall, irrespective of the nationality of such persons, be totalised by each such institution…

The Convention requires, that a person has been covered by at least two Member States' social security systems in order for an aggregation to take place. However, the ILO Convention does not make the aggregation dependent upon insurance periods stemming from both Member States, in order for an aggregation to take place.

The underlying explanation for the Regulation's lacuna with regard to illogical aggregation is the fact that in the early 1900s, it was not possible to be covered by a social insurance without being employed. This way, Article 2 of the ILO Convention makes sense; one cannot (in fact) invoke aggregation before actually having worked in two countries, and as soon as one has worked in two countries, one also has completed periods from two countries.

Just as in the case of the ILO Convention, Article 72 of Regulation 1408/71 presupposes that the person in question is covered by two or more countries' insurance. However, under Regulation 883/2004 and its widened personal scope a person can be covered by a national insurance on the basis of residence alone and the classic aggregation construction breaks down. Now a person can be covered by a Member State's social security without having worked there.

The EU has not taken this fact into account, and therefore 1+0 is an aggregation in the Regulation's meaning.

4.3.3. Finally: *Öberg* + *Bergström* = True?

The preliminary rulings in *Öberg* and *Bergström* have several similarities in addition to the fact that Ulf Öberg was the lawyer in the *Bergström* case.

With regard to the preliminary rulings, the *Öberg* case was similar to *Bergström*: Öberg had only worked abroad, and therefore could not claim aggregation on incomes from two Member States. However, in the *Öberg* case, Regulation 1408/71 was not applicable, as Öberg's completed periods stemmed from an EU institution and the Regulation foresees a migration between two Member States; instead, the preliminary ruling was based on the Treaty where the CJEU ruled that the Swedish law could hinder the free movement of workers. In the *Bergström* case, Regulation 1408/71 was applicable, and the outcome of the case was instead based on applying its Article 72.

Notwithstanding the fact that EU law does not detract the powers of the Member States to organise their social security systems, the *Bergström* case shows that the Regulation's framework limits national eligibility requirements.[89] The *Öberg* case, on the other hand, shows that also the primary law limits the same national requirements, see further Chapter 5.2.

From a national perspective, the legal position can be summarised as follows: Sweden has to pay work-based parental allowance, despite the fact that neither Bergström nor Öberg had worked in Sweden and thereby contributed to the national social security system.

In summary, it can be concluded that the preliminary ruling of the *Bergström* case and the court's current understanding of the equal treatment of facts challenges national notions of solidarity based upon contributing to solidarity after one's ability. In an internal market context, the free movement of people takes precedence over solidarity; an individual right comes before the collective.

4.4. CONCLUSION

The principle of equal treatment is central to forming a well-functioning internal market. Allowing the Member States to impose different requirements on identical situations would lead to an uneven playing field. However, under the Regulation and the principle of coordination, EU law respects the powers of the Member States to organise their social security systems. This is a delicate balancing act, where EU law only takes precedent where the free movement of workers is hindered.

The essential question is therefore under what circumstances a hindrance is deemed to exist? The evolution of a case law within the field of free movement of workers with regard to the principle of equal treatment shows a direction from direct discrimination towards a focus on impact where the market access lowers the understanding of when there is a hindrance. However, it turns out, perhaps somewhat surprisingly, that this evolution has not affected national social security models in a significant way, as the Regulation is based on the idea of market access.

The analysis in section 4.2.2 shows that any directly discriminating national legislation is neutralised by Article 4 of the Regulation. Hence the case law which concerns direct discrimination within the social security area, is limited, and primarily concerns obsolete national requirements of citizenship or omissions of the Regulation rules. As a paradox, direct discrimination has also occurred with regard to the Regulation itself. Such outcomes are difficult to predict and the CJEU therefore proceeded for instance in *Petroni* with a principle of best outcome overruling a direct discrimination resulting from the Regulation.

[89] eg Case C-70/95 *Sodemare SA, Anni Azzurri Holding SpA and Anni Azzurri Rezzato Srl v Regione Lombardia* [1997] ECR I-3395.

With regard to indirect discrimination, this involves complex causality evaluations, which goes deeper into national competence. These deal with the application of national rules, where differences occur only after a more thorough comparison between a Member States citizens and migrating workers. It can for example concern qualification requirements that are easier for national citizens to fulfil. Through the principles of aggregation and exportability, Regulation 883/2004 has come to term with indirectly discriminatory national rules. Aggregation means that the Member States have to take into consideration completed periods from other Member States and aggregate (add them together), when applying national eligibility requirements. Furthermore, the principle of exportability of benefits means that national benefits cannot be made conditional on residence within the country.

Indirect discrimination, just as direct discrimination, depends on a causal link between nationality/residence and a different outcome. If such a casual link is missing there can be no unequal treatment. In an assessment based on market access, no causal assessment is needed, as the national legislation or rather its outcome can be considered as a hindrance *in itself*. Therefore, from an integration perspective, this broader approach affects national legislation more. However, as shown in section 4.2.4, the market access model is already present as an important component in the Regulation context. This can be explained by the Regulation's aggregation rules that stem from the fact that independent national social security systems differ in terms of qualifications and that they, as such, therefore can lead to outcomes that can hinder the free movement. The CJEU however, as shown in *van Munster* and *Leyman*, has applied the principle of market access also to situations not covered by the Regulation. This tendency to expand the market principle has led and will lead to a reversal in the rules of the game when Member States have to defend their national social security model in a wider internal market context.

The exit model represents the final piece of the CJEU's equal treatment principle. Situations that fall within the Regulation are covered by its rules for aggregation with regard to access as well as exit. The analysis of the case law in section 4.2.5 shows that the exit model is applied to situations not covered by the Regulation's ambit, and hence goes beyond the context of the Regulation.[90]

Similarly, the Court challenges the outer limits of the Regulation in *Bergström* when it assumes a far-reaching understanding of aggregation and equal treatment of facts. The preliminary ruling thus challenges both current national notions of solidarity and Member States' competence to develop their social security systems.

True, the Member States, in order to support the free movement of persons, have limited their autonomy with regard to their social security systems in situations covered by the Regulation's coordination. However, when the CJEU applies the overarching primary law to situations *not* covered by the Regulation, the

[90] When a situation is covered by the regulatory framework, it neutralises the situation in the same way as with market access, through preventative legislation of 'the home state' through the Regulation's aggregation and exportability principles.

national social security systems are affected in unexpected ways. When the Court applies primary law, as in *De Cuyper, Nikula* or *Öberg,* the Regulation lurks in the shadows. The CJEU has glanced in these cases at the Regulation's solution. Thus, a parallel analogy of applying the Regulation rules has occurred. In these situations, the Member States have to justify their welfare models in a broader market context, even though these situations should stay within the competence of the Member States as they do not fall under the Regulation.[91]

Nevertheless, one cannot ignore the fact that the Member States' social security systems operate within the internal market. Situations will arise where the Regulation is not applicable and where the CJEU will be compelled to intervene. What can be criticised, however, is that in these situations, the Court has chosen to apply the market access model. Davies argues that the Court makes things a little too easy for itself.[92] Such considerations should be particularly important when it comes to such a sensitive area as social security.

[91] *De Cuyper* could have been decided based on the Regulation framework: M Dougan, 'Expanding the Frontiers of EU Citizenship by Dismantling the Territorial Boundaries of the National Welfare States', in C Barnard and O Odudu (eds), *The Outer Limits of European Union Law* (Oxford, Hart, 2009) 137.

[92] G Davies, *Nationality Discrimination in the European Internal Market* (Haag, Kluwer, 2003), ch 6, 'Discrimination is Better than Market Access'.

5

Treaty Before the Regulation

5.1. INTRODUCTION

THE STARTING POINT for EU law is that it is a coherent logical system within which new legislation correlates with existing legislation but also with the founding Treaties, Article 7 TFEU. The CJEU, in accordance with this, has stated that secondary legislation shall be interpreted according to the EU treaties and the general principles of law.[1] As seen in Chapter 3, the CJEU has used this starting point and interpreted the Regulation in an internal market context. Chapter 5 analyses how the CJEU has decided on cross-border social security issues not regulated by the Regulation's rules on coordination.

Chapter 5 picks up where Chapter 4 ended and indicates the emergence of a shadow effect in situations outside the Regulation's personal as well as material scope, where the CJEU applies the principle of non-discrimination in its broadest sense and by analogy clings to the Regulation's structure and rules in order to come up with a solution that is in line with promoting the free movement of workers.

Chapter 5 consists of two parts: one part where social security systems not covered by the Regulation have been dealt with by primary law, and another where another free movement makes its entry in what was perceived as the Regulation's exclusive material scope. This latter part, which covers cross-border healthcare, analyses how primary law affects the Regulation framework as well as the balance between the internal market and the Member States' autonomous systems in this regard.

5.2. SOCIAL SECURITY SYSTEMS NOT COVERED BY REGULATION 883/2004

5.2.1. Employees of European Institutions

When a person is employed by any of the European institutions and moves to another Member State for work, there is obviously a cross-border element, but the person in question is not moving between two states' social security systems,

[1] cf Case C-98/91 *Herbrink v Minister van Landbouw* [1994] ECR I-223, 9.

cf Articles 2.1 and 3.1, Regulation 882/2004. The Regulation therefore does not apply to these situations as Regulation 883/2004 coordinates between Member States.

With regard to employees of EU institutions, the CJEU put the individual's migrating movement into a larger context and has therefore applied both the principle of sincere cooperation as well as the primary law, Article 45 TFEU, rather than just noting that the Regulation is not applicable, as previously.[2]

In the first preliminary ruling marking this change of direction, *Gregorio My*,[3] the case concerned a pure intrastate relationship. The issue was about a provision of the Belgian national retirement pension arrangements, according to which the years a person had worked for one of the EU institutions were not taken into consideration.[4] My had partially worked as an employee in Belgium, and partially as an employee at one of the EU institutions. This led to neither Regulation 1408/71 nor the general Regulation 1612/68 on migrating workers being applicable; employees at the institutions were not covered by Regulation 1408/71, and as Gregorio My had worked only in Belgium, there was no cross-border element making Regulation 1612/68 applicable.

The CJEU argued that the principle of sincere cooperation in Article 10 (Article 4.3 TFEU) applied to national legislation which failed to take into account completed periods at an EU institution. Hence Belgium had to take into consideration My's completed EU periods for aggregation with the national completed periods.[5]

In a joint note[6] the Commission and its legal service attempted to calm the upset Member States by emphasising that they had no intention to suggest opening up the Regulation for the benefit of EU officials, in light of the *Gregorio My* case. On the contrary, they stressed that this was a special case, with no general applicability.[7]

The principle of sincere cooperation ended up cutting the Gordian knot in this particular case.[8] The outcome shows a CJEU which cares strongly about the free

[2] See Case C-411/98 *Angelo Ferlini and Centre hospitalier de Luxembourg* [2000] ECR I-8081, 41.

[3] Case C-293/03 *Gregorio My v Office National des Pensions* [2004] ECR I-12013.

[4] At the time of the preliminary rulings, the EU was still a community. I have therefore chosen to use the expressions community and community citizens.

[5] Case C-293/03 *Gregorio My v Office National des Pensions* [2004] ECR I-12013, 49.

[6] Joint note from the Secretariat and the Legal Service of 9 September 2005, *Impact of the My judgment—Taking into account periods of employment with the European Communities*, CA SP TM 247/05, EMPL/1801/05, 09/09/2005.

[7] The Court had previously ruled that a community national working in a Member State different from his or her own would not lose status as a worker as per Art 45 TFEU, because he/she is employed within an international organisation, even if the terms for arrival and stay in the employment country have been regulated in a specific way in an international convention. Joined Cases 389/87 and 390/87 *GBC Echternach and A Moritz v Minister van Onderwijs en Wetenschappen* [1989] ECR 723, 11; Case C-310/91 *Hugo Schmid v Belgium represented by the Minister van Sociale Voorzorg* [1993] ECR I-3011, 20; and Case C-411/98 *Angelo Ferlini v Centre hospitalier de Luxembourg* [2000] ECR I-8081, 42.

[8] The Court has recently confirmed *My* in the preliminary ruling in *Melchior*, where the principle of sincere cooperation has now been extended to contract workers at EU institutions, Case C-647/13 *Office national de l'emploi v Marie-Rose Melchior*, EU:C:2015:54.

movement of workers, even in cases where an individual has not, in a legal sense, moved between two Member States. The CJEU focused on the importance of citizens in Belgium being able to work at an EU institution without ending up in less favourable situations. The preliminary ruling, however, has logical flaws. The Regulation explicitly states, as confirmed in *Ferlini*,[9] that the Regulation cannot be applied even if a cross-border element did exist. Notwithstanding this fact, the CJEU ruled that Belgium had to apply, by analogy, the aggregation principle of the Regulation. In this way a shadow effect of the Regulation emerged in an intrastate setting. It was therefore only a matter of time before a similar situation would arise at the CJEU, but where an actual crossing of borders had taken place. The CJEU decided *Rockler*[10] and *Öberg*,[11] barely a year after *My*, on this issue.

Amy Rockler had been covered by Swedish social insurance, working for a Swedish airline up until 1996. After that, she worked as a secretary at the Commission in Brussels until the end of 1997. She was then again covered by Swedish social insurance while working as a flight attendant in Sweden. Rockler had a daughter in July 1998. *Försäkringskassan* (the Swedish Social Insurance Agency) decided that parental allowance at the higher working based level could not be paid for the first 180 days of Rockler's parental leave. The reason given was that Rockler had not been insured for sickness benefits for at least 240 consecutive days in Sweden prior to the expected delivery date, nor had she completed any period of insurance according to any other Member State's legislation.[12] Rockler appealed the ruling and the Swedish Administrative Court decided, in its review, to place the proceedings on hold and requested the CJEU to deliver a preliminary ruling.

Ulf Öberg worked at the CJEU from 1995 to 2000. During his time in Luxembourg he became the father of a son. Back in Sweden, Öberg applied for parental allowance. *Försäkringskassan* again decided that parental allowance at the higher working based level[13] could not be paid for the first 180 days of Ulf Öberg's parental leave. The reason given was that Öberg had worked at the CJEU during the period prior to the birth of his son, instead of in Sweden. Furthermore, the Agency stated that Regulation 1408/71 was not applicable. Ulf Öberg appealed this decision before the Stockholm County Administrative Court, which turned to the CJEU with a request for a preliminary ruling.

The CJEU chose to rephrase the national courts' questions essentially to whether the free movement of workers required that Swedish law should take into account

[9] Case C-411/98 *Angelo Ferlini and Centre hospitalier de Luxembourg* [2000] ECR I-8081.

[10] Case C-137/04 *Amy Rockler v Försäkringskassan* [2006] ECR I-1441.

[11] Case C-185/04 *Ulf Öberg v Försäkringskassan* [2006] ECR I-1453.

[12] If Amy Rockler had worked in another EU Member State, she would have qualified for the Swedish working based parental allowance according to the rules of the Regulation. Such insurance periods in another Member State would have been aggregated with the Swedish insurance period and thereby result in the required 240 days, entitling Amy Rockler to the family allowance at the higher level.

[13] In comparison to Amy Rockler, Ulf Öberg had not been insured in Sweden at all but had returned to Sweden after the birth of his son. Even if Öberg had worked in another EU country instead of at the CJEU, he would not have qualified for the higher level of the family allowance, as he did not have insurance periods for aggregation but only a foreign insurance period, however cf Bergström, section 4.3.2.

periods during which a worker was covered by a European institution's health insurance system, when applying the Swedish qualification rules on the level of family allowances.[14]

The CJEU first found that Regulation 1408/71 could not be applied, as the Regulation applies between Member States only.[15] The CJEU continued, however, by stating that notwithstanding this, the fact remained that any Member State national who has exercised his or her right to move freely for work and who has worked in another Member State, falls within the scope of Article 39 EC (Article 45, TFEU)[16] and according to former case law, an official within the European Communities is considered a migrant worker.[17] The CJEU underlined that the purpose of the Treaty's provisions for the free movement of persons is to make it easier for nationals of Member States to pursue all kinds of professional activities throughout the whole Union and to prevent measures which may discriminate against these citizens when they wish to work in another Member State. The CJEU hereafter found that provisions preventing or deterring nationals of Member States from leaving their country to exercise their right to free movement may constitute an obstacle, even if those rules apply, irrespective of nationality.[18] In light of this, the Court found that the Swedish national provision constituted an obstacle to the free movement of persons under Article 39 EC as such hindering effects was a fact.[19] During the subsequent review, the Swedish argument that the national legislation should be accepted in order to avoid an increased financial burden was rejected.[20] The periods during which Rockler and Öberg were covered by the European institutions' social security systems would thereby have to be taken into account in the Swedish calculations.

The CJEU confirmed the *Rockler* and *Öberg* rulings in *Gardella*,[21] where it established that a Union citizen working in a Member State other than the state of origin and who is employed by an international organisation is covered by Article 45 TFEU. The Court referred to Regulation 883/2004, finding that the Regulation would not require the possibility of transferring the capital value, which Gardella had earned within the Italian pension system, to the European Patent Office pension system. Therefore the Court reasoned that thereby by analogy the primary law of free movement of persons was not threatened. The CJEU then emphasised, however, that Gardella, as a migrating worker, could not be

[14] Case C-137/04 *Amy Rockler v Försäkringskassan* [2006] ECR I-1441 13, and Case C-185/04 *Ulf Öberg v Försäkringskassan* [2006] ECR I-1453, 10.

[15] Art 2.1 Regulation 883/2004.

[16] Case C-385/00 *FWL de Groot v Staatssecretaris van Financiën* [2002] ECR I-11819, 76.

[17] Joined Cases 389/87 and 390/87 *GBC Echternach and A Moritz v Minister van Onderwijs en Wetenschappen* [1989] ECR 723.

[18] Case C-385/00 *FWL de Groot v Staatssecretaris van Financiën* [2002] ECR I-11819, 78.

[19] Case C-137/04 *Amy Rockler v Försäkringskassan* [2006] ECR I-1441 19, resp Case C-185/04 *Ulf Öberg v Försäkringskassan* [2006] ECR I-1453, 16.

[20] Case C-137/04 *Amy Rockler v Försäkringskassan* [2006] ECR I-1441 24, resp Case C-185/04 *Ulf Öberg v Försäkringskassan* [2006] ECR I-1453, 21.

[21] Case 233/12 *Simone Gardella v Istituto nazionale della previdenza sociale (INPS)*, EU:C:2013:449.

deprived of the right to aggregate the insurance periods in a future consolidation calculation.[22] Thus, just as in *Öberg* and *Rockler*, a primary law aggregation of the insurance periods occurred, despite the absence of applicable secondary law.[23] In a more recent case in Belgium, the CJEU confirmed the case law with regard to employees at the EU institutions, as found in *Wojciechowski*.[24]

What puzzles one is that there is a Regulation that coordinates the social security systems between the Member States. However, the CJEU has argued that this does not mean that the regulatory framework is exclusive and exhaustive. A situation can thus still fall under primary law. A comparison can be made by looking at the Court's way of reasoning in *van Munster*,[25] where the Regulation was applicable but the result did not promote the freedom of workers, and where Belgium was asked to make sure that the national rules were interpreted in such a way that free movement was secured. In *Rockler*, *Öberg* and *Gardella* a primary law reading is applied, which shadows the Regulation even when it is not applicable.[26]

A paradox has evolved; the secondary legislation supports and clarifies the principles of primary law regarding the freedom of workers. However, primary law cannot be ignored in cases where the secondary legislation is not applicable.[27] In these situations, the primary law is seemingly inspired by the Regulation. This way, the primary law has an impact with regard to the competence of the Member States on a material scope which does not fall under the Regulation, *as if* the Regulation was applicable.

A trend towards increased protection for migrant workers directly based on the primary law of the EU Treaty will place greater demands on the authorities administrating the social security and may burden the welfare systems of the Member States in unanticipated ways. The question here is who will cover these additional expenses for the insured or even ineligible individuals who have not contributed to the Member State's social insurance by paying contributions?

5.2.2. A Special System for Civil Servants

The above rulings deal with the EU's social security systems not coordinated by the Regulation. Such situations, however, have also occurred with regard to certain social security systems within a Member State, which have been exempted from coordination as laid down in the Regulation. One example of such a situation is social security schemes for civil servants.

[22] ibid,. 45–46.

[23] In *Gardella* a parallelism has emerged, where the Regulation rules regarding aggregation affected the Court's judgment in situations where the Regulation is not applicable.

[24] Case C-408/14 *Aliny Wojciechowski v Office national des pensions (ONP)*, EU:C:2015:591.

[25] Case C-165/91 *Simon JM van Munster v Rijksdienst voor Pensioenen* [1994] ECR I-4661. See section 3.6.4.

[26] cf Case C-522/10 *Doris Reichel-Albert v Deutsche Rentenversicherungs Nordbayern*, EU:C:2012:475.

[27] G De Búrca and P Craig, *EU Law—Text, Cases and Materials* (Oxford, Oxford University Press, 2011) 108 ff.

A Greek doctor, Vougioukas, was a civil servant covered by Greek state social insurance. During a period of his professional life, Vougioukas had worked in a German state hospital and in 1988 he requested to have these completed periods taken into account in Greece. However, the Greek social security agency held that the Regulation was not to be applied as Vougioukas was covered by the Greek state social insurance, which did not fall under the scope of the Regulation. According to Greek national legislation, completed periods at foreign hospitals could not be considered as pensionable income. Vougioukas was therefore in a similar situation to Öberg and Rockler, as his state social insurance was exempt from the Regulation and its rules regarding coordination in cross-border situations.

The CJEU found in its preliminary ruling in *Vougioukas*[28] that the Member States are free to decide on their own social security systems for government employees,[29] but:

> 40. When it is stipulated in the national legislation that only work periods completed at the national state hospitals are approved as pensionable, while corresponding periods completed at state hospitals in other Member States are not approved, it creates [such] a deterrent effect on the workers.
>
> 41. Such a legislation creates a difference in treatment between the workers who have not exercised their right to free movement and the migrant workers, to the detriment of the latter, since it is only for the workers exercising the right to free movement the question arises, regarding the approval of the completed periods in other Member States within the community.[30]

In the light of the ruling in *Vougioukas*, the outcome of *Öberg* and *Rockler* was not particularly surprising; the free movement of workers must not be restricted by national law, even in situations when the Regulation does not apply. What is surprising, however, is that in its reasoning in *Öberg* and *Rockler* the Court did not refer to *Vougioukas*, which was delivered in 1995. The situations were almost identical and the solution the same: the Regulation cannot be viewed in isolation, and social security systems—which lie outside the scope of the Regulation—still fall under the primary law and where the underlying idea of a coordinative Regulation leads to a coordination and aggregation of the insurance periods between the systems based on primary law rather than secondary law.

The finding in *Vougioukas* that Article 48 TFEU is directly applicable was confirmed in *The Commission v Cyprus*,[31] where the CJEU established that relying on Articles 45–48 TFEU is possible without applying the coordination rules in Regulation 883/2004.[32] This means an expansion of the personal scope in its absolute broadest sense has been confirmed and where migrating workers can claim coordination of social security irrespective of the Regulation being applicable or not.

[28] Case C-443/93 *Ioannis Vougioukas v Idryma Koinonikon Asfalisseon (IKA)* [1995] ECR I-4033.
[29] ibid, 26.
[30] ibid, 40–41.
[31] Case C-515/14 *Commission v Cyprus*, EU:C:2016:30.
[32] ibid, 35.

5.3. CROSS-BORDER HEALTHCARE

5.3.1. Introduction

With regard to healthcare the EU lacks competence. True, the Maastricht Treaty introduced a limited competence where the Union could complement and coordinate Member States' healthcare policy, Article 129 EG.[33] This competence was limited, however, mainly to issues regarding public health.[34] Therefore, this competence has been and still is only complementary to the Member States' exclusive competence.[35]

Healthcare has, however, been a part of the coordination of social security systems since Regulation 3/58.[36] The coordination of the Member States' healthcare focused primarily on the need of migrating workers and their families for healthcare in various situations when a worker lives in one Member State and works in another, or when the family members stay behind while the worker works and lives in the country of employment. In addition to these rules, a possibility for the Member States to independently decide on providing planned cross-border healthcare was introduced by 1408/71 under Article 22.1.c.

Given this limited EU competence, the doctrine has therefore criticised the CJEU for circumventing the Regulation's control by opening up national healthcare systems for a patient mobility based on the free movement of services.[37] The monograph's starting point, as described in section 5.3.2 below, is however, that cross-border healthcare cannot be based on the free movement of workers.[38] Hence, it cannot be argued that there is a parallel primary legal conflict when the free movement of services was applied to cross-border healthcare by the CJEU.[39]

[33] E Szyszczak, 'Patients' Rights: A Lost Cause or Missed Opportunity?' in JW van den Gronde, E Szyszczak, U Neergard and M Krajewski (eds), *Legal Issues of Services of General Interest—Health Care and EU Law* (Haag, Asser, 2011) 105.

[34] T Hervey and J McHale, *Health Law and the European Union* (Cambridge, Cambridge University Press, 2004) 72 ff.

[35] With the Lisbon Treaty, the Member States clarified their competences by specifically enumerating the areas that are exclusive to the Member States, Art 168(7) TFEU. Further, in the Lisbon Treaty's protocol on Services of General Interest, Art 2 reinforces this by stressing that the Treaties in no way restrict the Member States' competences to offer and organise non-financial services of a general character.

[36] See Art 19, Regulation 3/58.

[37] HEGM Hermans, 'Cross-border health care in the European Union: recent legal implications of Decker and Kohll' [2000] *Journal of Evaluation in Clinical Practice* 431–39; VG Hatzopoulos, 'Killing National Health and Insurance Systems but Healing Patients? The European Market for Health Care Services After the Judgments of the CJEU in Vanbraekel and Peerbooms' [2002] *CMLR* 683; VG Hatzopoulos, 'Health Law and Policy: the Impact of the EU', in G De Búrca (ed), *EU Law and the Welfare State: In Search of Solidarity*, (Oxford, Oxford University Press, 2005); P de la Rosa, 'The Directive on Cross-border Healthcare or the Art of Codifying Complex Case Law' [2012] *CMLR* 15.

[38] cf R Giesen, 'Case C-120/95 *Nicolas Decker and Caisse de maladie des employés privés* [1998] ECR I-1831; Case C-158/96 *Raymond Kohll v Union des caisses de maladie* [1998] ECR I-1931' [1999] *CMLR* 841.

[39] cf AP van der Mei, 'Cross-Border Access to Health Care within the European Union: Recent Developments in Law and Policy' (2003) 10 *European Journal of Health Law* 369, 376, which establishes

In accordance with this reasoning, the CJEU has in fact not expanded cross-border healthcare in the true sense from the Regulation's system to a free movement of services. Instead, the healthcare rules in Regulation 883/2004 are meant as an exception, the free movement of services being the general rule.

5.3.2. The Background to the Inclusion of Healthcare in the Regulation

The original six Member States regard healthcare as part of social security, and closely tied to the worker.[40] In the original Regulation 3/58, the coordination of the healthcare focused on situations where a migrant worker ended up with no healthcare, or restricted access. Article 19 Regulation 3/58 dealt with situations equivalent to today's 'blue card'[41] and Article 20 addressed situations when workers and their family members lived in a Member State other than the competent Member State.

As a result of Regulation 1408/71 more precise rules were enacted, where migrant workers and their family could obtain healthcare in either the state of residence or work. In addition to this, a new possibility in Article 22.1.c was introduced, which made it possible for the Member States to offer planned healthcare in another Member State when unable to provide its own healthcare within a reasonable amount of time:[42]

Article 22

1. A worker or business owner satisfying the conditions for the competent State's legislation to receive benefits, when appropriate taking into consideration the provisions of Article 18, and

   …

   (c) who, after authorization from the competent institution, travels to another Member State's territory to receive treatment required by their health condition,

The person who came to challenge the Member States' view that the planned cross-border healthcare system was for the Member States to decide was Mrs Pierik, an early retiree who lived in the Netherlands and covered by the Dutch social security system.

that the Member States themselves wished to develop the mobility of patients before a court-driven development emerged. See also M Cousins, 'Patient Mobility and National Health Systems' (2007) 34 *Legal Issues of Economic Integration* 183, 192.

[40] The social security systems for the original EU6 are all based on the Bismarck model: P Roberts, 'A Short History of Social Security Coordination', in Y Jorens (ed), *50 Years of Social Security Coordination; Past—Present—Future*, Report of the conference celebrating the 50th Anniversary of the European Coordination of Social Security, Prague, 7 & 8 May 2009 (EU Commission, DG Employment, 2009) 19.

[41] Art 19 Regulation 883/2004.

[42] In the light of the strong reaction by the Member States to the *Pierik* saga, there are reasons to believe that the Member States did not intend to introduce an individual right for Member States' citizens.

Mrs Pierik had back pain, which made it impossible for her to work and therefore she had retired early. A couple of times, she had travelled to Germany to receive treatment, which improved her condition considerably. Similar treatment unfortunately was not available in the Netherlands. The treatment had initially been paid for by the Dutch authorities, but later on the responsible social security agency refused to pay, based on the fact that the treatment was not covered by Dutch legislation. Mrs Pierik had worked in the Netherlands her entire career and there was no cross-border element before her travelling to receive the German healthcare. The CJEU's reasoning followed the reasoning in the early preliminary rulings *Unger v Bestuur*[43] and *Hessische Knappschaft*.[44] In these preliminary rulings, the CJEU established that the applicability of the Regulation was not dependent upon whether a worker was in another Member State to work, or was there for other reasons (for example tourism). A cross-border movement had taken place and the Regulation was therefore applicable. The CJEU reasons in the same manner in *Pierik* when it finds that Article 22.1.c is applicable to individuals who fall under the Regulation's personal scope, as a cross-border movement takes place on the basis of the approval of healthcare. The Court ruled thereafter that the wording of Article 22.1.c 'to receive treatment required by their health condition', focused on the condition of the individual rather than on whether the treatment was given by the competent state.[45]

This fact in combination with the vague wording of Article 22.2—that such permission for a treatment 'cannot be denied if the treatment cannot be offered to the individual in question in the Member State [where] he/she resides', in combination with the fact that also 'stationary' persons had this right for treatment—resulted in an unexpected ruling. The outcome of the preliminary rulings in *Pierik I* and *Pierik II* thereby opened up the possibility for extensive cross-border healthcare.

The original EU6, with the introduction of Article 22.1.c, had aimed at introducing cross-border healthcare when Member States themselves could not offer healthcare within a reasonable amount of time. The Member States thereby challenged the case law by introducing Regulation 2793/81.[46] Article 22.2, second paragraph of the new Regulation came to read as follows:

> Permits according to paragraph 1 c cannot be denied, *if the treatment is a benefit given* according to the legislation within the Member State where the individual resides and if he/she cannot receive treatment within that State *within the period of time*, taking into

[43] Case 75/63 *MKH Unger, married to R Hoekstra v Bestuur der Bedrijfsvereniging voor Detailhandel en Ambachten te Utrecht* [1964] ECR 177.

[44] Case 44/65 *Hessische Knappschaft v Maison Singer et fils* [1965] ECR 965.

[45] Case 117/77 *Bestuur van het Algemeen Ziekenfonds Drenthe-Platteland v G Pierik* [1978] ECR I-825, 15.

[46] Council Regulation (EEC) No 2793/81 of 17 September 1981 amending Regulation (EEC) No 1408/71 on the application of social security schemes to employed persons and their families moving within the Community, and Regulation (EEC) No 574/72 fixing the procedure for implementing Regulation (EEC) No 1408/71, [1981] OJ L 275.

account his/her current health condition and the probable progression of the illness, that *is normal* for the treatment in question. [Emphasis added.]

The Member States thereby intended to limit the damage inflicted by *Pierik* by civil disobedience, concealed by new secondary legislation. The new wording produced a possibility rather than an obligation for the Member States' healthcare systems, in such cases where their own systems were unble to provide the care in question.[47]

Thereby, the Regulation came to include a possibility of cross-border healthcare, which did not focus on promoting the free movement for workers. This restriction to cross-border healthcare was challenged by Raymond Kohll, whose daughter was in dire need of expert dental care when the Luxembourg dental care was unavailable during the summer.

In *Kohll*,[48] the question arose whether the social security agency in Luxembourg, *Union des caisses de maladie* (UCM), could refuse Raymond Kohll's daughter specialist dental care in the German border town of Trier instead of in Luxembourg. The UCM rejected the application for care in Trier on the grounds that there was no urgent need for treatment and on the fact that the treatment could have been given in Luxembourg. Raymond Kohll did not accept the rejection and argued that the Treaty articles on free movement of services provided that a prior authorisation from the UCM was not needed for dental care performed in another Member State.

In *Luisi & Carbone* and *Grogan*,[49] the CJEU had found that healthcare is to be regarded as a service. In *Kohll* the Court underlined that the special nature of a service does not prevent healthcare from being considered a service.[50] The Court then had to consider two opposing interests: the free movement of services and the Member States' competence with regard to their healthcare systems. The Court respected this competence, and held that in the absence of harmonisation at Community level, it would be for the legislature of each Member State to determine the terms and conditions for their social security systems,[51] but also the conditions for entitlement of benefits.[52] The Court concluded, however, that irrespective of this

[47] For a critical pre-*Kohll* analysis see R Cornelissen, 'The Principle of Territoriality and the Community Regulations on Social Security (Regulations 1408/71 and 574/72)' [1996] *CMLR* 439, 464 ff. Cf also AP van der Mei, 'Recent Legal Developments—The New Directive on Patients' Rights in Cross-Border Healthcare' [2011] *Maastricht Journal of European & Comparative Law* 382, 383.

[48] Case C-158/96 *Raymond Kohll v Union des caisses de maladie* [1998] ECR I-1931. I have chosen not to analyse *Decker*, as this ruling regards free movement of goods and has no further bearing on the relationship between workers and services.

[49] Case C-159/90 *The Society for the Protection of Unborn Children Ireland Ltd v Stephen Grogan et al* [1991] ECR 21.

[50] Case C-158/96 *Raymond Kohll v Union des caisses de maladie* [1998] ECR I-1931, 20.

[51] cf Case 110/79 *Una Coonan v Insurance Officer* [1980] ECR 1445, 12; Case C-349/87 *Elissavet Paraschi v Landesversicherungsanstalt Württemberg* [1991] ECR I-4501, 15. Cf also Case C-275/96 *Anne Kuusijärvi v Riksförsäkringsverket* [1998] ECR I-3419 29.

[52] See Joined Cases C-4/95 and C-5/95 *Stöber and Piosa Pereira v Bundesanstalt für Arbeit* [1997] ECR I-511, 36.

finding, the Member States should still comply with EU law when exercising their exclusive competence in the healthcare sector.[53]

It is this specific EU legal context that makes the crucial difference between an instrument of international law and an intergovernmental instrument under the EU umbrella.[54]

Having determined this 'conditional independence' for the Member States, the CJEU held that the fact that the case concerned a dental treatment that was part of a social security system did not exclude the treatment from falling under the free movement of services. In light of this, the CJEU ruled that:

> 29. The dispute before the national court concerns treatment provided by an orthodontist established in another Member State, outside any hospital infrastructure. That service, provided for remuneration, must be regarded as a service within the meaning of Article 60 of the Treaty, which expressly refers to activities of the professions.

Given the fact that the treatment was to be considered to be a service within the meaning of the Treaty, the CJEU examined whether the requirement for a prior authorisation by the UCM could constitute a hindrance to the freedom to provide services. Previous case law had held that national restrictions regarding payments were considered to hinder the free movement of services.[55] The Court ruled in light of this that having to apply for prior authorisation constituted a hindrance to the free movement of services.

However, according to EU law, a Member State can, by referring to an objective justification, justify national measures that hinder the free movement of services. Luxembourg, along with the intervening Member States, argued that if patients could start choosing between care in the competent state and in another Member State, this possibility would seriously affect the economic sustainability of national healthcare systems, as many would start taking advantage of this right. Such a fact, according to the Court, could constitute an overriding public interest, which can justify a Member State's restriction of freedom of movement through a system of prior authorisation for cross-border healthcare.[56] The Court ruled, however, that neither the UCM nor the intervening governments had presented any facts that such restrictive national measures were necessary to ensure medical and hospital

[53] This right of Member States to decide over their own system is conditioned by the larger European legal context. Cf Case C-135/99 *Ursula Elsen v Bundesversicherungsanstalt für Angestellte* [2000] ECR I-10409, 33; Case C-227/03 *AJ van Pommeren-Bourgondiën v Raad van bestuur van de Sociale verzekeringsbank* [ECR] 2005 I-6101, 39. See also Joined Cases C-225/02 & C-306/03 *Rosa García Blanco v Instituto Nacional de la Seguridad Social (INSS) and Tesorería General de la Seguridad Social (TGSS) and Cristalina Salgado Alonso v Instituto Nacional de la Seguridad Social (INSS) and Tesorería General de la Seguridad Social (TGSS)* [2005] ECR I-523, 27.

[54] See section 2.3.3, where this distinction is discussed in more detail.

[55] See Joined Cases 286/82 and 26/83 *Graziana Luisi and Giuseppe Carbone v Ministero del Tesoro* [1984] ECR 377 and Case C-204/90 *Hanns-Martin Bachmann v Belgium* [1992] ECR I-249, 31.

[56] Art 52 TFEU enables the Member States the possibility to limit the free movement of services in order to be able to provide medical and hospital care to the extent, in consideration of public health and even the survival of the population, that it is essential to maintain a treatment capacity or a healthcare competence within the national territory.

care in Luxembourg,[57] and therefore the prior authorisation requirement constituted an obstacle to the free movement of services.[58]

The preliminary rulings in *Kohll*[59] and *Decker*[60] stirred up very strong feelings throughout the EU.[61] Patients now had the right to compensation for healthcare, in its capacity as a service, and with this healthcare also followed a right to the related goods obtained in another EU country.[62] This was notwithstanding the fact that the right to planned healthcare was already regulated in Regulation 1408/71.

Dougan has called the initiated legal development 'a conceptual transformation in the territorial identity of the Welfare State'.[63] The nationally regulated healthcare opened by these rulings up for a cross-border competition which could come to challenge the economic sustainability of the social security systems of the Member States.[64]

Major debate broke out among the competent authorities, hospital economists, politicians and academics[65] because the Regulation already had a well-developed

[57] Especially in the light of the Luxembourg system issuing a dental care check for care by a Luxembourg dentist; the system in itself was thus not subjected to destabilisation in a first stage.

[58] The CJEU avoided, however, explaining in detail the difference between the national prior authorisation ruling and Regulation of 1408/71 for prior authorisation procedure in *Kohll*: P Cabral, 'Cross-border medical care in the European Union—bringing down a first wall' [1999] *European Law Review* 387, 392.

[59] Case C-158/96 *Raymond Kohll v Union des caisses de maladie* [1998] ECR I-1931

[60] Case C-120/95 *Nicolas Decker and Caisse de maladie des employés privés* [1998] ECR I-1831.

[61] The former German Minister of Health, Seehofer, invited the Member States to amend the Treaty and was of the opinion that Germany should not obey case law that represented a severe threat to the German healthcare economy: D Sindbjerg Martinsen, *EU for the Patients—Developments, Impacts, Challenges* (SIEPS, 2007) 6, 21.

[62] Free movement of goods was found possible by the Court to be applicable in parallel in Case C-120/95 *Decker*. However, the free movement of goods dimension with regard to healthcare has not developed in any subsequent case law. The main reason is that healthcare is carried out for the most part by health services and not through the issuance of goods. Prostheses and other technical aids could, however, be covered by the *Decker* principle.

[63] M Dougan, 'Expanding the Frontiers of Union Citizenship by Dismantling the Boundaries of National Welfare States?' in C Barnard and O Oduduo (eds), *The Outer Limits of European Union Law* (Oxford, Hart, 2009) 121.

[64] Belgium introduced guidelines that permitted open healthcare in cross-border situations, but only up to a total of 18,500 BF (approximately 400 EUR): A Baeyens, 'Free Movement of Goods and Services in Health Care: a Comment on the Court Cases Decker and Kohll from a Belgian Point of View' [1999] *European Journal of Health Law* 373, 380 ff. These restrictions from the Belgian side were in breach of Union law but were never challenged until more recent case law made the guidelines obsolete. The initial Spanish reaction was that *Kohll* and *Decker* could not be applied to the special Spanish conditions (a recurring argument from many of the Member States: G Strban, *Patient mobility in the European Union: between social security coordination and free movement of services* (ERA Forum, 2013) 391, 397), see C Garcia de Cortazar, 'Kohll and Decker; or That is Somebody Else's Problem. The Challenge Facing Spain' [1999] *European Journal of Health Law* 397. The Dutch government, on the other hand, was more amenable to the case law and found that the Dutch system was already largely consistent: J Van Thiel and T Lugtenberg, 'Decker and Kohll and the Dutch System of Social Health Insurance' [1999] *European Journal of Health Law* 389.

[65] cf eg P Cabral, 'Cross-Border Medical Care in the European Union: Bringing Down a First Wall' [1999] *European Law Review* 387; 'Looking beyond Kohll and Decker', Eurohealth special issue, www.lse.ac.uk/LSEHealthAndSocialCare/pdf/eurohealth/vol7no4.pdf; and VG Hatzapoulos, 'Killing National Health and Insurance Systems but Healing Patients? The European Market for Health Care Services After the Judgments of the ECJ in Vanbraekel and Peerbooms', [2002] *CMLR* 683.

system where it was determined when, and under which conditions, the Member States could allow their patients to receive treatment abroad.[66] The national healthcare systems already faced major challenges in the form of increased costs as a result of an increasingly demanding and aging population. A failure to reform the healthcare systems could also gave rise to national alternative private solutions which would challenge the principle of a healthcare for all.[67] Would the Member States' domestic problems now open up to a cross-border service market as well?

What was forgotten in this heated debate was the fact that the CJEU, in the joined cases of *Luisi & Carbone*,[68] had already ruled that healthcare was to be seen as a service in a cross-border situation.[69] *Kohll* was thus a natural extension to these decisions, in which the CJEU considered that even a state social security system which included healthcare could fall within the scope of the free movement of services.[70]

[66] cf Guidance note of the Commission services on the relationship between Regulations (EC) Nos 883/2004 and 987/2009 on the coordination of social security systems and Directive 2011/24/EU on the application of patients' rights in cross border healthcare, EMPL/-/12, AC 246/12.

[67] W Sauter, 'The Proposed Patients' Rights Directive and the Reform of (Cross-Border) Healthcare in the European Union' [2009] *Legal Issues of Economic Integration* 109, 110.

[68] Joined Cases 286/82 and 26/83 *Graziana Luisi and Giuseppe Carbone v Ministero del Tesoro* [1984] ECR 377.

[69] The understanding of a service was clarified in Case C-211/08 *European Commission v Spain* [2010] ECR I-5267, where the CJEU made a distinction between healthcare as a service one travels to obtain and healthcare one obtains in the case of an accident in another Member State: Tourist healthcare is regulated in Regulation 883/2004 and reimbursement of payments take place between the Member States when healthcare is performed at the expense of the insurance country for emergency healthcare in the country of stay. In *Commission v Spain* the Commission argued that Art 56 TFEU was to also apply 'where such services have become necessary during the connected persons temporary visit in another Member State', ibid, 39, and that Spain could not limit compensation for their insured solely to the regulatory framework of Regulation 1408/71. In the case, the CJEU, however, limited the free movement of services by making a distinction between planned healthcare and healthcare that has been 'unscheduled'—ie the need has arisen during a stay in another Member State. The CJEU, in *Commission v Spain*, tried to establish a logic around the package of services for cross-border healthcare; one always has to see what the basis for the healthcare is—is it ongoing treatment, or is it a sudden illness during a temporary stay in another Member State? Neither Verschueren nor van der Mei find the Court arguing convincing. See H Verschueren, 'The EU social security co-ordination system: A close interplay between the EU legislature and judiciary', in P Syrpis (ed), *The Judiciary, the Legislature and the EU Internal Market* (Cambridge, Cambridge University Press, 2012) 199 ff; AP van der Mei, 'Cross-border Access to Healthcare and Entitlement to Complementary "Vanbraekel Reimbursement"' [2011] *European Law Review* 431, 437 ff; J Baquero Cruz, 'The Case Law of the European Court of Justice on the Mobility of Patients: An Assessment' in JW van de Gronden et al (eds), *Health Care and EU Law* (Haag, Asser, 2011) 83; P de la Rosa, 'The Directive on Cross-border Healthcare or the Art of Codifying Complex Case Law', [2012] *CMLR* 15 19.

[70] After a first far-reaching ruling, normally a calibration process is performed. Cf N Rennuy, 'The Emergence of a Parallell System of Social Security Coordination' [2013] *CMLR* 1221, 1235. See Case C-368/98 *Abdon Vanbraekel et al and Alliance nationale des mutualités chrétiennes (ANMC)* [2001] ECR I-5363; Case 157/99 *BSM Smits, married Geraets v Stichting Ziekenfonds VGZ and HTM Peerbooms v Stichting CZ Groep Zorgverzekeringen* [2001] ECR I-5473; Case C-385/99 *VG Müller-Fauré and Onderlinge Waarborgmaatschappij OZ Zorgverzekeringen UA, and between EEM van Riet and Onderlinge Waarborgmaatschappij ZAO Zorgverzekeringen* [2003] ECR I-4509; Case C-56/01 *Patricia Inizan, and Caisse primaire d'assurance maladie des Hauts-de-Seine* [2003] ECR I-12403; Case C-372/04 *The Queen, at the request of Yvonne Watts v Bedford Primary Care Trust, Secretary of State for Health* [2006] ECR I-4325; Case C-8/02 *Ludwig Leichtle and Bundesanstalt für Arbeit* [2004] ECR I-2641; Case

Based on the case law that followed *Kohll*,[71] one can summarise the standing of the law that when one applies for prior authorisation in accordance with Regulation 883/2004, only healthcare provided within the framework of the public healthcare system in the other Member State can be considered. In the case of the healthcare provided as a service, a health service can be offered by the state as well as private healthcare providers.[72] Prior authorisation, under Regulation 883/2004, entails that the insured does not have to pay for the healthcare, but has to pay the patient fee of the other country. As regards healthcare under the treaty and the free movement of services, a Member State can maintain or establish a system of prior authorisation in terms of hospital care. However, such prior authorisation may not go beyond what is necessary to maintain a national healthcare system which is adequate from a public health perspective. With regard to non-hospital services, however, the Member States cannot establish a condition of prior authorisation.

In case a Member State *does not* have a requirement for prior authorisation for hospital care based on the Treaty, the patient must pay out of their own pocket, to be subsequently reimbursed by the competent authority. Should the competent authority, however, find that the received healthcare is not covered by the national healthcare system, the insured will have to pay for the healthcare. Here, there is a large degree of uncertainty and the Commission has argued that the absence of a prior authorisation for hospital care may in itself constitute a barrier to the free movement of services.

The Patient Mobility Directive, which is intended to consolidate the development of the case law, reflects clearly the long and difficult road to the final Directive, with its 64 recitals in the preamble appearing in sharp contrast to only 23 Articles.[73] The Patient Mobility Directive takes a broader approach to cross-border healthcare than Regulation 883/2004 and the CJEU case law; it regulates not only when cross-border healthcare can occur, but also introduces a health cooperation

C-444/05 *Aikaterini Stamatelaki v NPDD Organismos Asfaliseos Eleftheron Epangelmation (OAEE)* [2007] ECR I-3185; Case C-512/08 *Commission v France* [2010] ECR I-8833; Case C-173/09 *Georgi Ivanov Elchinov v Natsionalna zdravnoosiguritelna kasa* [2010] ECR I-8889; Case C-255/09 *Commission v Portugal* [2011] ECR I-10547; Case C-268/13 *Elenea Petru v Casa Judeteană de Asigurări de Sănătate Sibiu and Casa Natională de Asigurări de Sănătate* EU:C:2014:2271.

[71] See Case C-444/05 *Aikaterini Stamatelaki v NPDD Organismos Asfaliseos Eleftheron Epangelmation (OAEE)* [2007] ECR I-3185, 22.

[72] See Case C-385/99 *VG Müller-Fauré and Onderlinge Waarborgmaatschappij OZ Zorgverzekeringen UA, and between EEM van Riet and Onderlinge Waarborgmaatschappij ZAO Zorgverzekeringen* [2003] ECR I-4509, 98 and 106–08.

[73] The large number of recitals was one of many tactics to be used in the negotiations in order to get the Member States to reach agreement on the Directive. Cf E Szyszczak, 'Patient's Rights: A Lost Cause or Missed Opportunity', in JW van den Gronde, E Szyszczak, U Neergard and M Krajewski (eds), *Legal Issues of Services of General Interest—Health Care and EU Law* (Haag, Asser, 2011) 118 ff; P de la Rosa, 'The Directive on Cross-border Healthcare or the Art of Codifying Complex Case Law' [2012] *CMLR* 15, 28.

aimed at improving the quality and safety of cross-border healthcare, and establishing cooperation on a general level.[74]

The main purpose of the Patient Mobility Directive is however to codify the case law on cross-border healthcare areas, even if this is not expressed in the preamble or in any of the articles of the Directive.[75] The Directive stresses, however, that it only clarifies the current status of the law; therefore, it introduces no new rules in relation to the possibility of obtaining cross-border healthcare.[76] The national competence, in terms of organisation and the provision of healthcare, is thus maintained according to Article 1(1) of the Directive. However, at the same time the Article indicates that the provisions of the Directive should make it easier to obtain access to cross-border healthcare. Article 1(1) reflects, in this way, (again) the built-in conflict between the Member States' desire for an autonomous system and the impact on the internal market and in this case the free movement of services. The legal basis of the Directive with both Article 114 TFEU (internal market) and Article 168 TFEU (social dimension) can be seen as a further indication of these opposing interests—it is not only the principles of the internal market that lay the groundwork of the legislation. Finally, the preamble stresses in reasons 3, 5, and 21 that the Directive should respect common values such as universality, access to quality healthcare, equality and solidarity.[77] Thus, the individual rights continue to challenge the Member States' collective endeavours.[78]

Regarding the relationship between the free movement of services and Regulation 883/2004, the Patient Mobility Directive has aimed to build bridges as regards certain definitions, while the major stumbling block—the relationship between these instruments—is still unresolved. However, the question is whether it can be solved as the Regulation is based on the free movement of persons, and the case law on the cross-border healthcare is based on the free movement of services. What complicates a future approach for the two legislative frameworks is that Regulation 883/2004 and its predecessors never focused on strengthening the free movement of persons through an opportunity for cross-border healthcare after certain conditions have been met. Instead, the Regulation has mainly been seen as an option for the Member States to use healthcare in other Member States

[74] The Patient Mobility Directive introduces five areas of cooperation which have been the subject of the Intergovernmental Open Method of Co-ordination: Mutual Assistance and Co-operation, Art 10; Recognition of Prescriptions, Art 11; the European Reference Networks, Art 12; e-health, Art 14; and Cooperation on the Evaluation of Medical Technology, Art 15. See PL Greer and B Vanhercke, 'The hard politics of soft law: the case of health', in E Mossialos, G Permanand, R Baeten and T Hervey (eds), *Health systems governance in Europe: the role of European law and policy* (Cambridge, Cambridge University Press, 2010) 186, 200 ff.

[75] cf P de la Rosa, 'The Directive on Cross-border Healthcare or the Art of Codifying Complex Case Law' [2012] *CMLR*, 15, 17 ff.

[76] See recital 33; cf ibid. 29.

[77] cf P de la Rosa, 'The Directive on Cross-border Healthcare or the Art of Codifying Complex Case Law' [2012] *CMLR* 15, 34.

[78] cf C Newdick, 'Citizenship, Free Movement and Health Care: Cementing Individual Rights by Corroding Social Solidarity' [2006] *CMLR* 1645, 1653 ff.

where their own healthcare was not sufficient or where the assessment had been made that it would have been cheaper to purchase healthcare in another Member State.[79] We cannot reconcile apples and oranges; the Regulation does and continues to offer cross-border planned healthcare based on a Member State's perspective, while the free movement of services is based on an individual's and company's right to receive and provide cross-border services.

5.4. CONCLUSION

Chapter 5 shows how the CJEU has acted when deciding cases based on the Treaty, together with the consequences that this has had.

When ruling in EU staff cases the CJEU has examined Regulation 883/2004, albeit not finding it applicable. The Court has thereby created a kind of a shadow effect where the Court applies a primary law 'coordination' of the social security systems, however with the principles as to be found in the Regulation.

Regulation 883/2004 is rooted in an unspoken understanding that a de-territorialisation of the national social security systems in a migratory context normally requires contributions being paid when migrating workers are being welcomed into a state's welfare system. However, as seen in section 5.2, the fact that the internal market is the larger context in which the Member States' social security systems have to operate, this has led to a situation where the Member States have to foot the bill for the EU staff who fall entirely outside the Regulation. This understanding of the internal market shows how the primary legislation affects national welfare systems, but also how the internal market has no answers for how this new solidarity will be financed in the long term unless new ways of thinking are developed that are no longer based on transnational solidarity.

In the same way, the case law with regard to the planned cross-border healthcare challenges the territorial concept of a welfare and solidarity of states. The case law beginning with *Kohll* shifts its focus from a collective solidarity towards an individual right in a market context. But what if money runs out? How long can an individual's right be given priority over collectivity?[80] At the same time the CJEU pointed out in *Elchinov*[81] a possibility for a Member State to regain control by strictly defining the healthcare that is provided, and by doing so limiting the cross-border healthcare. Such a bureaucratisation of healthcare can be done, paradoxically, at the expense of the patient—in this case, the focus is on the definition of the healthcare, rather than providing good and efficient healthcare.

[79] Luxembourg is an example of the latter, where it was decided to buy cross-border healthcare and on a relatively large scale: D Sindbjerg Martinsen, *EU for the Patients: Developments, Impacts, Challenges* (SIEPS, 2007) 6, 14.

[80] cf T Erhag, 'The Impact of Residence on Social Security and Taxation', in R Langer and M Sakslin (eds), *Co-ordinating Work-based and Residence-based Social Security* (Helsinki, Forum Iuris, 2004).

[81] Case C-173/09 *Georgi Ivanov Elchinov v Natsionalna zdravnoosiguritelna kasa* [2010] ECR I-8889.

The codification of the CJEU case law in the area of cross-border healthcare has evolved far more than could have been predicted when the CJEU 'introduced' the free movement of services in a Regulation context, but many fundamental questions on solidarity, and the system's sustainability, remain unanswered.

The Patient Mobility Directive has not only regulated cross-border healthcare, but has also established new cooperation structures which are intended to benefit both cross-border patients as well as domestic patients.[82] So, gradually, closer cooperation will evolve between the Member States in the area of healthcare, which may even overshadow *Kohll*.[83] Can it then be said that Robert Schuman's dream of a joint health project—*le Pool Blanc*—has finally begun to take shape, not as a result of legal battles, but through medical cooperation?[84]

[82] cf M Peeters, 'Free Movement of Patients: Directive 2011/24 on the Application of Patients' Rights in Cross-Border Healthcare' [2012] *European Journal of Health Law*, 29, 60.

[83] cf W Sauter, 'Harmonisation in healthcare: the EU patients' rights Directive' (2011) Tilburg Law and Economics Centre Research paper 2011/06, 24.

[84] See further about the 1950s visions of close health cooperation, in P de la Rosa, 'The Directive on Cross-border Healthcare or the Art of Codifying Complex Case Law' [2012] *CMLR*, 15 15 ff.

6

The Impact of Union Citizenship

6.1. INTRODUCTION

WITH THE INTRODUCTION of Union citizenship, the EU has started to move away from purely economic purposes to an arrangement in which Union citizenship is intended to be the 'fundamental status of nationals of the Member States',[1] and where national welfare models and the territorial idea of solidarity[2] are being challenged. The legislative process as regards the issue of Union citizenship has been the subject of rather heated debate.[3]

Legislative developments have to a large extent been codified in Directive 2004/38,[4] which had to be incorporated into the national legislation of the

[1] Case C-34/09 *Gerardo Ruiz Zambrano v Office national de l'emploi (ONEm)* [2011] REG I-1177, 41.

[2] cf P Ploscar, *The Principle of Solidarity in EU Internal Market Law* (Antwerpen, Universiteit Antwerpen, Faculteit Rechten, 2013); JW van den Gronde, E Szyszczak, U Neergard and M Krajewski, M. (eds), *Legal Issues of Services of General Interest—Health Care and EU Law* (Haag, Asser, 2011); M Ross and Y Borgmann-Prebil (eds), *Promoting Solidarity in the European Union* (Oxford, Oxford University Press, 2010); G de Búrca (ed), *EU Law and the Welfare State—In Search of Solidarity* (Oxford, Oxford University Press, 2005); C Barnard and O Odudu, *The Outer Limits of European Law* (Oxford, Hart, 2009); E Spaventa and M Dougan (eds), *Social Welfare and EU Law* (Oxford, Hart, 2005).

[3] cf C Caliess, 'The Dynamics of European Citizenship: from Bourgeois to Citoyen', in A Rosas, E Levits and Y Bot (eds), *The CJEU and the Construction of Europe: Analyses and Perspectives on Sixty Years of Case Law* (Haag, Asser, 2012); F Wollenschläger, 'A New Fundamental Freedom beyond Market Integration: Union Citizenship and its Dynamics for Shifting the Economic Paradigm of European Integration' [2011] *European Law Journal* 1; N Nic Shuibhne, 'The Outer Limits of EU Citizenship: Displacing Economic Free Movement Rights?' in C Barnard and O Odudu (eds), *The Outer Limits of EU Law* (Oxford, Hart, 2009); E Spaventa, 'Seeing the Woods despite the Trees? On the Scope of Union Citizenship and its Constitutional Effects' [2008] *CMLR* 13; M Dougan, 'The Constitutional Dimension to the Case Law on Union Citizenship' [2006] *European Law Review* 613. Lenaerts describes a development that goes beyond a 'fifth mobility' due to the ruling of the Court in Case C-34/09 *Gerardo Ruiz Zambrano v Office national de l'emploi (ONEm)* [2011] ECR I-1177, Case C-434/09 *Shirley McCarthy v Secretary of State for the Home Department* [2011] ECR I-3375 and Case C-256/11 *Murat Dereci mfl v Bundesministerium für Inneres* [2011] ECR. I-11315; K Lenaerts, 'The concept of EU citizenship in the case law of the European CJEU' (2013) 13 *ERA Forum* 569.

[4] Directive 2004/38/EC Of The European Parliamentand Of The Council of 29 April 2004 on the right of citizens of the Union and their family members to move and reside freely within the territory of the Member States amending Regulation (EEC) No 1612/68 and repealing Directives 64/221/EEC,68/360/EEC, 72/194/EEC, 73/148/EEC, 75/34/EEC, 75/35/EEC,90/364/EEC, 90/365/EEC and 93/96/EEC, [2004] OJ L158.

Member States by 1 May 2006. However, case law continue in parallel, in areas where the Directive is not applicable.[5]

As far as this text is concerned, it is relevant to follow these developments from two angles: first, what impact does the right of (permanent) residence included in Union citizenship have on the social security systems which are partly based on residence-based benefits, and secondly, what does not being a burden on the country of residence actually mean? Are social security benefits included in this concept?

6.2. BACKGROUND

Until the mid-1990s, EU legislation and case law in the area of the free movement of persons focused on supporting the free movement of workers. This was because the Union was essentially all about economic cooperation. With the ruling in *Martínez Sala*,[6] however, CJEU started developing the idea of the free movement of persons based on citizenship and not necessarily linked to economic activity.

The development, through case law, of Union citizenship and access to the welfare system with regard to residence have been controversial among academics and politicians ever since the Maastricht Treaty[7] introduced the concept Union citizenship in 1992.[8] The concept was a Spanish initiative during the negotiations and was part of an attempt to highlight all things positive with the EU, by strengthening the political rights of the individual in a limited EU context.[9] The idea was not to introduce any far-reaching substantial changes.[10] The changes that were

[5] Case C-135/08 *Janko Rottmann v Freistaat Bayern* [2010] ECR I-1449 and Case C-34/09 *Gerardo Ruiz Zambrano v Office national de l'emploi (ONEm)* [2011] ECR I-1177 can be seen as points of departure for this parallel evolution.

[6] Case C-85/96 *María Martínez Sala v Freistaat Bayern* [1998] ECR I-2691.

[7] Treaty of Maastricht on European Union [1992] OJ C 191.

[8] See eg D Kochenov and R Plender, 'EU Citizenship: From an Incipient Form to an Incipient Substance?' [2012] *European Law Review* 369; F Wollenschläger, 'A New Fundamental Freedom beyond Market Integration: Union Citizenship and its Dynamics for Shifting the Economic Paradigm of European Integration' [2011] *European Law Journal* 1; S Giubboni, 'A Certain Degree of Solidarity? Free Movement of Persons and Access to Social Protection in the Case Law of the European CJEU', in Y Borgmann-Prebil and M Ross (eds), *Promoting Solidarity in the European Union* (Oxford, Oxford University Press, 2010) 166; K Hailbronner, 'Union Citizenship and Access to Social Benefits' [2005] *CMLR* 1245.

[9] In Kochenov and Plender's view, the introduction of Union citizenship was not really anything new, as a quasi-citizenship already existed through case law like Case 186/87 *Ian William Cowan v Trésor public* [1989] ECR 195, and the introduction of Directive 2004/38 for senior citizens 'playboys': D Kochenow and R Plender, 'EU Citizenship: From an Incipient Form to an Incipient Substance?' [2012] *European Law Review* 369.

[10] cf H Lokrantz Bernitz, *Medborgarskapet i Sverige och Europa—Räckvidd och rättigheter* (Uppsala, Iustus, 2004) 220 ff.

made were modest and did not challenge the national states to any great extent.[11] Apart from providing a set of political rights, the wording was only a confirmation of the rights that were already included in the Treaty.[12]

Today, the situation is entirely different now that Union citizenship has been given more substance through the expansive development of case law, although after *Brey*[13] and *Dano*[14] this expansion is being balanced with restrictions that are the result of Directive 2004/38. Union citizenship is not an entirely logical creation, in that it gives rise to rights but not really any far-reaching obligations. It is a creation that questions the accepted view of citizenship, solidarity and the territorial limitations of welfare systems.[15]

The coordination of the social security systems has not been entirely unaffected by developments in the area of Union citizenship. With Regulation 883/2004, the legislator has also started to take the evolution of Union citizenship into account in such a way that the personal scope of the Regulation was expanded to also include Union citizens, Article 2.1.[16] Some legal experts in the field have claimed that the fact that Union citizens were included in Regulation 883/2004 does not really constitute a major change, but instead should only be seen as a symbolic gesture.[17]

It is true, that if you take a closer look at the rights or benefits that a Union citizen, who is not a worker, may enjoy in accordance with Regulation 883/2004, it is really not much more than access to planned care and tourist care. Most of the coordination procedure continues to be with regard to the parts of the social security system that traditionally have been seen as work-related insurance, like sick pay and unemployment benefits. The question remains, however, whether

[11] The right to vote in municipal elections in the place of residence was introduced, although that right already existed in many Member States, Art 20.2 b) TFEU. Moreover, the right to stand as a candidate in elections to the European Parliament at a person's place of residence was also introduced, Art 20.2 b) TFEU. The consular rights of Union citizens were reinforced for travel abroad, in that a Union citizen could turn to the diplomatic and consular authorities of another Member State if the Member State of which the Union citizen was a national was not represented in the country he/she was visiting/working in, Art 20.2 c) TFEU. Weiler describes the introduction of Union citizenship as 'little more than a cynical exercise in public relations on the part of the High Contracting Parties': J Weiler, 'Citizenship and Human Rights', in JA Winter, DM Curtin, AE Kellerman and B de Witte (eds), *Reforming the Treaty on European Union* (Haag, Kluwer, 1996) 57, 68.

[12] H Lokrantz Bernitz, *Medborgarskapet i Sverige och Europa—Räckvidd och rättigheter* (Uppsala, Iustus, 2004) 246 ff.

[13] Case C-140/12 *Pensionsversicherungsanstalt v Peter Brey*, EU:C:2013:565.

[14] Case C-333/13 *Elisabeta Dano and Florin Dano v Jobcenter Leipzig*, EU:C:2014:2358.

[15] Giubboni is highly critical: S Giubboni, 'A Certain Degree of Solidarity? Free Movement of Persons and Access to Social Protection in the Case Law of the European CJEU', in Y Borgmann-Prebil and M Ross (eds), *Promoting Solidarity in the European Union* (Oxford, Oxford University Press, 2010) 166.

[16] The Commission proposed, due to the development of the case law in the area of Union citizenship, an expansion of the personal scope to include Member State citizens who have been insured in accordance with national legislation; see Proposal for a Council Regulation (EC) on the coordination of the social security systems, 1999/C 38/08, 12.02.1999 10.

[17] For a discussion see Y Jorens and F van Overmeieren, 'General Principles of Coordination in Regulation 883/04' [2009] *European Journal of Social Security* 47 ff.

this change of direction might still entail a further step towards the erosion of sovereignty regarding national social security systems, partly through the recognition of Union citizens as eligible recipients of certain social security benefits thanks to their status as Union citizens. But perhaps above all because Union citizenship has an indirect impact on residence-based social security systems.

6.3. THE UNDERSTANDING OF THE CJEU OF THE CONCEPT OF UNION CITIZENSHIP

In order to understand the impact that Union citizenship has on Regulation 883/2004, it is important to analyse how the CJEU perceives the right of residence of Union citizenship. This right of residence may in turn have an impact on the concept of residence in Regulation 883/2004. Case law on cross-border situations for Union citizens is today consolidated in Directive 2004/38[18] as a Union citizen is, in parallel, still regulated by primary law.[19]

If you only look at the wording, the changes that came with the Maastricht Treaty were not terribly dramatic. It is true that according to the wording of Article 20.2 TFEU, a Union citizen shall enjoy the rights and obligations stipulated in the Treaty, but that the right to free movement is expressly limited through Article 21.1 TFEU:

> subject to the limitations and conditions laid down in the Treaties and by the measures adopted to give them effect.

Union citizenship as the basis for free movement came thus to be limited by both the Treaty and secondary law. The rules on European citizenship, probably due to the consensus above, were inconspicuous in the case law of the CJEU during the first five years. Until 1998, the CJEU only once referred to Union citizenship in a preliminary ruling. In the preliminary ruling in *Skanavi*,[20] the national court had raised a question about the interpretation of Article 8a in the EC Treaty (Article 21.1 TFEU). The Court, however, stated that since the circumstances of the case were also covered by Article 52 EC (Article 49 TFEU), the Court saw no reason to express a view about the interpretation of Union citizenship.

[18] Directive 2004/38/EC.

[19] K Lenaerts, 'The concept of EU citizenship in the case law of the European CJEU' [2013] *ERA Forum* 569; F Schulyok, 'The scope of application of EU Citizenship and EU Fundamental Rights in wholly internal situations' [2012] *Europarättslig Tidskrift* 448; K Lenaerts, '"Civis europaeus sum": from the cross-border link to the status of citizen of the Union' [2011] *FMW*—Online Journal on free movement of workers within the European Union, Publications Office of the European Union, Luxemburg, 6. For a critical analysis see J Schwarze, 'Balancing EU Integration and National Interests in the Case-Law of the CJEU' in *The CJEU and the Construction of Europe: Analyses and Perspectives on Sixty Years of Case-law—La Cour de Justice et la Construction de l'Europe: Analyses et Perspectives de Soixante Ans de Jurisprudence* (Haag, Asser, 2013) 268 ff.

[20] Case C-193/94 *Criminal proceedings against Sofia Skanavi and Konstantion Chryssanthakopoulos* [1996] ECR I-929.

It was only in 1998 with *Martínez Sala*[21] that the CJEU took the opportunity to develop the importance of Union citizenship for individual rights. The preliminary ruling concerned a Spanish woman, María Martínez Sala, who was legally resident in Germany. Martínez Sala was unemployed when she applied for an allowance to care for her child. According to the Court, there was no doubt that the allowance in question should have been regarded as both a family benefit according to Regulation 1408/71 and a social benefit according to Article 7.2 in Regulation 1612/68. Thus, the childcare allowance fell within the material scope of application for Community law and was subject to the principle of equal treatment in Article 6 EC Treaty (Article 18 TFEU). The CJEU left it to the German court to determine whether the provisions in the Regulations could be applied to Martínez Sala as a migrant worker,[22] but went on to examine whether a person in Martínez Sala's situation could be deemed to be covered by Community law on other grounds as well.

In this context, the CJEU stated that as a citizen of a Member State, legally resident in another, she was included in the personal scope and that the rules on European citizenship were applicable. According to the CJEU, such a person was subject to Article 17.2 EC (Article 20.2 TFEU), to which the right not to be discriminated against on the grounds of nationality is linked, Article 6.1 EC (Article 18.1 TFEU) applying in all situations which materially fall within the scope of Community law. Since the childcare allowance fell within the material scope of EU law, a bridge between this material right and the principle of equal treatment could be built; Martínez Sala was a Union citizen who was residing legally in another Member State, the childcare allowance fell within the material scope of Community law and Martínez Sala was not being treated in the same way as a German national.

However, what the CJEU overlooked (on purpose?) was that the material scope of EU law varies. Access to social benefits in accordance with the Regulations in place at the time, 1612/68 and 1408/71, was de facto dependent on actually being included in the personal scope. The fact that Martínez Sala resided legally in Germany alone could not, in the strict sense of the law, mean that the material scope for migrant workers could automatically be applied to her. The focus of a Regulation for migrant workers is economically active persons. To take a Regulation that is applicable to apples and claim that even oranges can be covered by these principles might be regarded as going a step too far. The doctrine, not entirely surprisingly, was also critical to this unprovoked expansion.[23] Even if the CJEU's bridge between the legal area and the non-discrimination principle in the Martínez Sala case is debatable, the fact remains that the ruling extended the scope of the ban on discrimination to cover all Union citizens *legally residing* in another Member State.

[21] Case C-85/96 *María Martínez Sala v Freistaat Bayern* [1998] ECR I-2691.

[22] ibid, 28, 34 and 45.

[23] cf K Hailbronner, 'Union Citizenship and Access to Social Benefits' [2005] *CMLR*, 1254 ff.

Martínez Sala resided legally in Germany and the question of whether Article 18.1 EC (Article 21.1 TFEU) could in itself entail an independent right to residence never arose. Therefore, this question as well as the question regarding the direct impact of the Article remained unanswered after the ruling. The question of the direct impact of Union citizenship and a person's right to claim an independent right to residence in the country of stay was instead answered in *Baumbast*.[24] The core issue in the case boiled down to clarifying whether a Union citizen, who could no longer be regarded as a migrant worker, had a direct applicable right, based on Union citizenship, to residence in another Member State under Article 18.1 EC (Article 21 TFEU). The CJEU stated that every Union citizen's right to move and reside freely in the territory of the Member States that had previously primarily been linked to an economic activity, was now to be regarded against the background of the provisions on Union citizenship in the Treaty. The CJEU stated that the aim was that the Union citizen status was to be the fundamental status of nationals of the Member States[25] and that it was not possible to ascertain from the Treaty whether there was a specific requirement regarding professional activity as a condition for being able to enjoy or maintain the rights conferred through Union citizenship. The CJEU subsequently stated that the right to reside in the territory of another Member State was directly conferred to every Union citizen and clearly provided for in Article 21.1 TFEU. According to the CJEU, the Article therefore had direct application. Subsequently, the CJEU balanced the preliminary ruling by pointing at the limitations that ensue from both primary and secondary law. The Directive in question[26] included the requirement not being a burden on the host state and the CJEU deemed that that requirement was reasonable. The preliminary ruling in *Baumbast* thus developed the legal position in *Martínez Sala*, who already resided legally in another Member State, to allowing a Member State to impose conditions on stay through secondary law with regard to not being a burden on the host state by having sufficient resources and being fully covered by medical insurance.

In *Trojani*[27] the CJEU developed the fundamental question: what is the outer limit for rights linked to the equal treatment of migrant Union citizens? It is interesting to note that *Trojani* is about social assistance, and not benefits that fall under social security.

The legal situation can be summarised as follows: if you are not a burden on the host state with regard to social assistance, you have a legal right to reside in the country (right of residence). If you have a right of residence, the logical

[24] Case C-413/99 *Baumbast and R* [2002] ECR I-7091.

[25] cf Case C-184/99 *Rudy Grzelczyk v Centre public d'aide sociale d'Ottignies-Louvain-la-Neuve* [2001] ECR I-6193, 31 and Case C-34/09 in Case C-34/09 *Gerardo Ruiz Zambrano v Office national de l'emploi (ONEm)* [2011] ECR I-1177 41.

[26] Council Directive 90/364/EEC of 28 June 1990 on the right of residence, [1990] OJ L 180.

[27] Case C-456/02 *Michel Trojani and Centre public d'aide sociale de Bruxelles (CPAS)* [2004] ECR I-7573.

consequence is that you enjoy the right to equal treatment as regards the EU's material scope.

Would it subsequently be possible to envisage a situation where the principle of equal treatment of Union citizenship could be applied for the enjoyment of residence based welfare systems of the host state? Can Union citizenship lead to social benefits, or does every application for a social benefit, like for example, a social security benefit, lead to being perceived as a burden? The key question is thus which social benefits result in a Union citizen 'being a burden on the host state'? The CJEU has embarked upon an answer to the question in the preliminary rulings in *Brey* and *Dano*, which are discussed in more detail in section 6.6 below.

6.4. DIRECTIVE 2004/38

Case law continued to develop Union citizenship, but every preliminary ruling that answered a question on the subject resulted in further questions demanding answers. The legal area started to become difficult to grasp. Therefore, the active approach of the CJEU regarding Union citizenship put pressure on the Member States to compile the case law in the area through legislation. A Free Movement Directive, Directive 2004/38—emanating from the directives of the 1990s[28] and the developed case law of the CJEU in the area of Union citizenship—was therefore drawn up and incorporated by the Member States by the end of April 2004. The aim of the new Directive was not only to codify the legal situation, but also to enhance the free movement of Union citizens within the Union, to gain a greater clarity regarding the conditions and formalities and to simplify the rules.[29] Hence, the Directive regulates the right for *all Union citizens* to travel to and reside both temporarily and permanently in other Member States other than the Member State of which the person in question is a national.

To start with, it is important to note that the Directive covers both the rights of those who are economically active and those who are not in the same legal act. This is an important difference compared to previous Regulations where there has been a sharp dividing line between those who are economically active covered by Regulation 1612/68 and 1408/71 respectively and all other groups of persons with right of residence directives with conditions.

Directive 2004/38 is based on the principle that the longer you stay in a Member State, the stronger your connection with that state. There are three timelines in the Directive under which the non-economically active Union citizens' fall:

1. *For up to three months.* Article 6 of the Directive provides the right for all Union citizens and their family members to reside freely in another Member State

[28] Council Directive 90/365/EEC of 28 June 1990 on the right of residence for employees and self-employed persons who have ceased their occupational activity, [1990] OJ L 180, and Council Directive 93/96/EEC of 29 October 1993 on the right of residence for students, [1993] OJ L 317.

[29] See recital 4, Directive 2004/38/EC.

for three months. However, the Directive has excluded the non-economically active Union citizens from social assistance for the first three months. Thus, union citizens residing in another Member State for up to three months cannot apply for social assistance in the visiting state.

2. *Three months to five years.* Residence for longer than three months applies not only to migrant workers and the self-employed who are given a right to reside automatically, but also to students who are enrolled in a recognised educational establishment and Union citizens who are not economically active but who have sufficient financial resources for themselves and their family members and are covered by a comprehensive sickness insurance. The right to reside in another Member State is conditional; the right to reside applies as long as a person does not become a burden on the social assistance system of the host state.[30]
3. *After five years.* Union citizens and their family members, who have remained and resided legally in another Member State in accordance with the conditions of Directive 2004/38, shall according to Article 16 have the right to permanent residence. The conditions that have applied prior to that stage no longer apply when a person has received permanent residence; ie the conditions for right of residence regarding economic activity, sickness insurance and sufficient resources etc. Hence, the person gains a strong position in the host state, akin to that of the nationals of that Member State, and the person may pose a burden on the state under the same conditions as the nationals of that Member State.

6.5. THE LINK BETWEEN BEING A BURDEN AND NATIONAL SOCIAL SECURITY SYSTEMS

The legal situation and Directive 2004/38 are based on the preliminary rulings *Martínez Sala*, *Baumbast* and *Trojani*. For the purpose of this article, it is interesting to note that the only issue dealt with in *Trojani* is that of whether a Union citizen can be regarded as being a burden and can lose his/her right to residence when he/she applies for social assistance; it is not about social benefits in a broader sense. What about benefits that are not regarded as social assistance? What about benefits that are covered by social security? Is it possible to say that you have sufficient resources, and thus—paradoxically supported by the host state—have the right to residence if your resources actually stem from the social security systems of the host state?[31] Or do you become a burden on the host state because you enjoy

[30] cf Case C-413/99 *Baumbast and R* [2002] ECR I-7091 and Case C-200/02 *Kunqian Catherine Zhu, Man Lavette Chen and Secretary of State for the Home Department* [2004] ECR I-9925.

[31] The CJEU in Case C-200/02 *Kunqian Catherine Zhu, Man Lavette Chen and Secretary of State for the Home Department* [2004] ECR I-9925, 45 arrived at the conclusion that where the economic resources come from is of no relevance.

the benefits of the welfare system in general? The preliminary ruling in *Martínez Sala* opened up the social security systems to those who were already residing legally in the country, but can a Union citizen claim these benefits merely on the basis of Union citizenship?

Both the previous Free Movement Directive and Directive 2004/38 include one basic requirement: the right to free movement is linked to a person at least not being a burden on the host state. In other words, the person shall have sufficient resources to survive and not be a burden on the healthcare system of the host state. These requirements have been included to avoid a situation where the welfare systems of the Member States are destabilised because of 'undesired' beneficiaries who would otherwise 'pour in' from poorer Member States to lead a 'comfortable and carefree existence' in the richer Member States without contributing to the welfare system through work and taxes.[32]

It is therefore important in this context to highlight that Directive 2004/38 only states that as a Union citizen you shall not be a burden on the social assistance system, Article 7.1b). In other words, the social security of a Member State, literally cannot be regarded as being included in the list of social benefits that would lead to a Union citizen losing the right to residence were he/she to apply for them.

The welfare societies of today are complex in structure and no longer consist only of social assistance. The systems consist instead of a wide range of different benefits and support schemes. Paradoxically, the relevant question is thus whether a Union citizen can maintain his/her right to residence by being a burden on the host state from a macro perspective. Being a burden in the sense that you are a burden on the welfare system but not the parts of the system that have to do with the social assistance system.

This question has gained in importance for social security systems that include residence-based benefits.[33] Regulation 882/2004 includes residence as its final ground for the determination of the applicable legislation. If you are regarded as being resident in the country of stay in accordance with Regulation 883/2004, you are covered by the social security system of the host state. If we toy with the idea that the social security system of the host state includes fairly comprehensive residence-based benefits, the question will arise regarding whether the Union citizen may apply for these benefits based on his/her residence. Since these benefits do not constitute social assistance, a state's social security might thus support the right to residence of a Union citizen in that the citizen would not burden the social

[32] cf the political debate in the UK; 'Up to 70,000 Romanian and Bulgarian migrants a year "will come to Britain" when controls on EU migrants expire', *Daily Mirror*, 17 January 2013; '"Don't come here, it's not very nice"—Ministers plan campaign to put off Romanians and Bulgarians migrants', *The Telegraph*, 27 January 2013.

[33] The residence-based benefits are based on a welfare model where persons who are not in employment are also covered by the social security system. Cf the Beveridge model and the Nordic model.

assistance system of the host state. This theoretical model sounds improbable, but *Brey* and *Dano* indicate that such a 'sponsor agreement' is fully possible.

6.6. BRIDGE OVER TROUBLED WATER

6.6.1. The Link Between Regulation 883/2004 and Directive 2004/38

Around Europe, opinions regarding the desire to protect national welfare systems have been voiced increasingly loudly. The free movement for non-economically active Union citizens has been set against this.

These conflicting interests have led to four preliminary rulings: *Brey*,[34] *Dano*,[35] *Alimanović*[36] and *García-Nieto*[37] where the CJEU has trimmed its sails in this current ungenerous wind and is now suggesting a full retreat. Not only are the outer boundaries of Union citizenship being withdrawn in this almost panicked retreat, but also unfortunately the coordination of social security in EU law.[38]

Legally, as we have seen above, the situation is such that Directive 2004/38[39] makes it possible to limit access to social assistance for non-economically active Union citizens. The coordination of the social security systems of the Member States through Regulation 883/2004, has no such limitation: benefits are paid in accordance with national legislation without any unequal treatment.

The four preliminary rulings in question touch upon welfare benefits, also known as special non-contributory cash benefits, which are in the borderland between social assistance and social security benefits. Thus, good arguments can be cited claiming that it is not reasonable that the formal name of a social benefit

[34] Case C-140/12 *Pensionsversicherungsanstalt v Peter Brey*, EU:C:2013:565.

[35] Case C-333/13 *Elisabeta Dano and Florin Dano v Jobcenter Leipzig*, EU:C:2014:2358.

[36] Case C-67/14 *Jobcenter Berlin Neukölln v Nazifa Alimanovic and Others*, EU:C:2015:597.

[37] Case C-299/14 *Vestische Arbeit Jobcenter Kreis Recklinghausen v Jovanna García-Nieto and others* EU:C:2016:114.

[38] The Doctrine has mainly focused on the outer boundaries for Union citizenship, rather than on the bridging between Regulation 883/2004 and Directive 2004/38; D Thym, 'The Elusive Limits of Solidarity: Residence Rights of and Social Benefits for Economically Inactive Union Citizens' [2015] *CMLR* 17; N Nic Shuibhne, 'Limits Rising, Duties Ascending: the Changing Legal Shape of Union Citizenship' [2015] *CMLR* 889; R Zahn, '"Common sense" or a threat to EU integration? The court, economically inactive EU citizens and social benefits' [2015] *Industrial Law Journal* 573; S Peers, 'Benefits for EU citizens: a U-turn by the CJEU?' [2015] *Cambridge Law Journal* 195. For an analysis on the interrelationship between these two legal instruments see H Verschueren, 'Preventing "Benefit Tourism" in the EU: a Narrow or Broad Interpretation of the Possibilities offered by the CJEU in Dano?' [2015] *CMLR* 363; see also H Verschueren, 'Free Movement of benefit Tourism: the Unreasonable Burden of Brey' [2014] *European Journal of Migration and Law* 147 and B Spiegel, 'Anspruch auf Leistungen der sozialen Sicherheit von nicht aktiven Personen—wer fürchtet sich vor "Sozialtourismus"? Neue EuGH Fälle: C-140/12, Brey, und C-333/13, Dano' [2014] *ERA Forum* 339.

[39] Directive 2004/38/EC of the European Parliament and of the Council of 29 April 2004 on the right of citizens of the Union and their family members to move and reside freely within the territory of the Member States amending Regulation (EEC) No 1612/68 and repealing Directives 64/221/EEC,68/360/EEC, 72/194/EEC, 73/148/EEC, 75/34/EEC, 75/35/EEC,90/364/EEC, 90/365/EEC and 93/96/EEC, [2004] OJ L158.

is the deciding factor when determining whether it should be limited or not. The CJEU finds therefore in *Brey*, *Dano*, *Alimanović* and *García-Nieto* that national benefits can be regarded both as social security benefits as provided for in Regulation 883/2004 and social assistance which can be made conditional on residence in accordance with the provisions in Directive 2004/38.[40]

From a purely legal point of view, the line of reasoning of the CJEU has its flaws, when the Court links Regulation 883/2004 and Directive 2004/38 without taking into account the different aims of the Regulation and Directive and their different structures, where social security benefits are insurance solutions while social assistance constitutes financial aid.

The flaws in this legal line of reasoning would have far-reaching consequences if the same point of view were to be put across as regards social security benefits per se. It is therefore worrying that the CJEU held in *European Commission v United Kingdom and Northern Ireland* claimed that it is be possible to introduce a right of residence condition on purely residence-based social security benefits, as regards non-economically active Union citizens.[41]

Against this background, the monograph critically analyses two questions:

1. Is it possible, as found by the CJEU in *Brey*, *Dano* and *Alimanović*, to perceive the special non-contributory benefits in the Regulation as social assistance in accordance with Directive 2004/38?
2. Can the preliminary rulings of the CJEU in *Brey*, *Dano*, *Alimanović* and *García-Nieto* also be used to extend the concept of social assistance to also include pure social security benefits and what would be the consequence of this on the coordination of the social security systems of the Member States in general?

6.6.2. The EU Legal Regulation of Special Non-Contributory Cash Benefits and Social Assistance

Special non-contributory cash benefits are social security benefits with a flavour of social assistance as they are intended to meet special needs and are normally based on residence. As benefits under the Regulation they would be exportable. However, Member States were not keen on the fact that these special national benefits were to be exported according to the exportability principle of the Regulation. As a result, Article 70 of the Regulation states that special non-contributory cash benefits that satisfy the criteria laid down in Article 70 do not need to be exported.

[40] Directive 2004/38 is based on the notion that non-economically active Union citizens may not become a burden on the social assistance system of the host Member State. The right of residence is thus, according to Art 7.1(b), made conditional upon the Union citizen having sufficient resources and comprehensive sickness insurance.

[41] Case C-308/14 *European Commission v United Kingdom and Northern Ireland*, EU:C:2016:436.

Ever since the ruling of the CJEU in *Piscitello,*[42] there have been discussions on how far the Member States may limit the export of social security benefits that are closely linked to the living conditions in the Member State. A derogation was thus introduced through Regulation 1247/92:[43] when a social security benefit is listed as a special non-contributory benefit it can be limited to only being granted within the borders of the country. The rule thus entails a deviation from the general principle of the Regulation, that when you are covered by the social security system of a Member State, you have the right to these benefits regardless of whether you live in the country, commute from it or have your family in your country of origin.

The only derogation in Regulation 1247/92 is the one on the export principle of Regulation 883/2004.[44] The special non-contributory cash benefits are thus covered by the other parts of the fundamental principles and provisions of the Regulation. The fact that special non-contributory cash benefits continue to be covered by the scope of the Regulation makes it difficult, however, for both the Member States and the CJEU. Similarly, the fact that the benefits are covered by the Regulation means that the provision of the Regulation, also in the future, shall be applied in reverse—when a person moves *to* another Member State. This, together with the fact that Regulation 883/2004 expanded the personal scope to also include Union citizens, has led to a situation whereby non-economically active Union citizens may, thanks to the construction of the Regulation, sneak in by the backdoor: if the host state is identified as the competent state in accordance with the provisions of the Regulation, ultimately through residence according to Article 11.3 e, this state shall grant the special non-contributory cash benefits also to residing non-economically active Union citizens.[45]

Both the previous Free Movement Directives[46] and case law,[47] on which Article 7.1 b of Directive 2004/38 is based, include an inherent balance between the free movement of persons and the interests of the Member States: The right to the free movement of persons is linked to the requirement that a Union citizen shall not be a burden on the host state as regards the social assistance system: if a person were to become dependent on social assistance for his/her livelihood, that person would no longer have the right to residence. As regards the social security systems of the Member States, there is no corresponding balance: the systems are

[42] Case 139/82 *Paola Piscitello v Istituto nazionale della previdenza sociale (INPS)* [1983] ECR 1427. See also F Pennings, *European Social Security Law*, 6th edn (Cambridge - Antwerp - Portland, Intersentia, 2015) 65ff.

[43] Council Regulation (EEC) No 1247/92 of 30 April 1992 amending Regulation (EEC) No 1408/71 on the application of social security schemes to employed persons, to self-employed persons and to members of their families moving within the Community, [1992] OJ L 136.

[44] Regarding the Regulation's export principle see F Pennings, *European Social Security Law*, 6th edn (Cambridge - Antwerp - Portland, Intersentia, 2015) 22.

[45] See also Art 10 a 3 and 10 a 4, Regulation 883/2004.

[46] Directives 64/221/EEC, 68/360/EEC, 72/194/EEC, 73/148/EEC, 75/34/EEC, 75/35/EEC,90/364/EEC, 90/365/EEC and 93/96/EEC.

[47] See, eg, Case C-413/99 *Baumbast and R* [2002] ECR I-7091 and Case C-200/02 *Kunqian Catherine Zhu, Man Lavette Chen and Secretary of State for the Home Department* [2004] ECR I-9925.

instead linked in cross-border situations through complex coordination procedures in order to strengthen the free movement of persons.

In other words, social security benefits are not included in the list of welfare benefits that would lead to a Union citizen risking losing his/her right to residence according to Directive 2004/38. Instead it would seem that the principle of equal treatment in Article 4 of the Regulation may lead to a situation whereby residence-based security benefits would become accessible to non-economically active persons with residence.

In this way, the requirements in the Regulation stipulating that the persons for whom the rules are applicable shall have the same rights as nationals of the state in question are pitted against the desires of the Member States to limit access to social benefits by introducing conditions.[48]

6.6.3. The CJEU Rulings in Brey, Dano, Alimanović and García-Nieto

The question that the CJEU was trying to find an answer to in *Brey*, *Dano Alimanović* and *García-Nieto* is whether a Union citizen may be a burden to the host state by applying for social security benefits that lie in the borderland between social assistance and pure social security benefits.

The preliminary ruling in *Brey*[49] is one of the most important but also one of the most complex preliminary rulings that the CJEU has delivered in the area of social security in recent years.

The background to *Brey* was that an increasing number of pensioners (ie non-economically active Union citizens) were moving to Austria where they were applying for a compensatory supplement to top up rather scant pensions from their respective countries.[50] This compensatory supplement had already been registered as a special non-contributory benefit by Austria and was thus exempted from export. In order to further limit payment of the compensatory supplement, Austria introduced a requirement that Union citizens should have right of residence before the compensatory supplement could be granted.[51]

The CJEU found that the fact that the Austrian compensatory supplement was registered as a special non-contributory benefit did not necessarily affect the assessment of right to residence according to Directive 2004/38, since the Regulation has other aims than the Directive.[52] The aim of the Regulation is that the migrant Union

[48] Case C-333/13 *Elisabeta Dano and Florin Dano v Jobcenter Leipzig*, EU:C:2014:2358, 54.

[49] Case C-140/12 *Pensionsversicherungsanstalt v Peter Brey*, EU:C:2013:565.

[50] There was a twofold increase in the number of applicants over three years, albeit from a very low figure: from 498 in 2009 to 940 in 2012. Opinion of the Advocate General, 29 May 2013, Case C-140/12 *Pensionsversicherungsanstalt v Peter Brey*, EU:C:2013:337, fn 4.

[51] The Austrian legislator made the national benefit conditional upon a right of residence in Austria as of 1 January 2011.

[52] Case C-140/12 *Pensionsversicherungsanstalt v Peter Brey*, EU:C:2013:565, 50.

citizen should be able to retain certain social security benefits, while Directive 2004/38 gives the host state the possibility of limiting the granting of social assistance.[53]

The CJEU thereafter introduced a broad perspective when it established that social assistance systems should be seen as:

> all assistance introduced by the public authorities, whether at national, regional or local level, that can be claimed by an individual who does not have resources sufficient to meet his own basic needs and the needs of his family and who, by reason of that fact, may become a burden on the public finances of the host Member State during his period of residence which could have consequences for the overall level of assistance which may be granted by that State.[54]

A social benefit thus does not have to come under the social assistance legislation in a Member State for it to be regarded as social assistance. A social benefit can just as well be managed by a social insurance authority; it is the substance of the benefit which is the determining factor, not the authority that manages the benefit.

The CJEU motivated this broad view by stating that the opposite interpretation would lead to 'an unjustifiable difference' because of the way the different welfare systems of the Member States are organised; similar social benefits would either be covered by Regulation 883/2004 and would thus be granted, or fall under Directive 2004/38 and thus could be conditional upon the right to residence.[55]

In the light of the line of reasoning above, the CJEU found that special non-contributory cash benefits fall under Directive 2004/38 and can therefore be conditional upon the right to residence.

As regards Regulation 883/2004, and the position of its special non-contributory cash benefits in relation to Directive 2004/38, *Dano* confirms the line of reasoning in *Brey*.

Germany's *Grundsicherung* had been listed by Germany as a special non-contributory cash benefit that does not need to be exported in accordance with the provisions in Regulation 883/2004. The German court underlined in its request for a preliminary ruling that the German benefit was covered by the provisions of the Regulation. In the light of this connection, the CJEU was asked to indicate whether Article 4 in the Regulation on equal treatment would prevent German legislation from differentiating between German nationals and Union citizens as regards the access to *Grundsicherung*.[56]

The CJEU confirmed that the coordination in Regulation 883/2004 included special non-contributory cash benefits and that no derogation from the principle of

[53] See the Court's reasoning on pp 51–57.

[54] ibid, 61.

[55] ibid, 59.

[56] Case C-333/13 *Elisabeta Dano and Florin Dano v Jobcenter Leipzig*, EU:C:2014:2358, 45.

equal treatment was made for these benefits.[57] The CJEU subsequently reinforced the principle of equal treatment by referring to the fact that this interpretation corresponded to the aims of the legislator[58] that special non-contributory cash benefits must be granted in the country of residence without discrimination on grounds of nationality.[59]

Thus the CJEU prepared for a wrecking ball in order to state that unauthorised unequal treatment was taking place as the German national legislation stipulated additional requirements for residing Union citizens compared to German nationals.

The CJEU avoided game set and match, by rewording the German court's question on the requirement in the Regulation regarding equal treatment to also include the limitations of the principle of equal treatment that follows from Directive 2004/38.[60] The CJEU was thereby able to confirm *Brey* by rewording the question and stating that special non-contributory cash benefits can be regarded as social assistance as in Directive 2004/38, and that the Member States can thus differentiate between Union citizens and the nationals of the Member State in question who are in the same situation as regards access to social assistance.

The CJEU reinforced its line of reasoning by stating that material conditions can be introduced since the Regulation Article in question (Article 70.4) was a rule regarding the determination of applicable legislation. Thus, the requirement of equal treatment in the Regulation cannot be invoked since a rule on the determination of applicable legislation only identifies which state is competent and does not stipulate any more detailed qualification requirements. In the light of the above, the CJEU found that: 'It follows that there is nothing to prevent the grant of such benefits to Union citizens who are not economically active from being made subject to the requirement that those citizens fulfil the conditions for obtaining a right of residence under Directive 2004/38'.[61]

According to the third preliminary ruling of relevance *Alimanović*, 'such benefits (special non-contributory cash benefits) are also covered by the concept of "social assistance" within the meaning of Article 24(2) of Directive 2004/38'. Thus the Grand Chamber in *Alimanović* consolidated the view of the CJEU regarding the dual role of special non-contributory cash benefits. This has also been confirmed in *García-Nieto*.

[57] ibid, 48–51.

[58] See Recital 7 of Council Regulation (EEC) No 1247/92 of 30 April 1992 amending Regulation (EEC) No 1408/71 on the application of social security schemes to employed persons, to self-employed persons and to members of their families moving within the Community, [1992] OJ L 136.

[59] Case C-333/13 *Elisabeta Dano and Florin Dano v Jobcenter Leipzig*, EU:C:2014:2358, 52–53.

[60] cf K Voss, 'But that's not what I asked! The reformulation of questions asked in preliminary rulings' [2015] *Europarättslig Tidskrift* 939.

[61] Case C-333/13 *Elisabeta Dano and Florin Dano v Jobcenter Leipzig*, EU:C:2014:2358, 83.

6.6.4. A Worrying Shift in Perspective—or the Question Warrants the Answer?

It is important to note at the outset that the point of departure of the CJEU differs in *Brey* and in *Dano*.[62] In *Brey*, the CJEU had to answer a single question:[63] the question about whether Directive 2004/38 restricts the national legislation. The two introductory questions of the German court in *Dano* were instead focused on whether the provisions in Regulation 883/2004 would allow a German special non-contributory cash benefit to be conditional.

The facts of the *Dano* case were unusually clear and provocative: Dano was a non-economically active Union citizen who had not completed her schooling in her home country of Romania. During her time in Germany she had not made any attempts to make a living herself by looking for work but had instead applied for and received national social benefits. She was the very epitome of a benefits tourist.[64] It was therefore too great a temptation for the Grand Chamber of the CJEU to set an example with *Dano* and clarify the limits for the solidarity of the host state vis-à-vis non-economically active Union citizens by means of a strict literal interpretation of Directive 2004/38 that followed from *Brey*.[65] This temptation and the zeal of the Court, however, led to the CJEU not paying attention to the fact that the national courts' request for a preliminary ruling differed as regards the question raised, and that the bridge constructed between Regulation 883/2004 and Directive 2004/38 in *Brey* entailed five serious flaws.[66]

6.6.4.1. Social Security Benefits are not Social Assistance

Regulation 883/2004 is a legislative product stemming back to the beginning of the twentieth century when migrant labour was in focus, and it still is in focus today. Union citizenship, on the other hand, is a much younger legal construction, the very essence of which is more unclear than ever, where case law has tried

[62] The German national court asked whether the principle of equal treatment under Art 4 of the Regulation would also apply to the special non-contributory cash benefits, Case C-67/14 *Jobcenter Berlin Neukölln v Nazifa Alimanovic and Others*, EU:C:2015:597, 38.

[63] The CJEU reformulated the question posed irrespective of the fact that the Austrian Administrative Authority had issued Brey an EEA citizen registration certificate, Case C-140/12 *Pensionsversicherungsanstalt v Peter Brey*, EU:C:2013:565, 32. However, as the right of residency might change over time this certificate is of no legal value, but no mention of this fact was made by the CJEU.

[64] The *Daily Mail* tracked down Elisabeta Dano in Leipzig and made her the archetype of social tourism: www.dailymail.co.uk/news/article-2835442/The-Roma-gipsy-sparked-crackdown-benefit-tourism-Elisabeta-Dano-25-tracked-German-city-finding-centre-landmark-welfare-case.html.

[65] cf N Nic Shuibhne, 'Limits Rising, Duties Ascending: the Changing Legal Shape of Union Citizenship' [2015] *CMLR* 889.

[66] See also Verschueren, who is of the opinion that the CJEU does not take into account the aspect that the limitation of the export of the special non-contributory cash benefits, as a consequence, leads to the giving out of the benefits in the state of residence. H Verschueren, 'Free Movement of benefit Tourism: the Unreasonable Burden of Brey' [2014] *European Journal of Migration and Law* 162 ff.

to balance the right of non-economically active Union citizens to stay in a state, against the host state's need to safeguard its welfare system.[67]

As Union citizenship developed through the case law of the CJEU, the need to consolidate this development grew. The development was codified in Directive 2004/38 in the spring of 2004. Almost simultaneously,[68] the modernisation of Regulation 1408/71 was achieved after 12 years of negotiations.[69] This modernisation, in the shape of Regulation 883/2004, took consideration of Union citizenship by expanding the personal scope of the Regulation to also include Union citizens who are or who have been covered by the social security system of a Member State, Article 2.1.[70]

With the expansion of the personal scope of the Regulation in April 2004, there were suddenly two EU legal instruments that overlapped as regards the personal and material scope.

When legal instruments have points of contact with each other, the legislator may pay attention to this fact by regulating and clarifying the relationship between the instruments. As regards Regulation 883/2004, this was done with Regulation 492/2011.

The aim of this Regulation, just as with Regulation 883/2004, is to promote the free movement of workers through detailed secondary legislation.[71] The relationship between these two Regulations is regulated in Article 36.2 in Regulation 492/2011, which gives Regulation 883/2004 precedence when the regulations are applicable in parallel.[72] Such a regulated order of priority does not exist between Regulation 883/2004 and Directive 2004/38.

It may seem odd that two major legislative projects within the EU that have strong points of contact were not reconciled.[73] One explanation could be that the legislative processes were led by different DGs within the Commission. The Advocate General found in line with this in his Opinion to the ruling in *Brey* that the drafting of the two pieces of legislation had not been synchronised.[74]

[67] N Nic Shuibhne, 'Limits Rising, Duties Ascending: the Changing Legal Shape of Union Citizenship' [2015] *CMLR* 889, 896 ff.

[68] Regulation 883/2004 and Directive 2004/38 were adopted within just a day of each other at the very end of April 2004, before the enlargement of the EU with 10 new Member States took place.

[69] The European Summit in Edinburgh 1992 made the decision to modernise Regulation 1408/71: E Eichenhofer, 'How to Simplify the Co-ordination of Social Security' [2000] *European Journal of Social Security* 231, 232.

[70] See further Proposal for a Council Regulation (EC) on coordination of social security systems, 1999/C 38/08, 12.02.1999.

[71] P Starup and MJ Elsmore, 'Taking a logical step forward? Comment on Ibrahim and Teixeira' [2010] *European Law Review* 571.

[72] This can be seen in eg Case C-206/10 *European Commission v Federal Republic of Germany*, EU:C:2011:283, 39.

[73] H Verschueren, 'Free Movement of benefit Tourism: the Unreasonable Burden of Brey' [2014] *European Journal of Migration and Law* 162, fn 66.

[74] The Opinion of the AG in Case C-140/12 *Pensionsversicherungsanstalt v Peter Brey*, EU:C:2013:337, 42.

Moreover, it is the case that the distinction between social aid schemes and social security benefits in the Regulation has been added to differentiate between the different areas, not to lead to specific legal outcomes, as is the case with the concept of social assistance as it is used in Directive 2004/38.[75]

Social assistance refers to different types of benefits that are granted to a person who has not reached a reasonable standard of living through for example work, a pension or student grant. Social assistance is normally funded through taxes.

In other words a social safety net, there to help in situations where a person is unable to make a living.

Social security is instead based on the payment of social contributions. This is a collective solution where individuals, by paying social contributions, have access to various state or state-regulated insurance solutions like parental benefits, sick pay and pensions. Social security has, depending on the historical context but also political influences, developed in different directions, where two main tracks can be observed: work-based social security and residence-based social security. Work-based social security is dependent on income and contributions paid. This type of social security only encompasses a state's workers and their family members. The rest of the population has to rely on other, less comprehensive, welfare solutions.

Residence-based social security differs from work-based social security in that there is an ambition as regards redistribution policy and solidarity, which is built into the system. It is not, however, based on an individual means test, which is the case with the tax-based social assistance schemes. Instead this is an insurance solution with an element of solidarity within the territory of a state.

This view as regards social security is shared and reinforced by the fact that the Member States register social benefits in line with the provisions of the Regulation on special non-contributory cash benefits. The Member States do not question that these residence-based benefits are covered by the scope of the Regulation, but request a derogation from the export principle of the Regulation since the benefits are said to have a special link with the state in question.[76]

Regardless of this situation, the CJEU established in *Brey* that a special non-contributory cash benefit could in parallel be regarded as social assistance by introducing an EU legal definition of social assistance that is so broad that a large majority of the benefits of a welfare state are covered by the term.[77] A social security benefit can thus be conditional on one EU regulation regardless of whether another EU regulation is based on equal treatment.

[75] For a lengthy analysis see the Opinion of the Advocate General in Case C-140/12 *Pensionsversicherungsanstalt v Peter Brey*, EU:C:2013:337, 35 ff.

[76] cf Case 35/77 *Elisabeth Beerens v Rijksdienst voor Arbeidsvoorziening* [1977] ECR 2249, where the CJEU has established that when a Member State has informed the Commission that it considers that a social benefit constitutes a social security benefit that should be included in the coordination, there is no right to withdraw it.

[77] Case C-140/12 *Pensionsversicherungsanstalt v Peter Brey*, EU:C:2013:565, 61.

The current situation is reminiscent of the situation after *Nonnenmacher*,[78] where the CJEU established that the original provision in Regulation 3/58 regarding applicable legislation did not prevent the payment of parallel social security benefits.[79] The Member States suddenly found themselves in a situation where, based on their own national legislation, they had to pay social security benefits despite the fact that the Regulation identified another Member State as the competent state. In this way, *Nonnenmacher* led to a situation where security benefits were paid without a reciprocal receipt of social contributions. Therefore, the Member States clarified the rule on applicable legislation in the new Regulation 1408/71 so that it was made clear that the rule had exclusive effect; the state that was identified as the competent state and all other Member States were thus prevented from paying national benefits. The CJEU noted where the winds were blowing from and confirmed in *Ten Holder*[80] that the new wording was to be regarded as good law. The Member States were thus able to invoke the Regulation in order to avoid the obligations stipulated in the national legislation.

The negative impact on the free movement of persons that was caused by *Ten Holder* was subsequently considered by the CJEU in a number of preliminary rulings, the first of which was *Bosmann*,[81] which established that eligibility for national social security benefits that are residence-based, regardless of whether another state is the competent state, shall not be regarded as preventing the free movement that the Regulation is intended to support. The CJEU underlined that the aim of the Regulation is to support the free movement of persons not to regulate the conditions according to which national benefits can be paid (or rather not be paid).

The situation that has arisen due to *Brey* allows the Member States to instead invoke Directive 2004/38 in order to avoid the obligations of the Regulation. The outcome is thus the best possible for the Member States; benefits will not have to be exported when they have been included in the annex as a special non-contributory cash benefit in accordance with Regulation 883/2004. Nor do they have to be paid to non-economically active Union citizens residing in the country in accordance with Directive 2004/38. The free movement of persons is suddenly limited in both directions. Derogations and limitations reinforce each other logarithmically without a comprehensive view of EU law, which is rather worrying.[82]

[78] Case 92/63 *M Th Nonnenmacher, widow of HE Moebs v Bestuur der Sociale Verzekeringsbank* [1964] ECR 281.

[79] The rules for determining the legislation applicable determine which national social security system is applicable. The underlying idea is to ensure that a migrant will always be covered by a social security system. See N Rennuy, 'The Emergence of a Parallell System of Social Security Coordination' [2013] *CMLR* 1221, 1222 ff.

[80] Case 302/84 *AA Ten Holder v Bestuur van de Nieuwe Algemene Bedrijfsvereniging* [1986] ECR 1821.

[81] Case C-352/06 *Brigitte Bosmann v Bundesagentur für Arbeit–Familienkasse Aachen* [2008] ECR I-3827.

[82] cf N Nic Shuibhne, 'Limits Rising, Duties Ascending: the Changing Legal Shape of Union Citizenship' [2015] *CMLR* 889, 934 ff. Nic Shuibhne paints a picture where the primary law understanding of the Union citizenship has now been replaced by a textual reading of secondary legislation.

What distinguishes the two situations is that *Bosmann* and the subsequent cases *Hudzinski* and *Wawrzyniak*[83] were about migrant workers being refused national security benefits invoking the provisions in the Regulation on applicable legislation. In *Brey*, it was not a matter of workers but instead non-economically active Union citizens. Should this alter the preconditions?

It should not, since Regulation 883/2004 now, according to Articles 2.1, also includes this group of persons. The remaining question is instead about the position of the EU regulations vis-à-vis each other: can Directive 2004/38 be applied on special non-contributory cash benefits which are regulated by Regulation 883/2004?[84] This question leads us to the second part of the CJEU building a bridge between Regulation 883/2004 and Directive 2004/38.

6.6.4.2. *The Focus of Regulation 883/2004 is to Do Away with Potential Obstacles in Both the Previous State and the (New) Competent State*

When the CJEU built the bridge between Regulation 883/2004 and Directive 2004/38 in *Brey* (at pp 51–56), it did it in the light of a peculiar shift in perspective.

At p 52, the CJEU establishes that the aim of Regulation 883/2004 is to ensure that certain social security benefits that have been granted by the country of origin can be kept during a cross-border movement, while Directive 2004/38 mainly gives the receiving state the possibility to limit access to social assistance.[85]

Here, the CJEU is guilty of a gross simplification of the Regulation. The Regulation aims not only to guarantee that it will be possible to continue to receive benefits from previous competent states. The aim of the Regulation is perhaps above all, taking the principle of equal treatment into account, to reinforce the free movement of persons by ensuring that a person who is covered by the Regulation is treated by the (new) competent state in the same way as the nationals of that state. The Regulation thus regulates the right to benefits that have been earned in the state of origin *as well as* the obligations of the competent state.[86]

[83] Joined cases Case C-611/10 *Waldemar Hudzinski v Agentur für Arbeit Wesel—Familienkasse* and Case C-612/10 *Jaroslaw Wawrzyniak v Agentur für Arbeit Mönchengladbach—Familienkasse* EU:C:2012:339.

[84] It is important to bear in mind that special non-contributory cash benefits are not in the social assistance twilight zone per se. Special non-contributory cash benefits can also be aimed at supporting people with disabilities, Case C-299/05 *Commission of the European Communities v European Parliament and Council of the European Union* [2007] ECR I-8695, or have a focus on supporting specially adapted work, Case C-287/05 *DPW Hendrix v Raad van Bestuur van het Uitvoeringsinstituut Werknemersverzekeringen* [2007] ECR I-6909.

[85] The CJEU recognises that the purpose of Directive 2004/38 is twofold, but focuses on the possible restrictions rather than the Directive's aim supporting the free movement of persons, see Case C-140/12 *Pensionsversicherungsanstalt v Peter Brey*, EU:C:2013:565, at 53–56. Cf Case C-480/08 *Teixiera v London Borough of Lambeth* [2010] ECR I-1107, 60 and case C-310/08 *London Borough of Harrow v Nimco Hassan Ibrahim and Secretary of State for the Home Department*, EU:C:2010:80 49. See also N Nic Shuibhne, 'Limits Rising, Duties Ascending: the Changing Legal Shape of Union Citizenship' [2015] *CMLR* 889, 896 ff.

[86] cf F Pennings, *European Social Security Law*, 6th edn (Cambridge - Antwerp - Portland, Intersentia, 2015) 8 ff.

As regards *Brey*, it is not about Germany refusing to pay the pension that Brey has earned, but instead it is about the competent state, Austria, introducing qualification requirements for access to the compensatory allowance. Hence, it is odd that the CJEU based its ruling on a purpose that is not relevant in the context at hand.

When this erroneous perspective is put forward, there is no overlapping of Regulation 883/2004 and Directive 2004/38.[87] It is therefore irrelevant for the preliminary ruling how the terms 'social aid in the Regulation' and 'social assistance in Directive 2004/38' relate to each other. Thus, it is possible for the CJEU, without an in-depth line of reasoning, to establish in *Dano* that 'the "special non-contributory cash benefits" as referred to in Article 70(2) of Regulation No 883/2004 do fall within the concept of "social assistance" within the meaning of Article 24(2) of Directive 2004/38'.[88]

Hence, the CJEU does not either have to take a stance as to whether the principle of equal treatment in the Regulation might limit the possibility of Directive 2004/38 to treat Union citizens unequally. This is, however, a very relevant question. In particular against the background of the fact that special non-contributory cash benefits have been registered as social security benefits.[89] This is why it is unfortunate that the CJEU chose to reword the question of the national court in *Dano* to include equal treatment as stipulated both in the Regulation and Directive 2004/38.[90]

The principle of equal treatment in EU law is a general legal principle, but is also included in primary law through Article 18 TFEU. In *Dano*, the CJEU stated that this principle of equal treatment was further defined in Article 24 in Directive 2004/38 and Article 4, Regulation 883/2004.[91] The principle of equal treatment as such does not differ therefore. What does differ is the possibility to depart from this principle. Article 24.2 of Directive 2004/38 allows, under certain conditions, unequal treatment in the light of the fact that the legislator wishes to balance the obligations of the Member States vis-à-vis non-economically active Union citizens.

The aim of the expansion of the personal scope of Regulation 883/2004 was not to lead to comprehensive substantial changes.[92] It may be inferred by the fact that the persons who are covered or have been covered by the social security system of a

[87] The referral to the Member States' intervention is a non-argument, as the Member States are ever keen to evade the requirements of Regulation 883/2004, Case C-140/12 *Pensionsversicherungsanstalt v Peter Brey*, EU:C:2013:565, 50.

[88] Case C-333/13 *Elisabeta Dano and Florin Dano v Jobcenter Leipzig*, EU:C:2014:2358, 63. This parallel track has been confirmed in *Alimanović*, where the Grand Chamber simply refers to the reasoning in *Dano;* Case C-67/14 *Jobcenter Berlin Neukölln v Nazifa Alimanovic and Others*, EU:C:2015:597, 44.

[89] cf the notification procedure according to Art 9 of the Regulation 883/2004 where there is no opt-out possibility once a benefit has been registered as a social security benefit. Case 35/77 *Elisabeth Beerens v Rijksdienst voor Arbeidsvoorziening* [1977] ECR 2249.

[90] Case C-333/13 *Elisabeta Dano and Florin Dano v Jobcenter Leipzig*, EU:C:2014:2358, 56.

[91] cf ibid, 61.

[92] cf Y Jorens and F van Overmeieren, 'General Principles of Coordination in Regulation 883/2004' [2009] *European Journal of Social Security* 47 ff.

Member State but who are non-economically active are only covered by two areas in Title III in the Regulation: sickness, maternity and equivalent paternity benefits in Chapter 1, and grant where a death has occurred in Chapter 3. The structure of the Regulation thus continues, regardless of the expansion of the personal scope, to be based on the migrant worker where the majority of the coordination rules in the Regulation are with regard to this latter group of persons. Regulation 883/2004 therefore still departs from the fundamental structures of the Regulation that are based on a coordination of the social security benefits for migrant workers and in line with this absolute equal treatment.

The uncomfortable outcome for the Member States as regards social security benefits, where non-economically active Union citizens can claim equal treatment when they are residents, arises with the expansion of the personal scope.[93] But is this fact a legitimate reason not to apply the Regulation? Is this relationship a legitimate reason for the CJEU to confuse the issue and erase the boundaries between two very different parts of the welfare state? Should not the situation that has arisen instead be subject to a revised regulation where we revert to the original personal scope and where the special characteristics of social security benefits are respected?

6.6.4.3. The Rules in the Regulation must be Understood in the Light of the Principle of Equal Treatment in EU Law

Whatever the situation regarding this fundamental question, the CJEU, to be on the safe side, in its obiter dicta in *Brey* (39–45), claimed that Regulation 883/2004 does not prevent the Member States from having supplementary qualification requirements after the Regulation has determined the state as the competent state.

The CJEU referred at this point to *Dumont de Chassart,* where the Court established that the rules regarding applicable legislation in Regulation 883/2004 only determines a Member State as the competent state.[94] The competent state is therefore not required to automatically grant social security benefits. Instead the Member State is free to maintain or adopt national qualification requirements that shall be fulfilled if an applicant shall have access to the benefits. This finding is correct and in line with the fact that Regulation 883/2004 is based on coordination. The Member States continue to have legislative competence.[95]

What the CJEU chose to disregard in its reasoning is the reservation that almost always arises in EU law contexts: freedom under responsibility. This freedom under responsibility has been highlighted in recital 17a in the Regulation, which in fact stipulates that:

[93] cf the Gender Perspective: V Paskalia, 'The (In)Visibility of Gender in the New Regulation [2005] *European Journal of Social Security* 197.

[94] Case C-619/11 *Patricia Dumont de Chassart v Office national d'allocations familiales pour travailleurs salariés (ONAFTS)*, EU:C:2013:92, 39–41. See also Case C-179/13 *Raad van bestuur van de Sociale verzekeringsbank v LF Evans*, EU:C:2015:12, 45.

[95] cf F Pennings, *European Social Security Law*, 6th edn (Cambridge - Antwerp - Portland, Intersentia, 2015) 6 ff.

> Once the legislation of a Member State becomes applicable to a person under Title II of this Regulation, the conditions for affiliation and entitlement to benefits should be defined by the legislation of the competent Member State.

However, this freedom entails a responsibility where the second part of recital 17a emphasises that it shall be done 'while respecting Community law'. This rather wing-clipped freedom was also emphasised in *Dumont de Chassart*. The CJEU established, further into the ruling, that the national qualification requirements must be the same vis-à-vis all persons, both nationals of the state in question and migrant workers.[96] Thus, the national rules, which take precedence when a Member State has been determined as the competent state by the rules on applicable legislation in the Regulation, cannot be drawn up without taking consideration of the comprehensive principle of equal treatment in EU law. The obiter dicta of the CJEU are therefore self-defeating.

6.6.4.4. *The Consequences of the EU Having Limited Legislative Competence in the Area of Social Policy*

In *Brey*, the CJEU also pursued a line of reasoning that a different outcome would:

> lead to unjustifiable differences in treatment between Member States, according to how their national social security systems are organised[97]

The CJEU chose to ignore the fundamental fact that Regulation 883/2004 is based on coordination. The basic principle is that the Member States determine their own social security systems.

In line with this the Regulation entails no provisions on the harmonisation of legislation on social security in the Member States. With regard to workers, Article 51 only stipulates that the Member States' legislation shall be coordinated. The differences concerning content and procedure between different social security systems in each and every Member State, and consequently between the entitlement of the people that work in them, are therefore not affected by this provision.[98]

With Regulation 883/2004, the personal scope was expanded to encompass all citizens in a Member State that are or have been covered by the social security

[96] Case C-619/11 *Patricia Dumont de Chassart v Office national d'allocations familiales pour travailleurs salariés (ONAFTS)*, EU:C:2013:92 41. See also Case C-388/09 *Joao Filipe da Silva Martins v Bank Betriebskrankenkasse-Pflegekasse* [2011] ECR I-5737, 71 for further case law. See also Case C-347/10 *A Salemink v Raad van bestuur van het Uitvoeringsinstituut werknemersverzekeringen*, EU:C:2012:17, 39–41 and Case C-106/11 *MJ Bakker v Minister van Financiën*, EU:C:2012:328, 32–34.

[97] Case C-140/12 *Pensionsversicherungsanstalt v Peter Brey*, EU:C:2013:565 59.

[98] Case C-393/99 *Hervein et al* [2002] ECR I-02829, 50. Cf Case C-41/84 *Pietro Pinna v Caisse d'allocations familiales de la Savoie* [1986] ECR 1, 20; Case C-340/94, *EJM de Jaeck v Staatssecretaris van Financiën* [1997] I-461, 18; Case C-221/95 *Institut national d'assurances sociales pour travailleurs indépendants (Inasti) v Claude Hervein and Hervillier SA* [1997] I-609, 16. See also N Rennuy, 'The Emergence of a Parallell System of Social Coordination' [2013] *CMLR* 1225 ff.

system of a Member State. Consequently, the same principle continues to also apply to this expanded personal scope regardless of the fact that the outcome of certain specific situations might be perceived as unfair.

Therefore, the Regulation cannot be used to justify the claim of an indirect harmonisation of the social benefits of the Member States by starting to equate social security benefits with social assistance at the general level.

As regards primary law, there is the fact that the competence of the EU as regards a common social policy is very limited. Although Article 151 TFEU stipulates that within the field of social policy the EU shall promote employment, improve living and working conditions, achieve satisfactory social protection and combat social exclusion. The action that the EU can take is, however, very limited according to Article 153 TFEU, as the measures that can be taken at the EU level in the area of social policy may only be supportive in nature and shall be a complement to the legislation of the Member States. Moreover, this supportive action can only be taken with unanimity in accordance with the specific legislative procedure. In this light, you could say that the EU has not been awarded competence regarding how the Member States choose to organise their social benefits; whether it is a matter of social assistance or social security.

It is thus possible to establish that Union law respects the authority of the Member States to organise their welfare systems both specifically (Regulation 883/2004) and in general (the way the Member States organise their welfare systems). In this way, an 'unjustifiable' difference cannot arise. The differences are instead a natural consequence of the fact that the social security systems and the social assistance systems of the Member States are coordinated without any harmonisation.

As has been shown above, the expansion of the personal scope of the Regulation to include a large majority of all Union citizens has led to a situation whereby non-economically active Union citizens might gain access to national special non-contributory cash benefits on the basis of residence, by claiming equal treatment. This leads to unexpected and uncomfortable outcomes. But is it the task for the CJEU to correct these outcomes, and thus harmonise the social welfare systems of the Member States by the back door and by disregarding the coordination procedure and the fact that the EU lacks the legislative competence in this particular area?

6.6.4.5. Does Directive 2004/38 Have an Advantage over Regulation 883/2004?

How should we handle the fact that it is not always self-evident what should be perceived as a special non-contributory cash benefit and what should be perceived as a 'pure' social security benefit? In line with the current development of case law in the shape of *Brey*, *Dano*, *Alimanović* and *García-Nieto* the dividing line will be much more important since it will be possible to impose a residence condition on the special non-contributory cash benefit for a Union citizen. In the future, will we start seeing a CJEU assessing the benefits that the Member States include on the list of special non-contributory cash benefits with greater alacrity than has previously been the case? *The Commission v The Council and the European Parliament*[99] is one of a series of rulings where the CJEU established that registered special non-contributory cash benefits should be viewed as social security benefits.[100] The stance of the CJEU has been that the nature of the benefit is decisive, and not the classification as a special non-contributory cash benefit. This restrictive view of special non-contributory cash benefits on the part of the CJEU has opened up the welfare systems to migrant workers living in another state than the competent state: an export according to the rules of the Regulation has thus become possible. Will the balance now tip over to the side where free movement of persons is limited, the free movement that the Regulation is intended to support, because the CJEU dances to the tune of the Member States to withhold certain social security benefits from non-economically active Union citizens resident in any particular Member State?

Without priority rules in place regarding the Regulation and the Directive, it is difficult to see that the overarching aim of the Regulation with regard to the free movement of persons can be limited concerning special non-contributory cash benefits, solely on the ground that certain outcomes as regards non-economically active Union citizens may be seen as tricky.

6.6.5. Can a Residency Condition be Added to all Social Security Benefits? Case C-308/14 *The Commission v The UK*

Brey, *Dano*, *Alimanović* and *García-Nieto* all deal with national social security benefits that are classified as special non-contributory cash benefits according to Regulation 883/2004. In *Brey*, the CJEU held that such special non-contributory cash benefits could be regarded, in parallel, as social assistance in the meaning

[99] Case C-299/05 *Commission of the European Communities v European Parliament and Council of the European Union* [2007] ECR I-8695.

[100] The Commission stated in Case C-299/05 that certain Swedish, Finnish and British benefits included in the revised Annex for special non-contributory cash benefits through Regulation 657/2005 ([2005] OJ L 117) should be regarded as social security benefits and not non-contributory benefits. As regards Sweden, the CJEU stated that even if the special derogation in the Regulation with regard to certain disability schemes were linked to a person's social conditions in Sweden, the purpose of the care allowance is mainly medical in nature. The purpose is thus covered by the scope of the Regulation, 'sickness benefits'. The main purpose of the disability allowance, according to the CJEU, is to cover the risks of the illness, which caused the disability. Thus, both benefits lacked the mixed character that is necessary to be exempt from export. It can also be said that the EU Regulation and the Swedish disability policy are not aligned. The Regulation does not recognise benefits that include social security benefit features but that have a further underlying aim, for example, integration into society. Moreover, it is very provocative indeed, from the perspective of Swedish disability policy, to regard disability as an illness. The preliminary ruling thus gives rise to further questions than just financial ones. If the CJEU were in the future to revise its view on these benefits and instead class them as special non-contributory cash benefits, the delicate issue for Sweden concerning whether a residence condition should be introduced with regard to persons with disabilities who are non-economically active Union citizens resident in Sweden would arise.

of article 7.1 b of Directive 2004/38. Hence applying for such a social security benefit could be seen as burdening the social assistance system according to Directive 2004/38.

The latest in a line of preliminary rulings that addresses the boundaries of transnational solidarity is the case C-308/14, *Commission v United Kingdom*.[101] The ruling deals with 'pure' social security benefits where Directive 2004/38 is not applicable.

Irrespective of this fact the preliminary ruling sent a clear signal to the United Kingdom only days ahead of its referendum held on June 23, 2016.[102] The signal was that Regulation 883/2004 enables additional discriminatory national legal requirements with regard to access to residence based social security benefits.[103]

6.6.5.1. *Background to the Infringement*

The background to the infringement case against the UK was that in 2008, the UK had made access to national family benefits conditional. Child Benefit and the Child Tax Credit (tax relief for families with children) were, after a national amendment to the law, only granted if a migrant Union citizen had a right to residence. The situation was similar to that in *Brey*, *Dano*, *Alimanović* and *García-Nieto*, where social security benefits had become conditional on the right to residence.

There is, however, a decisive difference: the British benefits have been registered and classified as family benefits in the meaning of the Regulation[104] and not as special non-contributory cash benefits with a flavour of social assistance.

Social security benefits that have been registered by a Member State as benefits covered by the scope of the Regulation do not fall under Article 3.5 of the Regulation where social assistance is defined. With a purely textual interpretation it is therefore clear that if a residence-based benefit is registered as a social security benefit, it will not be possible to invoke Directive 2004/38, since the Directive is only aimed at benefits that are perceived as social assistance.

With regard to this, the CJEU held that the British benefits *Child Benefit* and *Child Tax Credits* are to be understood as benefits in cash, even though financed by the tax system and not by social contributions.[105] The Court concluded that

[101] Case C-308/14, *European Commission v United Kingdom and Northern Ireland*, EU:C:2016:436.

[102] The Judgment was delivered 14 June 2016.

[103] However, the ruling did not have a decisive impact on the outcome of the referendum as the British tabloid press did not cover the story. The British daily press did cover but not extensively cf http://www.independent.co.uk/news/uk/politics/eu-court-backs-uks-ability-to-restrict-child-benefits-for-migrants-a7081046.html, see also http://www.theguardian.com/law/2016/jun/14/european-court-back-uk-limits-migrants-access-child-benefits, accessed 18 April 2017.

[104] Declaration by the United Kingdom pursuant to Art 9 of Regulation (EC) No 883/2004 of the European Parliament and of the Council of 29 April 2004 on the coordination of social security systems, http://ec.europa.eu/social/main.jsp?catId=868&intPageId=2285&langId=en.

[105] ibid, p 55.

since the British benefits are paid out automatically when a family fulfils certain criteria, the benefits are to be seen as social security benefits, covered by the Regulation's material scope.[106] Finally, the Court noted that these benefits have not been included in Annex X to Regulation 883/2004. Therefore, the benefits cannot be regarded as special non-contributory cash benefits.[107]

The Commission v United Kingdom case draws here a clear line: social security benefits, apart from special non-contributory cash benefits, that fall within the material scope of Regulation 883/2004 cannot in parallel fall under Directive 2004/38. Therefore, the Member States cannot claim an unequal treatment of union citizens that stems from Directive 2004/38's Articles 7.1 (b) and 24.2. Instead pure national social security benefits within the material scope of the Regulation 883/2004 are still covered by the Regulation and its rules on equal treatment in Article 4.

The crucial and decisive issue was therefore whether the United Kingdom had the right, according to the Regulation 883/2004, to introduce an additional requirement of a right to reside. This irrespective of the fact that Article 11.3 e of the Regulation already had determined the UK legislation as the applicable legislation and that under universal models the sheer residence in itself suffices for eligibility.

The CJEU found in its ruling that it is possible to introduce additional national requirements.[108] The Court stated that Article 11.3 e of Regulation 883/2004 is merely to be seen as a conflict of law rule, not a rule determining any material criteria with regard to the substantial right to social security benefits.[109] Thus additional national requirements, such as a right to reside as in *Brey*, with regard to residence-based benefits are possible.[110]

O'Brien criticises the introduction of the unreasonable burden test as a catch-all principle.[111] I agree with this criticism as the use of the Directive 2004/38's unreasonable burden-test was introduced to the special non-contributory cash benefits as the Directive's notion 'social assistance' was broadened in *Brey* to include these social security benefits. Hence, no new catch-all principle was introduced where all social benefits including social security benefits would be covered. On the opposite, the CJEU was at pains trying to argue that special non-contributory cash benefits were to be regarded as social assistance and thus falling under Directive 2004/38.[112]

[106] ibid, pp 58–60.

[107] ibid, p 56.

[108] Cf The Advocate General Cruz Villalón that argues that the national legislature is examining the lawfulness of a residence in connection with the grant of certain social benefits, the Opinion of the Advocate General, EU:C:2015:666, p 54. This understanding led the Advocate General straight on to an assessment of a possible discrimination under article 4 of the Regulation.

[109] Case C-308/14, *Commission v United Kingdom*, pp 64 and 65.

[110] ibid, p 68.

[111] O'Brien, C, 'The ECJ sacrifices EU Citizenship in vain: Commission v. United Kingdom', [2017] *CMLR* 209; p 219.

[112] Case C-140/12, Brey, p 50 ff.

As the Regulation 883/2004 applies in *Commission v UK* the non-discriminatory principle in Article 4 of Regulation 883/2004 applies in full.

The CJEU finds, with regard to this issue, that the United Kingdom's legislation gives rise to indirect discrimination, since the British requirement of residence is more easily fulfilled by British residents, '... who more often than not are habitually resident in the United Kingdom ...'.[113]

The finding of the CJEU is however not correct as, the British Immigration Act of 1971, Section 2, provides that a person has the right to reside and live in the United Kingdom if the person is a British citizen. *E contrario* a person being a citizen of another Member State has not such a right. The British Immigration Act makes a direct distinction between British citizens and those who are not British citizens.[114] It cannot therefore be the case of an indirect discrimination but direct discrimination.[115]

However, as a direct consequence of the Court seeing the British legislation as indirectly discriminatory is that the Court will not be restricted to the direct discrimination exceptions listed in Article 45.3 TFEU: public policy, public security or public health. Seeing the British Immigration Act as indirectly discriminatory the Court can therefore take into consideration the aim of securing economic sustainability with regard to social *security* as an objective justification in cases where market access has been at stake.[116]

The CJEU has in the recent infringement case *European Commission v Republic of Cyprus* of 21st January 2016 confirmed that a Member State has the possibility of unequal treatment if it can prove that it is motivated by ensuring the economic balance in the national social security system. This burden of proof means '... an objective, detailed analysis, supported by figures ...'[117] In *Commission v UK* the CJEU totally ignore the case law with regard to the burden of proof.[118] The Court simply moves on to a proportionality test where the CJEU finds that the British

[113] Case C-308/14, Commission v United Kingdom, pp 76 and 78.

[114] Cf O'Brien, C, 'The ECJ sacrifices EU Citizenship in vain: Commission v. United Kingdom', [2017] *CMLR* 209; 225.

[115] The Advocate General Cruz Villalón discusses the legitimacy of a requirement of a right to reside rather than whether the requirement is discriminatory, The Opinion of the Advocate General, EU:C:2015:666, p 58 ff. In doing so the Advocate General finds that it is not possible to uphold a distinction between two legislative acts. '... the EU legal order could hardly consist of a multiplicity of entirely separate compartments ...', p 72. However, as the Social policy is an area of limited competence the issue is rather whether the purpose of the EU law is to sweeten the (national) bitter pill or respect the EU legislation which has not connected Regulation 883/2004 and Directive 2004/38 as the legal bases differ, cf the Advocate General Wahl, Opinion in C-140/12, Pensionsversicherungsanstalt v Peter Brey, EU:C:2013:337, p. 56. See also O'Brien that states that '... legal principles and instruments should not simply be eclipsed by "natural" discriminatory instincts.', O'Brien, C, 'The ECJ sacrifices EU Citizenship in vain: Commission v. United Kingdom' [2017] *CMLR* 209; 225.

[116] Case C-158/96, *Raymond Kohll v Union des caisses de maladie*, EU:C:1998:171, p 41.

[117] Case C-515/14, *European Commission v Republic of Cyprus*, EU:C:2016:30. Cf O'Brien, C, 'The ECJ sacrifices EU Citizenship in vain: Commission v. United Kingdom' [2017] *CMLR* 209; 230.

[118] Ibid p 227 ff.

requirement of a right to reside is proportional, since the authority checks are not carried out in a systematic manner but only performed by the authorities in cases when it is not certain whether there is a right to reside or not.[119] This control can, however, only be done systematically since the HM Revenue & Customs has to follow national rules on good administration and decide on basis of complete information.[120]

6.6.5.2. *Analysis*

The residence-based models are based on a redistributive basic idea that stems from the early twentieth century with poor public health or [as in Sweden] an ageing population. With universal welfare systems, states quickly reached out to entire populations, rather than only the working population.

The universal residence-based model has, with the free movement of persons that goes with Union citizenship, been exposed in such a way that was impossible to predict in previous contexts with more limited mobility between states.

British social security is based on the Beveridge model.[121] This is a universal model, whereby everyone resident in the UK has access to social security benefits. Child Benefit and Child Tax Credits are paid to residents of the UK. When these universal residence-based benefits were exposed to a substantial Union citizenship with new rights but not the corresponding obligations, domestic political pressure arose to change the conditions of the benefits vis-à-vis non-economically active Union citizens.[122]

The initial issue is therefore the same as in *Brey*, *Dano*, *Alimanović* and *García-Nieto*: can access to social security benefits become conditional on a right to residence? There are, however, two major differences.

First, in the infringement case it is not a matter of special non-contributory cash benefits. It is instead about pure social security benefits. It is about social security benefits that are supposed to be coordinated through Regulation 883/2004. Secondly, *Brey*, *Dano*, *Alimanović* and *García-Nieto* are about universal islands in an otherwise Bismarckian landscape. They are about special derogations from otherwise national fundamental structures in place where work is the basis for social security benefits.

[119] Case C-308/14, Commission v United Kingdom, p 83.

[120] Cf Cousins: '… it is clear that there *is* systematic verification of the right to reside in *every* case—it is only the *degree* of verification that varies.' Cousins, M, 'The baseless fabric of this vision: EU citizenship, the right to reside and EU law' [2016] *Journal of Social Security Law* 89; 104, O'Brien, C, 'The ECJ sacrifices EU Citizenship in vain: Commission v. United Kingdom' [2017] *CMLR* 209; 228.

[121] The 1942 report on *Social Insurance and Allied Services*, known as the Beveridge Report, was an influential document in the founding of the welfare state in the United Kingdom: see B Abel-Smith, 'The Beveridge report: Its origins and outcomes' (1992) 1-2 *International Social Security Review* 5.

[122] cf S Giubboni, 'A Certain Degree of Solidarity? Free Movement of Persons and Access to Social Protection in the Case Law of the European CJEU', in Y Borgmann-Prebil and M Ross (eds) *Promoting Solidarity in the European Union* (Oxford, Oxford University Press, 2010); K Hailbronner, 'Union Citizenship and Access to Social Benefits' [2005] CMLR 1245.

If it is possible to start exempting the core of the social security benefits from the coordination of Regulation 883/2004 by referring to Directive 2004/38, what will there be left to coordinate? What has happened in *Commission v the UK*, is that the CJEU has de facto limited the personal scope of the Regulation to only encompass migrant workers. The principle of equal treatment in the Regulation has been invalidated by asserting the possibilities for unequal treatment, for the parts of the residence-based social security benefits that contain redistribution policy features vis-à-vis the non-economically active Union citizens. The Member States will therefore be free to set up a 'virtual' territoriality within the state and thus limit the residence-based benefits to their own nationals (and of course migrant workers).[123] A territoriality which is what the coordination of the social security systems of the Member States, according to recital 7 in the Regulation, has been put in place to dismantle.[124] It is about a coordination that with Regulation 883/2004 was expanded to cover more persons including all citizens that are or have been covered by a social security system of a Member State.

The situation is akin to when the CJEU opened Pandora's box in the area of cross-border healthcare. It is sufficient to take a peek into that box to realise how the complexity of the social security systems can interplay with, reinforce and/or prevent what the CJEU initially perceived as a neat way of resolving an unpredictable and rather tricky situation.

By drawing up parallel legal tracks in *Kohll*,[125] in that the Regulation was still applicable but supplemented with a free movement of services in the area of cross-border healthcare, the CJEU was able to ensure cross-border healthcare in the individual case. The situation in *Kohll* was, however, relatively uncomplicated where the healthcare cost for Luxemburg remained at the same level as the same cost of care that had been paid in Luxemburg that now had to be paid to the German caregiver. Some 15 preliminary rulings and one Patient Mobility Directive[126] later, the applicable law for cross-border healthcare can hardly be accused of unequivocally reinforcing cross-border healthcare.[127]

It can be said that, as opposed to *Kohll*, there is a desire on the part of the CJEU to limit (or rather balance) a fundamental freedom of movement to only encompass economically active Union citizens. It is thus a matter of contrary judicial activism from the part of the CJEU: an activism to limit EU law rather than reinforce

[123] Migrant workers have a right of residency as of day one, Art 7.1. a Directive 2004/38.

[124] Wyatt talks of the national models being complemented by 'provisions of Community Law designed to compensate for their territorial "shortcomings"'. D Wyatt, 'Social Security Rights of Migrant Workers and their Families' [1977] CMLR 411, 414.

[125] Case C-158/96 *Raymond Kohll v Union des caisses de maladie* [1998] ECR I-1931.

[126] Directive 2011/24/EU of the European Parliament and of the Council of 9 March 2011 on the application of patients' rights in cross-border healthcare, [2011] OJ L 88/45.

[127] E Szyszczak, 'Patient's Rights: A Lost Cause or Missed Opportunity', in JW van den Gronde, E Szyszczak, U Neergaard and M Krajewski (eds), *Legal Issues of Services of General Interest—Health Care and EU Law* (Haag, Asser, 2011) 118 ff.

it. Nonetheless, this judicial activism gives rise to the same question regarding the CJEU as a potential legislator:[128] but the question is instead whether it is up to the CJEU to limit and thus also reinstate, the persons covered to what was stipulated in Regulation 1408/71?

There are different ways of organising national welfare. To put it simply, you could say that social security benefits can either be based on residence or work. The fundamental idea of the Beveridge model was characterised by a territorial solidarity with people who were residents in the United Kingdom. The model is based on the idea of equal treatment where all residents have the same rights. The British amendments to the law that have been made were a step away from the basic principle of the Beveridge model. A difference has thus been introduced which leads to thoughts about the impact of harmonising EU law in the direction of the Bismarck system, at least in cross-border situations where work now gives rise to the right to social security benefits. The paradox in this context is that the Member States, in order to preserve their systems, are introducing residence requirements and are themselves driving this process forward.

6.7. CONCLUSION

The preliminary rulings in *Brey*, *Dano*, *Alimanović*, *García-Nieto* and *the Commission v the UK* cover the entire system of welfare and give rise to a number of questions on national welfare policy, solidarity, Union citizenship, fundamental rights, and not least strong feelings.

The national welfare models are normally based on solidarity that stems from a common history, values and identity.[129] This solidarity is above all regulated in laws that are based on a territorial solidarity.[130] This solidarity vis-à-vis the neediest is based on residence, since work, as a ground for qualification, does not enter into the equation to any great extent.[131]

With the expansion of the personal scope of the Regulation 883/2004 in the year 2004 to also include a majority of all Union citizens, it was possible for a new group of persons to gain access to the social security benefits that were already granted on the basis of residence. This situation together with the principle of equal treatment of Regulation 883/2004 led to unexpected (and for certain Member States) undesired results.[132]

[128] cf H Rasmussen, *On Law and Policy in the European CJEU—A Comparative Study in Judicial Policymaking* (Dordrecht, Martinus Nijhoff Publishers, 1986).

[129] K Tuori, 'European Social Constitution: Between Solidarity and Access Justice', in K Purnhagen and P Rott (eds), *Varieties of European Economic Law and Regulation, Liber Amicorum for Hans Micklitz* (Cham, Springer, 2014) 374 ff.

[130] cf Pieters, who refers to circles of solidarity normally to be found within the borders of a state. F Pieters, *Social Security: An Introduction to the Basic Principles*, 2nd edn (Haag, Kluwer, 2006) 21.

[131] G Esping-Andersen, *The Three Worlds of Welfare Capitalism* (London, Polity Press, 1990) 27 ff.

[132] For a discussion on solidarity, trans-solidarity and the outer boundaries thereof in the light of recent legal developments see, eg, D Schiek, 'Perspectives on social citizenship in the EU—from

The preliminary rulings in *Brey*, *Dano*, *Alimanović* and *García-Nieto* indicate that the CJEU is now trying to obtain a balance between the social rights, in a broad sense, of the non-economically active Union citizens and the demands for economic balance in the welfare systems of the Member States.[133]

One might think that it is not reasonable that a benefit of one Member State falls under the scope of Directive 2004/38, while the benefit of another is instead regarded as a social security benefit with far-reaching impact.

The CJEU has been sensitive to the problems and in its preliminary ruling in *Brey* constructed a bridge between Regulation 883/2004 and Directive 2004/38. This continued in *Dano* and could be said to have been consolidated in *Alimanović* and *García-Nieto*. This construction, however, as shown above, holds five serious flaws:

1. Social security benefits and social assistance have different underlying aims. For that reason, these types of benefits have been regulated in two separate EU law regulations with different perspectives as regards the free movement of persons.
2. In *Brey* the CJEU disregards the fact that the main focus of Regulation 883/2004 is the competent state and not the previous competent state.
3. The rules of the Regulation on applicable legislation indicate which state is the competent state, this does not mean, however, that the Member States may introduce supplementary national qualifications that do not take consideration of the principle of equal treatment in Article 4, Regulation 883/2004.
4. The EU has limited legislative competence in the social policy area, this is why the social welfare systems differ and so the outcomes differ, even if they may be regarded as 'unwarranted'.
5. Without mutual rules of priority between Regulation 883/2004 and Directive 2004/38 it is not self-evident that the overarching aim of the Regulation with regard to free movement of persons is only limited on the basis that certain outcomes as regards non-economically active Union citizens might be regarded as tricky.

As regards the status of the national special non-contributory cash benefits it is therefore difficult, to see how the smokescreens established by the CJEU, justify overlooking Regulation 883/2004. Moreover, the outcome in *Brey*, *Dano*, *Alimanović* and *García-Nieto* runs the risk of leading to far-reaching consequences not only as regards special non-contributory cash benefits but also the social security systems of the Member States in general as the CJEU has taken those preliminary rulings as a starting point in *Commission v The UK*.

status positivus to status socialis activus via two forms of transnational solidarity' in D Kochenov, *EU Citizenship and Federalism: The Role of Rights* (Cambridge, Cambridge University Press, 2016) and N Nic Shuibhne, 'Limits Rising, Duties Ascending: the Changing Legal Shape of Union Citizenship' [2015] CMLR 889.

[133] The issue of striking a balance between these interests were not at stake in *Dano*, as according to the German national court Elisabeta Dano did not have a right of residency.

The CJEU, when assessing this latter preliminary ruling, should have taken into account as it is expressed by Bengoetxea, MacCormick and Moral Soriano 'whether and by what considerations its decisions are justified, or at the very least, rationally justifiable.'[134]

Taking account of the current state of affairs in that light, it is clear that the underlying reason for the bridge decided by the CJEU is justifiable from the point of view put forward by the Advocate General in *The Commission v the UK* and it is a matter of a beloved child having many names: social security benefit, social assistance, social benefit. But then, as shown above, you disregard the fact that the benefits differ in a fundamental way and that it is still the Member States who decide and manage their respective systems since the EU lacks the competence in the area of social policy. Moreover, it is hardly justifiable that the CJEU, in its eagerness to build a bridge in *Brey* disregards the fact that the main focus of Regulation 883/2004 is the competent state and not the previous competent state. In this context, in the light of the free movement of persons, it is also important to take into consideration the long-term consequences the mix-up of the CJEU as regards welfare benefits.

As far as special non-contributory cash benefits are concerned, the complexity has increased, since in the future not only must there be a differentiation between economically active and non-economically active Union citizens, but also between special non-contributory cash benefits with social assistance features and special non-contributory cash benefits that instead have a different purpose for instance the integration of people with disabilities in society.

In *Commission v UK* CJEU accepts a national distinction being made between migrating workers and economically inactive union citizens as to the access to national residence-based social security benefits.

This is not surprising, given the previous case law and the fact that the Court plays the Social Tourism Card right at the beginning of its judgment where it states that Article 11.3 e could lead to residence based family benefits being requested by '… in particular, economically inactive persons.'[135]

It is difficult to disregard the fact that the CJEU delivered its judgment *Commission v United Kingdom* only days before the British referendum.[136] As shown, the CJEU substantially narrows the personal scope, despite the clear wording in Article 2 of the Regulation and, furthermore, introduces a catch-all principle as to unreasonable burden. However, the Court does that without the judgment

[134] J Bengoetxea, N MacCormick and L Moral Soriano, 'Integration and Integrity in the Legal Reasoning of the European CJEU', in C de Búrca and J Weiler, *The European CJEU* (Oxford, Oxford University Press, 2001) 43.

[135] Case C-308/14, Commission v United Kingdom, p 63.

[136] See also O´Brien who is of the opinion that the CJEU operated as a political actor releasing the judgment nine days before the referendum, O'Brien, C, 'The ECJ sacrifices EU Citizenship in vain: Commission v. United Kingdom' [2017] *CMLR* 209; 209.

being rationally justifiable. Instead, the judgment is at risk of being perceived as an odd interjection in the run-up to the referendum.

The judgment will inevitably lead to question the personal scope of the Regulation 883/2004 and raise the issue whether the scope should be limited to (once again) include only migrating economically active union citizens, thus better reflecting the current understanding of the outer boundaries to a transnational solidarity.

In other words, arguments for a return to the personal scope of the original Regulation 3/58 and Regulation 1408/71 could be brought to the fore. This option would, in my opinion, bring honesty, more clarity and foreseeability.

The Commission, however, tries to ignore this elephant in the room in its recent proposal to amend the Regulation 883/2004.[137] The Commission proposes that the current standing of (bad) case law should form the basis for an amended set of rules on applicable legislation. The proposal foresees an amendment of Article 4 of the Regulation on equal treatment by introducing the possibility for Member States to require legal residence as set out in Directive 2004/38 before granting residence based social security benefits.

I fear that such an amendment would not be in line with Article 18 TFEU and the primary law understanding of the equal treatment principle. Furthermore, the new wording would lead to even more confusion as what would happen, in fact, is that the personal scope of the Regulation would be limited by the proposed amendment.

[137] Proposal for a Regulation of the European Parliament and of the Council amending Regulation (EC) No 883/2004 on the coordination of social security systems and Regulation (EC) No 987/2009 laying down the procedure for implementing Regulation (EC) No 883/2004, COM(2016) 815.

7

The Charter of Fundamental Rights

7.1. INTRODUCTION

THIS MONOGRAPH EXAMINES three areas. The social security systems of the Member States have been coordinated in an internal market context, and the monograph has analysed how this context impacts national social security systems. The monograph then explores how Union citizenship and the Charter of Rights have affected the coordination of the national social security systems. Chapter 6 has shown how Union citizenship can enhance the free movement of persons, but also how a recent balancing vis-à-vis the Member States' concerns with regard to their systems sustainability has occurred. The third simultaneously acting area of law on which this chapter focuses, is the European Union Charter of Fundamental Rights (the Charter of Fundamental Rights, or the Charter).[1]

The Charter of Fundamental Rights became binding primary law in 2009 as part of the Lisbon Treaty. Court statistics show that the number of cases where the Charter of Fundamental Rights has been invoked has increased steadily, and that now the Court has referred to the Charter of Fundamental Rights in a total of more than 600 cases.[2]

Rosas has stated that, so far, the cases have had essentially four issues of concern: the applicability of the Charter of Fundamental Rights; references to the Charter in the case law where the Charter is used as an interpretational background; interpretation of Charter rights; and setting aside secondary legislation in light of the Charter of Fundamental Rights.[3]

[1] Charter of Fundamental Rights of the European Union, [2010] OJ C 83/389.

[2] *2015 Report on the application of the EU Charter of Fundamental Rights* (COM (2016) 265 final) and Staff Working Document on the Application of the EU Charter of Fundamental Rights in 2015, SWD (2016) 158 final, (COM (2016) 265 final) 6.

[3] Up to 2014 and for the most part, the Articles and rights of the Charter on which the CJEU had to take a position included Art 47 on the Right of Access to the Judicial System; civil rights including non-discrimination; Art 51 on the Charter's applicability; Art 52(1), (3) and (7) regarding the Charter's relationship with the ECHR and national constitutions; Art 52(5) on the division of rights and principles; and Art 53 of the ECHR as the starting point for the protection level. See A Rosas, *Four Years of Charter Case Law: Some Observations* (Oxford, Hart, 2015) and P Douglas-Scott, 'The Relationship Between the EU Charter and the ECHR I, Protecting the Internal Market from the Charter', in S de Vries, U Bernitz and S Weatherill (eds), *Five Years Legally Binding EU Charter of Fundamental Rights—What is the State of Play in the Protection of Fundamental Rights in the EU?* (Oxford, Hart, 2015).

The current chapter initially touches on Article 34 of the Charter and the right to social security in relation to other civil rights instruments. Thereafter, a background is given for the Charter, followed by a short description of its content and overall structure. The applicability of the Charter has been and still is a sensitive issue for the Member States, and therefore special attention is dedicated to it. The issue has particular bearing on the Charter's impact versus the national social security systems, not least because Regulation 883/2004 is an instrument of coordination. The chapter's conclusion provides an analysis of the substantive articles, including Article 34 and the Right to Social Security, to ascertain whether these rights can be of substantial independent nature and thereby impact on the Member States' national social security systems.

7.2. THE RIGHT TO SOCIAL SECURITY IN RELATION TO THE ECHR AND OTHER RIGHTS INSTRUMENTS UNDER THE CHARTER OF FUNDAMENTAL RIGHTS

A predominant issue raised is whether and how the European Convention on Human Rights (ECHR) catalogue of rights interacts with the Charter of Fundamental Rights.[4]

The Lisbon Treaty and Article 6 TFEU stipulate that the EU shall accede to the ECHR.[5] This process is now facing new challenges, following the CJEU's opinion of 18 December 2014, in which the Court stated that the accession treaty was not compatible with current EU legislation.[6] However, an accession would not add any substantive rights, to a significant extent, to national social security systems, in that the ECHR catalogue does not include any substantial rights to social security.[7]

[4] For a thorough overview, see L Besselink, *The Protection of Fundamental Rights post-Lisbon—The Interaction between the EU Charter of Fundamental Rights, the European Convention on Human Rights (ECHR) and National Constitutions*, Reports of the XXV FIDE Congress, Tallinn, 2012, Vol 1, 63–140.

[5] E Wennerström, 'EU Accession to the European Convention on Human Rights—the Creation of a European Legal Space for Human Rights or the Last Stand for the Normative Supremacy of the Strasbourg System?' [2013] *Europarättslig Tidskrift* 375; J Polakiewicz, 'EU Law and the ECHR: Will the European Union's Accession Square the Circle?' [2013] *European Human Rights Law Review*, 592; X Groussot, T Lock and L Pech, 'EU Accession to the European Convention on Human Rights: A Legal Assessment of the Draft Accession Agreement of 14th October 2011' [2011] 218 *Fondation Robert Schuman, European Issues.*

[6] Opinion pursuant to Art 218(11) TFEU—Draft international agreement—Accession of the European Union to the European Convention for the Protection of Human Rights and Fundamental Freedoms—Compatibility of the draft agreement with the EU and FEU Treaties, Opinion 2/13, EU:C:2014:2454.

[7] See Case 17371/90 *Gaygusuz v Austria*, 16 September, 1996. Gaygusuz had paid social security contributions in Austria but could not obtain the benefits because he was not an Austrian citizen. The ECtHR found that the Convention was applicable when there was a connection between the contributions being paid and a right to social security. According to ECHR Art 14 and its Protocol 1, Art 1 the situation posed an unlawful discrimination. See also M Dahlberg, 'Should Social Rights Be Included in Interpretations of the Convention by the European Court of Human Rights?' [2014] *European Journal of Social Security* 252. White notes that the ECHR does not in itself lead to a right to social security,

The declarations in respect of the Charter of Fundamental Rights[8] refer in particular to two instruments in the field of social security. The European Council's European Social Charter[9] contains wordings of relevance to national social security systems. These formulations, which are binding for the signatory states, however, go no further than what is already present in national legislation.[10] The second instrument, the Community Charter of Fundamental Social Rights of Workers,[11] has mainly been regarded as a declaratory document whose goals have subsequently been included in the EU Treaties.[12]

In light of the above, the current chapter focuses mainly on EU legal aspects of the Charter of Fundamental Rights and does not deal with the parallel rights instruments.

7.3. THE CONTENTS AND STRUCTURE OF THE CHARTER OF FUNDAMENTAL RIGHTS

Article 6.1 TEU establishes that 'The union should recognize the rights, freedoms and principles laid down in the European Charter of Fundamental Rights ... to have the same legal value as the Treaties'. The Charter of Fundamental Rights is thus primary law and now represents one of the foundations of EU law.[13]

The Charter includes not only a wide range of traditional freedoms and rights[14] but also social rights and a constitutionalisation of certain EU-specific legal rights, such as freedom of movement of persons and non-discrimination. In this way it

as the ECtHR's case law concern procedural issues in connection with the social security systems: R White, 'Art 34—Social Security and Social Assistance', in P Peers, T Hervey, J Kenner and A Ward (eds), *The EU Charter of Fundamental Rights; a Commentary* (Oxford, Hart, 2014) 930 ff.

[8] Explanations relating to the Charter of Fundamental Rights, [2007] OJ C 303/02.

[9] European Social Charter (ETS 35), http://conventionp.coe.int/Treaty/en/Treaties/Html/035.htm, and European Social Charter (Revised) (ETS 163), http://conventionp.coe.int/Treaty/en/Treaties/Html/163.htm.

[10] cf R White, 'Art 34—Social Security and Social Assistance', in P Peers, T Hervey, J Kenner and A Ward (eds), *The EU Charter of Fundamental Rights* (Oxford, Hart, 2014) 934.

[11] 'The Community Charter of Fundamental Social Rights for Workers' (May 1990) 6/90 *European File*, www.eesc.europa.eu/resources/docs/community-charter-en.pdf.

[12] See P Watson, *EU Social and Employment Law*, 2nd edn (Oxford, Oxford University Press, 2014) 44 ff. The Lisbon Treaty refers to this Charter in Chapter X of the EU's Social Policy, Art 151 TFEU.

[13] See however Pétursson, who is of the opinion that the Charter of Fundamental Rights can be seen as a "supra-constitutional" legal act: GT Pétursson, *The Proportionality Principle as a Tool for Disintegration in EU Law—of Balancing and Coherence in the Light of the Fundamental Freedoms* (Oxford, Hart, 2015) 118 ff.

[14] The Charter of Fundamental Rights bears traces of a more universal catalogue of rights that in part does not become actualised in the normal sense of the word. The Charter of Fundamental Rights contains, for example, a prohibition on the EU institutions to engage in torture and slavery. Zetterquist is of the opinion that these prohibitions cannot be actualised, as the Member States themselves, as assignees to the ECHR, cannot transfer such competence to the EU and its institutions. O Zetterquist, 'The Charter of Fundamental Rights and the European *Res Publica*', in G Di Federico, *The EU Charter of Fundamental Rights* (Berlin—Heidelberg, Springer, 2011) 12.

contains a broader catalogue of rights than the ECHR and thus certain rights have an independent EU law meaning.[15]

The Charter of Fundamental Rights contains two kinds of rights: negative rights, which EU institutions and the Member States shall respect when implementing EU law—the rights of freedom of expression, freedom of religion and freedom of association—and positive rights, such as social rights.[16]

Title I, Dignity, establishes that human dignity is inviolable, as is the right to life and integrity the Title also includes the prohibition of torture and slavery. The classic freedom of expression and freedom of religion, and also the more modern right to protection of personal data (Article 8) are covered in Title II (Articles 6-19) while the fundamental rights relating to equality, gender, children's rights and the rights of the elderly are contained in Title III (Articles 20–26). Title IV (Articles 27–38) deals with social rights that focus primarily on working life, but includes also a more general right to social security benefits and social services. Title V (Articles 39–46) establishes citizens' rights, such as the right to vote and to stand as a candidate for election to the European Parliament and in municipal elections, and the right to good administration. Title VI (Articles 47–50) confirms legal rights with regard to the administration of justice, such as the right to an effective remedy and a fair trial, and the principle of *ne bis in idem*. The Charter of Fundamental Rights concludes with Title VII, which contains general provisions relating to the fundamental issues of interpretation and application.[17]

7.4. APPLICATION OF THE CHARTER OF FUNDAMENTAL RIGHTS

7.4.1. Introduction

Articles 51–53 provide when and how the Charter is to be applied. Article 51 lays down when the Charter is applicable, Article 52 defines the scope of the fundamental rights, and Article 53 regulates the Charter of Fundamental Rights' relationship with the ECHR, national constitutions and international conventions.[18]

[15] cf T Kerikmäe, *EU Charter: Its Nature, Innovative Character, and Horizontal Effect*, in T Kerikmäe (ed), *Protecting Human Rights in the EU* (Berlin—Heidelberg, Springer, 2014) 8 ff. See also K Nyman-Metcalf, *The Future of Universality of Rights*, in T Kerikmäe (ed), *Protecting Human Rights in the EU* (Berlin—Heidelberg, Springer, 2014) 26 ff.

[16] See O Zetterquist, 'The Charter of Fundamental Rights and the European *Res Publica*', in G Di Federico (ed), *The EU Charter of Fundamental Rights* (Berlin—Heidelberg, Springer, 2011) 3.

[17] cf H Kailia, 'The Scope of Application of the Charter of Fundamental Rights of the European Union in the Member States', in P Cardonnel, A Rosas and N Wahl (eds), *Constitutionalising the EU Judicial System—Essays in Honour of Pernilla Lindh* (Oxford, Hart, 2012) 294 ff.

[18] cf Ward, who states that one must not misunderstand the purpose of the Charter. It is not a general human rights legal instrument, but is applicable only in the context of Union law and where its specific legal construction must be taken into consideration. A Ward, 'Remedies under the EU Charter of Fundamental Rights', [2016] *Europarättslig Tidskrift* 15.

7.4.2. Article 51

7.4.2.1. Introduction

Article 51 of the Charter states that the fundamental rights apply to the Union's institutions, and the Member States when they implement Union law.[19]

The Charter was negotiated relatively rapidly, during an intense year starting in December 1999. The key to the speed of the negotiations was the set of highly restrictive general Articles, including Article 51.[20]

Even if on paper the Charter does not extend the power of the Union or its competence, there were fears that the Charter of Fundamental Rights could de facto come to increase the power of the Union at the expense of the Member States.[21] The General Articles 51–53 were therefore added to limit the impact of the Charter. Furthermore, the preamble underlines that the Charter is a catalogue of already existing rights. This was also emphasised in the Conclusions of the presidency at the summit in Cologne.[22]

Initially, it can be noted that the linguistic expression of Article 51 differs in the various language versions. The English version refers to 'implement' and the French refers to the equivalent 'mise en oeuvre', while other language versions

[19] The personal scope which can invoke the Charter of Fundamental Rights is however wide: all those who reside in or are staying in the EU. The predominant part of the rights recognised by the Charter of Fundamental Rights is granted to "all", regardless of nationality. The rights according to Title V are reserved for the citizens of the Union, while the right to asylum is for obvious reasons directed towards third country nationals. Some social rights are reserved for workers (Arts 27–32). The personal scope of the Charter is of less importance since the relevant personal scope is determined by Regulation 883/2004 and Regulation 1231/2010 which extend the personal scope to the nationals of third countries who are legally resident in a Member State and where an EU law is applicable: Regulation 1231/2010 of 24 November 2010 on the extension of Regulation (EC) No 883/2004 and Regulation (EC) No 987/2009 to apply to third country nationals who solely, on the grounds of their nationality, are not covered by these regulations, [2010] OJ L 344/1.

[20] A Ward, 'Article 51: Field of Application', in P Peers, T Hervey, J Kenner and A Ward (eds), *The EU Charter of Fundamental Rights* (Oxford, Hart, 2014) 1424 ff.

[21] Earlier catalogues of rights in federal states have led to an enlargement of rights. This, notes Zetterquist, is the main reason why the United Kingdom and Poland negotiated an exception, Protocol 33, which underlines that the Charter should not affect British or Polish law or legal interpretation. O Zetterquist, 'The Charter of Fundamental Rights and the European Res Publica', in G Di Federico (ed), *The EU Charter of Fundamental Rights* (Berlin—Heidelberg, Springer, 2011) 12. Cf H Kailia, 'The Scope of Application of the Charter of Fundamental Rights of the European Union in the Member States', in P Cardonnel, A Rosas and N Wahl (eds), *Constitutionalising the EU Judicial System—Essays in Honour of Pernilla Lindh* (Oxford, Hart, 2012) 294, and C Barnard, *The Charter, the Court—and the Crisis*, University of Cambridge Faculty of Law Legal Studies Research Paper Series, Paper No 18/2013, August 2013, 5.

[22] H Kailia, 'The Scope of Application of the Charter of Fundamental Rights of the European Union in the Member States', in P Cardonnel, A Rosas and N Wahl (eds), *Constitutionalising the EU Judicial System—Essays in Honour of Pernilla Lindh* (Oxford, Hart, 2012) 294; see also K Lenaerts, 'Exploring the Limits of the EU Charter of Fundamental Rights' [2012] *European Constitutional Law Review* 375 ff. However, the Commission noted in its Communication on the legal nature of the Charter of Fundamental Rights of the European Union 10 that 'it is reasonable to assume that the Charter will produce all its effects, legal and others, whatever its nature'.

(eg Swedish and Finnish) instead use the much broader 'application'. The explanations relating to the Charter of Fundamental Rights[23] point in the direction that the Charter is applicable when EU law is applied, and not that it can be invoked only in the case of implementation; this, as the explanation of Article 51 indicates, means that the Member States are obliged to respect the fundamental rights when they make decisions within the scope of the application *or* when implementing Union law.[24]

Lenaerts points out three different situations where an assessment is required if Union law is to be applied in the meaning of the Charter:[25] a situation where EU law is not present at all, mainly in a domestic situation, as in *Annibaldi;*[26] a situation where Member States implement EU law, as in *Wachauf*[27] and *Karlsson;*[28] and a third situation where a Member State limits the impact of EU law, as in *ERT*.[29] *Lenaerts* is of the opinion, in light of the explanations for the Charter, that its application shall be for 'all situations where the Member States fulfil their obligations under the treaties as well as under secondary law'.[30]

The preliminary ruling in *Åkerberg Fransson*[31] confirmed Lenaerts' view that the concept of application is to be understood in a broad sense, as in *Åkerberg Fransson* the Court found that the Charter is applicable 'in all situations governed by European Union law',[32] and 'where national legislation falls within the scope of European Union law'[33] but also in the cases where 'a situation ... is not entirely determined by European Union law'.[34] This broad approach was confirmed in *AMS*[35]

[23] The explanations were developed as official memoranda *after* the Charter of Fundamental Rights was drawn up and adopted; J-P Jacqué, 'The Explanations Relating to the Charter of Fundamental Rights', in P Peers, T Hervey, J Kenner and A Ward (eds), *The EU Charter of Fundamental Rights* (Oxford, Hart, 2014) 1715. Notwithstanding the explanations' unorthodox creation, these do carry weight in the application, Art 52.7, the Charter of Fundamental Rights Article.

[24] Explanation of Art 51, para 2, *Explanations Relating to the Charter of Fundamental Rights*, [2007] OJ C 303/17.

[25] K Lenaerts, 'Exploring the Limits of the EU Charter of Fundamental Rights' [2012] *European Constitutional Law Review* 378.

[26] Case C-309/96 *Daniele Annibaldi v Sindaco del Comune di Guidonia and Presidente Regione Lazio* [1997] ECR I-7493.

[27] Case 5/88 *Hubert Wachauf v Bundesamt für Ernährung und Forstwirtschaft* [1989] ECR 2609.

[28] Case C-292/97 *Kjell Karlsson and others* [2000] ECR I-2737.

[29] Case C-260/89 *Elliniki Radiophonia Tiléorassi AE and Panellinia Omospondia Syllogon Prossopikou v Dimotiki Etairia Pliroforissis and Sotirios Kouvelas and Nicolaos Avdellas and others (ERT)* [1991] ECR I-2925.

[30] K Lenaerts, 'Exploring the Limits of the EU Charter of Fundamental Rights' [2012] *European Constitutional Law Review* 375, 378.

[31] Case C-617/10 *Åklagaren v Hans Åkerberg Fransson*, EU:C:2013:105.

[32] ibid, 19.

[33] ibid, 21.

[34] ibid, 29. Cf A Ward, 'Article 51: Field of Application', in P Peers, T Hervey, J Kenner and A Ward (eds), *The EU Charter of Fundamental Rights* (Oxford, Hart, 2014) 1427. See also K Lenaerts, 'The Court of Justice of the European Union and the Protection of Fundamental Rights' (2011) XXXI *Polish Yearbook of International Law* 79, 88 ff.

[35] Case C-176/12 *Association de médiation sociale v Union locale des syndicats CGT and others*, EU:C:2014:2, 42.

as well as in *Pfleger*.[36] Furthermore, it seems that EU law is applied when a Member State applies a Regulation: *ONEm*.[37]

7.4.2.2. Determination of Applicable Legislation—Application of EU Law?

Fundamental rights were very much present in the preliminary ruling of *Dano*.[38] The German court asked the CJEU, in its questions to the Court, whether Articles 1 and 20 of the Charter of Fundamental Rights on human dignity and equality before the law permitted German non-contributory benefits to be limited to financial support for repatriation of non-economically active Union citizens. The crucial question was: does Regulation 883/2004 lead to an application of EU law?

The Court emphasised in its ruling that the Charter of Fundamental Rights does not lead to an extension of the competence of the Union.[39] The Court further emphasised that the EU competence within the field of social security is limited to coordination.[40] The Court referred here to *Brey*,[41] where the Court ruled on Article 70, Regulation 883/2004, which regulates the special non-contributory benefits in a specific order, and which also includes a rule for determining the applicable legislation. The Court notes that such a rule points out the competent State without determining any eligibility requirements.[42]

The Court almost adopts in *Dano* a tunnel vision to avoid having to take into account the Charter of Fundamental Rights. The CJEU would otherwise have been forced to take a position, fill out and apply the vague and abstract terms of human dignity and equality before the law in a very politically sensitive case.[43] Such an assessment would also have seen the CJEU consider the Charter's Article 21 and Article 14, ECHR.[44] The Court would thus have had to consider the case law of the ECtHR in a balancing act concerning non-economically active union citizens, a situation which the ECtHR has not considered in its case law.

However, this tunnel vision meant that the Court disregarded its previous case law, according to which Regulation 883/2004, notwithstanding that it only coordinates, has been seen in a larger EU law context.[45] This starting

[36] Case C-390/12 *Proceedings brought by Robert Pfleger and Others*, EU:C:2014:281, 34.

[37] Case C-284/15 *Office national de l'emploi (ONEm) v M and M v Office national de l'emploi (ONEm) and Caisse auxiliaire de paiement des allocations de chômage (CAPAC)*, EU:C:2016:220. Cf A Ward, 'Remedies under the EU Charter of Fundamental Rights' [2016] *Europarättslig Tidskrift* 21.

[38] Case C-333/13 *Elisabeta Dano and Florin Dano v Jobcenter Leipzig*, EU:C:2014:2358.

[39] ibid, 88.

[40] ibid, 89 and 90.

[41] Case C-140/12 *Pensionsversicherungsanstalt v Peter Brey*, EU:C:2013:565, 41.

[42] ibid, 49; Case C-333/13 *Elisabeta Dano and Florin Dano v Jobcenter Leipzig*, EU:C:2014:2358, 89.

[43] cf Westens criticises the concept of equality before the law, as empty words. P Westen, 'The Empty Idea of Equality' [1981–82] *Harvard Law Review* 537.

[44] The interrelationship between the more general Art 20 on equality before the law and the more specific Art 21 on non-discrimination is unclear; M Bell, 'Art 20—Equality Before the Law', in P Peers, T Hervey, J Kenner and A Ward (eds), *The EU Charter of Fundamental Rights* (Oxford, Hart, 2014) 565.

[45] cf Case C-135/99 *Ursula Elsen v Bundesversicherungsanstalt für Angestellte* [2000] ECR I-10409; Case C-227/03 *AJ van Pommeren-Bourgondiën v Raad van bestuur van de Sociale verzekeringsbank*

point is present in a large number of cases and can be illustrated by *Dumont de Chassart*:[46]

> In the absence of harmonisation at the EU level, each member state remains competent that its legislation, *in compliance with the European Union law*, provides the conditions that will apply to granting benefits within the social security system.[47] [Emphasis added.]

This statement is in line with Regulation 988/2009,[48] which introduced an additional recital 17a to Regulation 883/04 to clarify that the Member States are free to determine the material conditions for affiliation and entitlement to benefits:

> Once the legislation of a Member State becomes applicable to a person under Title II of this Regulation, the conditions for affiliation and entitlement to benefits should be defined by the legislation of the competent Member State, while respecting Community law.

As seen in the previous chapters, any national social security law that makes it difficult or hinders a union citizen's right to free movement will be set aside by the CJEU. This can be illustrated by *Salemink*,[49] where the Court found that Article 45 TFEU does not allow any additional national residence requirements once a Member State has been pointed out by the Regulation rules on determining the applicable legislation. This restriction of additional national law has been confirmed in *Evans*.[50]

The Court's reasoning in *Dano* where it finds that determining the applicable legislation according to the Regulation is not to be seen as an application of EU law is not in line with the previous understanding that the EU law has a deep impact on the national social security systems. Although the rule of the Regulation to determine the applicable legislation is not comparable to a direct application of EU law, this is at least about a situation where the national legislation of a Member State is under surveillance of EU law. It could therefore be argued that such a situation covers 'the application' of EU law, as hindering national law can no longer be maintained with reference to the free movement of workers being supreme. The preliminary ruling in *ERT*[51] shows that a limitation of national competence can

[2005] ECR I-6101 and Joined Cases C-225/02 and C-306/03 *Rosa García Blanco v Instituto Nacional de la Seguridad Social (INSS) and Tesorería General de la Seguridad Social (TGSS) and Cristalina Salgado Alonso v Instituto Nacional de la Seguridad Social (INSS) and Tesorería General de la Seguridad Social (TGSS)* [2005] ECR I-523.

[46] Case C-619/11 *Patricia Dumont de Chassart v Office national d'allocations familiales pour travailleurs salariés (ONAFTS)*, EU:C:2013:92.

[47] ibid, 41.

[48] Regulation (EC) No 988/2009 of the European Parliament and of the Council of 16 September 2009 amending Regulation (EC) No 883/2004 on the coordination of social security systems, and determining the content of its Annexes, [2009] OJ L284/43.

[49] Case C-347/10 *A Salemink v Raad van bestuur van het Uitvoeringsinstituut werknemersverzekeringen*, EU:C:2012:17.

[50] Case C-179/13 *Raad van bestuur van de Sociale verzekeringsbank v LF Evans*, EU:C:2015:12. The Court adds in para 45 of the preliminary judgment that *Salemink* cannot be understood as if EU law is the only law governing the right to the membership of a national social security system.

[51] Case C-260/89 ERT [1991] ECR I-2925.

be seen as an application. This extensive understanding of 'application' is further confirmed by the previous case law, which stipulates that it is application of the Union law when 'a national legislation is covered by the scope of the Union law.[52]

EU law has, indirectly at least, an effect on national eligibility rules. The Member States have to take EU law into account when they apply their national law. Will this no longer be seen as an application of the Union law in the sense of the Charter of Fundamental Rights?

7.4.2.3. Application of EU Law—Concluding Remarks

The preliminary ruling in *ONEm*[53] suggests that if an issue relates to Regulation 883/2004's substantive rules, this will be seen as an application according to Article 51 of the Charter of Fundamental Rights, thus making the Charter applicable. This makes perfectly sense since the Member States' authorities then apply directly coordinative rules. The remaining question, however, is how the Court will understand the term 'application of the Union law' with regard to the rules on determining the applicable legislation.

In *Dano* it was difficult for the CJEU not to conclude that Elisabeta Dano was to be regarded as a resident with regard to Regulation 987/2009's rules on determining residence, as she had resided for some time in Germany. According to Regulation 883/2004, this should then have resulted in her being eligible for the German hybrid benefit (being a residence based benefit). As shown above in the concluding section of chapter 6, section 6.6, the CJEU, however, avoided this outcome by stating that a hybrid benefit is, in parallel, to be regarded as social assistance in the sense of Directive 2004/38. Therefore, the CJEU was able to restrict the access to hybrid benefits, since the right to social assistance can be made dependent upon a right to reside. If the CJEU, when answering the German court's fourth question on the possible application of the Charter, had followed its earlier extensive rulings in *Åkerberg Fransson*, *AMS* and *Pfleger* on 'application', it could have opened the door that had just been closed for non-economically active union citizens with regard to Directive 2004/38. This as an assessment of the Charter of Fundamental Rights, with regard to the case law of the ECtHR, could lead to an entitlement of benefits to Elisabeta Dano based on the principle of human dignity (but not in her capacity as a Union citizen).

As discussed above in section 6.6.3, it remains unclear whether the CJEU has ruled that all rules of the Regulation on determining the applicable legislation mean that there is no application of the EU law. Can these be seen as completely neutral, simply pointing out the competent state, or do we have to take into account the wider context of the Union law which certainly affects the national law?

[52] Case C-617/10 *Åklagaren v Hans Åkerberg Fransson*, EU:C:2013:105, 21; Case C-176/12 *Association de médiation sociale v Union locale des syndicats CGT and others*, EU:C:2014:2, 42; Case C-390/12 *Proceedings brought by Robert Pfleger and Others*, EU:C:2014:281, 34.

[53] Case C-284/15 *Office national de l'emploi (ONEm) v M and M v Office national de l'emploi (ONEm) and Caisse auxiliaire de paiement des allocations de chômage (CAPAC)*, EU:C:2016:220.

The situation has become as predicted by *Rosas*: the issue of whether a national situation concerns the application of the EU law must be decided from case to case where the decisive factor is whether a national application affects the functioning of EU law.[54] The recently delivered preliminary decision in *Poclava*[55] confirms this approach. According to *Poclava*, the EU's competence in the social law area is limited, and therefore the question of the application of EU law must be regarded with this taken into account.[56]

The CJEU, however, in doing this case-by-case assessment, must observe that the Charter of Fundamental Rights, according to the preamble, places the individual at the centre by emphasising Union citizenship. In addition, Article 1 of the Charter on human dignity makes no distinction between the economically active and non-economically active EU citizens.[57]

The balance is thus delicate; on one hand, the Charter of Fundamental Rights is not, to a large degree, based on a market-economic perspective, while on the other hand, it would be problematic if the Charter were to lead to a far-reaching economic solidarity vis-à-vis the non-economically active union citizens. *Dano* is perhaps one of the clearest examples so far in this conflict where the CJEU had to revise the concept of application of the Union law in order to achieve a balance in relation to the Member States and their need to limit the social benefits versus the non-economically active union citizens.

7.4.3. Article 52 and Article 53

The Charter of Fundamental Rights limits the applicability of the Charter to the extent that Article 52 limits the material scope, and Article 53 states that the Charter shall be applied in accordance with other international and national instruments in the field.

The Charter of Fundamental Rights makes a distinction, in accordance with Article 52.5, between rights and principles. This distinction was made while drafting the Charter, in order to meet the concerns of Member States.[58]

In order to be able to rely upon the Charter of Fundamental Rights before a national court, a fundamental right must be classified as a right and not a principle. The rights of the Charter have inherent strong values and can be said

[54] Case C-284/15 *Office national de l'emploi (ONEm) v M and M v Office national de l'emploi (ONEm) and Caisse auxiliaire de paiement des allocations de chômage (CAPAC)*, EU:C:2016:220.

[55] A Rosas, 'When is the EU Charter of Fundamental Rights Applicable at National Level?' [2012] *Jurisprudencija* 1269.

[56] Case C-117/14 *Grima Janet Nisttahuz Poclava v Jose María Ariza Toledano (Taberna del Marqués)* EU:C:2015:60 40–42.

[57] C Dupré, 'Art 1—Human Dignity', in P Peers, T Hervey, J Kenner and A Ward (eds), *The EU Charter of Fundamental Rights* (Oxford, Hart, 2014) 6 f.

[58] Ward, A., 'Article 51: Field of Application', in P Peers, T Hervey, J Kenner and A Ward (eds), *The EU Charter of Fundamental Rights* (Oxford, Hart, 2014) 1418.

to be autonomous.[59] Principles on the other hand, according to Article 52(5), can be claimed only after being implemented in additional Union law or national legislation.[60] A principle will thus be possible to invoke only after being filled with content.[61] Advocate General Cruz Villalón has found that, according to the current legal position, 'Public authorities must respect the individual legal situation guaranteed by "rights", but in the case of a "principle" the obligation is much more general'.[62] The principles can be seen as an imposition of the EU and/or Member States to promote and convert those principles to a substantial reality.

The division of rights and principles will certainly be an area which will be treated carefully by the CJEU, since according to Article 52(5), the fundamental rights will receive an almost equivalent direct effect and may start to be used by the eligible individual before the national courts. A broad interpretation of the concept of rights will thus lead to rights that can be invoked before the national courts. This fact will ultimately result in an increased number of preliminary rulings where the CJEU will be faced with highly politically sensitive issues.

Furthermore Article 52 along with Article 53 regulates the sensitive relationship between the Charter and the ECHR, the national constitutions and the international conventions.[63]

According to Articles 52.2, 52.3 and 52.6, the fundamental rights of the Charter must be interpreted in accordance with the common constitutional traditions of the Member States, as well as with the ECHR, by taking into account the national legislation and practice upon implementation of the Charter.[64] These references are intended to prevent an independent evolution of the Charter.

In close connection with these principles of the Charter's interaction with related legal instruments, Article 53 states that the Charter of Fundamental Rights cannot restrict or adversely affect the protection of fundamental rights that are

[59] cf K Lenaerts, 'Exploring the Limits of the EU Charter of Fundamental Rights' [2012] *European Constitutional Law Review* 375, 399 ff.

[60] cf the Opinion of the Advocate General in Case C-176/12 *Association de médiation sociale v Union locale des syndicats CGT and others*, EU:C:2013:491, 42–51.

[61] A Ward, 'Article 51: Field of Application', in P Peers, T Hervey, J Kenner and A Ward (eds), *The EU Charter of Fundamental Rights* (Oxford, Hart, 2014) 1417; cf K Lenaerts, 'Exploring the Limits of the EU Charter of Fundamental Rights' [2012] *European Constitutional Law Review* 375, 399 ff, and E Hancox, 'The meaning of 'implementing' EU law under Article 51(1) of the Charter: Åkerberg Fransson' [2013] *CMLR* 1411.

[62] The Opinion of the Advocate General in Case C-176/12 *Association de médiation sociale v Union locale des syndicats CGT and others*, EU:C:2013:491, 50.

[63] A new constitutional legal journey has begun with the ratification of ECHR, as provided by Art 6 of TEU. This will put focus on the relationship between the Charter of Fundamental Rights and the ECHR but also on the relationship between the CJEU and the ECtHR in relation to each other. Cf K Lenaerts, 'Exploring the Limits of the EU Charter of Fundamental Rights' [2012] *European Constitutional Law Review* 375; M Safjan, *Areas of Application of the Charter of Fundamental Rights of the European Union: Fields of Conflict?* EUI Working papers, Law 2012/22; F Fontanelli, 'The European Union's Charter of Fundamental Rights Two Years Later' (2011) 3 *Perspectives on Federalism*. This trip is currently beset with delays, see section 7.2 above.

[64] However, the Charter, compared with the ECHR, can ensure a stronger protection: Art 52.3, second sentence.

already recognised by Union law, international law, the ECHR and national constitutions. In line with this, the ECHR and the case law of ECtHR constitute thus the basis for the protection level of the Charter of Fundamental Rights.[65]

7.4.4. Summary

We can observe that:

- — the CJEU has adapted the understanding of 'application' in Article 51.1, case-by case;
- — the understanding of 'application' is a narrow one in *Dano* with regard to the regulation rules on determining the applicable legislation in terms of the hybrid benefits,
- — the CJEU has underlined that the Charter does not, in itself, extend the EU's competence;
- — the CJEU will be cautious in expanding the notion rights in the light of Article 52(5);
- — a general question that is still waiting to be solved is the relationship between the Charter, ECHR and the national constitutions.

Summing up, the President of the CJEU, Lenaerts, was of the opinion that 'the Charter marks a new stage in the process of European integration...'.[66] However, at the same time he stressed that Articles 51–54 of the Charter restrict the impact of the Charter and thereby meet the concerns of the Member States with regard to an ever-closer union.

7.5. NATIONAL SOCIAL SECURITY SYSTEMS AND THE SOCIAL RIGHTS OF THE CHARTER OF FUNDAMENTAL RIGHTS

7.5.1. Introduction

Social rights, such as social security[67] and social assistance, are characterised as positive rights in a fundamental right context. Positive rights—as opposed to negative rights where a state shall refrain from infringing rights—assume that a state shall guarantee certain foreseen freedoms and rights. Guaranteeing social rights cost, since the rights are based on a social policy and welfare models, which

[65] The European Court has been criticised for not recognising the ECHR's protection of competition law. See H Andersson, 'Dawn Raids under Challenge' [2014] *European Competition Law Review* 135.

[66] K Lenaerts, 'Exploring the Limits of the EU Charter of Fundamental Rights' [2012] *European Constitutional Law Review* 375.

[67] In the EU context, social security is the area defined in EC Regulation 883/2004, which mainly deals with security systems including family benefits, sickness and care benefits, and old-age benefits.

are funded via both taxes and social contributions that are paid within a state by a group of entitled people (*ratione personae*) regulated in national legislation.

Unlike political freedoms and rights, which to a large extent are understood in the same way in all Member States, views diverge as regards the position and essence of social rights.[68] Moreover, the construction and scope of welfare systems differ between Member States, due to various parameters like social development, political outlook and financial resources. Social rights have furthermore been regulated at different levels in the Member States, depending on constitutional traditions and political views.[69]

In an EU legal context, social rights have been regarded as an internal matter of Member States, because of the costs involved and because social rights are regulated and perceived differently in the various Member States. Until the ratification of the Charter, social rights therefore have languished in the EU, unless they have figured in an internal market context where they have been a complement to and promoted the free movement of workers.[70] A broader agenda as regards social rights has not been developed in the EU context since Member States have decided not to relinquish any general competence. Instead, the EU's social dimension has developed slowly and often in a roundabout way over time.[71]

The question that this chapter aims to answer is whether the Charter will change this relationship and whether an independent EU legal social right as regards social security will emerge; a social right which is a complement to or challenges the current EU legal coordination of the social security systems of the Member States.

[68] Member States' views on social security as a fundamental right differ; in some, social security is enshrined in the constitution, while others, like Sweden, take the view that social security cannot be regarded as a fundamental right but instead is determined by the political choices of a state which may change over time. Cf A-S Lind, *Sociala rättigheter i förändring—En konstitutionellrättslig studie* ['Changing Social Rights—A Constitutional Study'] (Uppsala, 2009).

[69] '...social rights are traditionally associated with a common history, homogeneity, and a common identity which goes hand in hand with a willingness to accept the redistribution of costs of social policies.': Y Borgmann-Prebil and M Ross, 'Promoting European Solidarity: Between Rhetoric and Reality?', in M Ross and Y Borgmann-Prebil, *Promoting Solidarity in the European Union* (Oxford, Oxford University Press, 2010) 5. Cf W Lamping, 'Mission Impossible? Limits and Perils of Institutionalizing Post-National Social Policy' in M Ross and Y Borgmann-Prebil, *Promoting Solidarity in the European Union* (Oxford, Oxford University Press, 2010). See also S Coppola, 'Social Rights in the European Union: The Possible Added Value of a Binding Charter of Fundamental Rights', in G Di Federico (ed), *The EU Charter of Fundamental Rights, Ius Gentium: Comparative Perspectives on Law and Justice* (Berlin, Springer, 2011) 200 ff.

[70] In these situations, Regulations 492/2011 and 883/2004 have included the welfare system of the state where the activity is pursued for these groups of persons. Cf S Coppola, 'Social Rights in the European Union: The Possible Added Value of a Binding Charter of Fundamental Rights', in G Di Federico (ed), *The EU Charter of Fundamental Rights, Ius Gentium: Comparative Perspectives on Law and Justice* (Berlin, Springer, 2011) 202. As regards migrant union citizens, however, a certain independent social solidarity has emerged for the state of residence. See C-184/99 *Rudy Grzelczyk v Centre public d'aide sociale d'Ottignies-Louvain-la-Neuve* [2001] ECR I-6193; Case C-456/02 *Michel Trojani and Centre public d'aide sociale de Bruxelles (CPAS)* [2004] ECR I-7573; Case C-209/03 *The Queen, at the request of Dany Bidar v the London Borough of Ealing and the Secretary of State for Education and Skills* [2005] ECR I-2119. This social solidarity has been codified as regards a Union citizen who legally resides in the state in Art 14(3) of Directive 2004/38 on the right to move and reside freely.

[71] P Watson, *EU Social and Employment Law*, 2nd edn (Oxford, Oxford University Press, 2014) ch 2.

7.5.2. The Right to Social Security Pursuant to Article 34 of the Charter; a (Directly Invocable) Right?

7.5.2.1. Introduction

Article 34 of the Charter expressly stipulates that social security is a fundamental right, as follows:

Article 34

Social security and social assistance

1. The Union recognises and respects the entitlement to social security benefits and social services providing protection in cases such as maternity, illness, industrial accidents, dependency or old age, and in the case of loss of employment, in accordance with the rules laid down by Union law and national laws and practices.
2. Everyone residing and moving legally within the European Union is entitled to social security benefits and social advantages in accordance with Union law and national laws and practices.
3. In order to combat social exclusion and poverty, the Union recognises and respects the right to social and housing assistance so as to ensure a decent existence for all those who lack sufficient resources, in accordance with the rules laid down by Union law and national laws and practices.

As this Article stipulates, the Charter regulates two different situations as regards social security. First, it recognises and respects the entitlement to social security in EU legal contexts. Secondly, it confirms the entitlement to social security in free movement situations. Since the wording is general in nature, it is therefore of utmost importance as regards the impact of the Article to decide whether it can be regarded as a *right* or whether it is a *principle* which is dependent on a more precise description in further legislation at the national or EU level.[72] If the Charter requires supplementary legislation when it comes to social security, its impact will only be in compliance with existing legislation and case law. Thus, a leverage effect is not possible where Article 34 itself would expand the area of social security. As regards the Member States, this means that 'Community law does not detract from the powers of the Member States to organise their social security systems…',[73] neither in situations where EU law is invoked on a general level, nor when there is only coordination.

At a more general level, the most important cases as regards the question of Article 34 as a right or a principle are *Kamberaj*[74] and *AMS*.[75]

In *Kamberaj* the issue was whether a regional housing benefit could be covered by Article 34.3 regarding the entitlement to social assistance. This case

[72] cf Art 52(5) of the Charter.

[73] Case C-158/96 *Raymond Kohll v Union des caisses de maladie* [1998] ECR I-1931.

[74] Case C-571/10 *Servet Kamberaj v Istituto per l'Edilizia sociale della Provincia autonoma di Bolzano (IPES) and others*, EU:C:2012:233.

[75] Case C-176/12 *Association de médiation sociale v Union locale des syndicats CGT and others*, EU:C:2014:2.

raised the issue of whether Italian legislation was in accordance with Directive 2003/109 concerning the status of third-country nationals who are long-term residents.[76] In its preamble, the Directive refers to the Charter, recital 3 of which stipulates that the Directive respects the fundamental rights. Against this background, the Court of Justice ruled that a Member State in its application of EU law and Directive 2003/109 must take special consideration of Article 34.3, stating that a Member State must 'recognise and respect the right to social assistance'.

The Court of Justice's line of reasoning follows a logic where Article 34.3 of the Charter is dependent on the existence of a Directive. The Court bases its decision on the fact that Article 34.3 stipulates that social assistance shall be understood 'in accordance with the rules laid down by Union law and national laws and practices.' In this way the Court of Justice reinforced the idea that Member States have to ensure an appropriate effect of the Directive. On the other hand, the case indicates that national legislation on social assistance cannot come under attack merely by referral to Article 34.3. The fact that the Court of Justice linked the Charter to a reference to the preamble of the Directive and did not explicitly make reference to Article 34.3 indicates thus that the right to social assistance in accordance with 34.3 is a principle and not a right.[77]

The subsequent preliminary ruling in *AMS* further confirms the Court of Justice's unwillingness to recognise the social rights in Article 34 as rights. True, the Court ruled on Article 27 in *AMS*, but the wordings of Articles 27 and 34 are similar and for that reason the ruling in *AMS* can also be said to have a bearing on whether Article 34 can be seen as a right.[78] In *AMS*, the Court of Justice found the wording in Article 27 of the Charter to be insufficiently precise to be understood as a right.[79] The Court ruled that it is clear that Article 27 must be complemented by secondary law or national law to ensure its full impact.[80] This, however, is not applicable—the Court of Justice ruled that the directive in question could not be linked to Article 27. Thus, it was not possible to invoke the Charter in *AMS*.[81]

[76] 2003/109/EC, [2004] OJ L 16-44.

[77] According to Peers, the fact that the Court of Justice chose to refer to Art 34 in itself indicates how important the Charter is. S Peers, 'The Court of Justice lays the foundations for the Long-Term Residents Directive: *Kamberaj, Commission v Netherlands, Mangat Singh*' [2013] *CMLR* 529, 542.

[78] Art 27 stipulates that a worker has the right to information and consultation 'in the cases and under the conditions provided for by Union law and national laws and practice.' This can be compared to the wording of Art 34.1 about the entitlement to social security being conditional by specifying the right 'in accordance with the rules laid down by Union law and national laws and practice'.

[79] Case C-176/12 *Association de médiation sociale v Union locale des syndicats CGT and others*, EU:C:2014:2, 44–45. Compare the Advocate General's line of reasoning at p 54. Advocate General Cruz Villalón's Opinion in Case C-176/12 *Association de médiation sociale v Union locale des syndicats CGT and others*, EU:C:2013:491.

[80] Case C-176/12 *Association de médiation sociale v Union locale des syndicats CGT and others*, EU:C:2014:2, 45. The wording 'fully effective', however, is an opening towards Art 27 having a certain impact, notwithstanding that it is a matter of a principle.

[81] The Court of Justice also takes the opportunity to state that freedom from age discrimination can be regarded as an independent right by referring in para 47 to the preliminary ruling in *Kücükdeveci*; see further section 7.6.3. below.

In light of the above, my assessment is that the Court of Justice will not regard the entitlement to social security as a right in the near future. This is especially true when one bears in mind that social security systems are regarded as being at the very heart of a Member State. Article 34 should therefore be seen as a principle that is dependent on supplementary legislation.

The Charter differentiates between the entitlement to social security, Article 34.1, and the right to social security in free-movement situations, Article 34.2. These two situations differ, and even the wording regarding references to Union law and national law differ to a certain extent as well.[82] These principles will thus be dealt with separately below.

7.5.2.2. *Article 34.1: The Entitlement to Social Security Benefits: Outside the Scope of* Ratione Materiae?

Article 34.1 of the Charter can be divided into two parts when it stipulates that the Union in the Charter 'recognises and respects the entitlement to social security benefits ... in accordance with the rules laid down by Union law and national laws and practices.'

The expression 'recognises and respects' in Article 34.1 is not very far-reaching, textually, and one might be tempted to draw the conclusion that Article 34.1 is a vague principle which is fully dependent on supplementary legislation created by a legislator. However, in *Kamberaj* the Court of Justice stated that the entitlement to social benefits in accordance with Article 34.3—here the wording is identical—could be used as a basis for interpretation and in that way could reinforce the substance of a directive. Hence, if the Court of Justice has to rule on a situation where social security can be claimed in an EU legal context, and there is relevant EU legislation that can be invoked, one could argue that Article 34.1 constitutes a lever just as it does in *Kamberaj*. However, there is a decisive difference that speaks against such an approach. Article 34.3 states expressly that its aim is to combat social exclusion and poverty. This specific aim constituted the Court of Justice's lever in *Kamberaj*. A corresponding lever is lacking in Article 34.1.

As regards the second part of Article 34.1, 'in accordance with the rules laid down by Union law and national laws and practices', the Court of Justice has established, as far as social security is concerned, in eg *Kohll* that '[in] the absence of harmonisation at Community level, it is therefore for the legislation of each Member State to determine, first, the condition concerning the right or duty to be insured with a social security scheme ... and second, the conditions for

[82] White claims that this relationship can hardly entail a decisive difference when ruling on whether the entitlement to social security can be perceived as a right or a principle; R White, 'Social Security', in S Peers and A Ward (eds), *The European Union Charter of Fundamental Rights*, (Oxford, Hart, 2009) 318.

entitlement to benefits.'[83] The Member States are thus free to determine both the *rationae personae* that may be entitled to the benefits foreseen by the respective social security schemes as well as the *ratione materiae*. Notwithstanding this fact, the Member States shall take account of Community law when exercising their national competence; the right to determine one's own system is therefore conditional in a broader EU legal context.[84]

A related issue is therefore whether the Charter may have an impact on the powers of the Member States to organise their social security systems: the Charter stipulates the benefits which Member States shall provide to the *rationae personae*. It may certainly be difficult for Member States to claim that the national social security schemes are not at all within the scope of EU law, as the EU has an indirect legislative competence through the free movement of persons and Regulation 883/2004 has the aim of coordinating national social security schemes. However, the social security systems of the Member States were not set up to incorporate Community legislation. Furthermore, Regulation 883/2004 in itself does not provide substantial rights or benefits. In *Annibaldi*[85] and *Dereci*[86] the Court established that the legislation of a Member State, which does not stem from a Member State's EU law obligations, does not fall within the remit of the Charter. Moreover, the Court ruled in *McB*[87] that the Charter's application is limited in those cases where an EU legislative act does not aim to make any substantial changes to the powers or tasks of the EU. For such situations 'the Charter should be taken into consideration solely for the purposes of interpreting the Regulation … and should be no assessment of national law as such.' The social security schemes of the Member States do not stem from EU legal obligations. However, the Member States have decided to coordinate security systems in order to reinforce the free movement of persons—but in accordance with *McB*, the Charter can only be asserted as regards Regulation 883/2004 itself and not with regard to the underlying national social security systems that it is coordinating. From a purely textual point of view, Article 34.1 lists the different social insurance benefits that

[83] Case 18. Compare with earlier Case 110/79 *Una Coonan v Insurance* Officer [1980] ECR 1445, 12; Case C-349/87 *Elissavet Paraschi v Landesversicherungsanstalt Württemberg* [1991] ECR I-4501, 15. See also Case C-275/96 *Anne Kuusijärvi v Riksförsäkringsverket* [1998] ECR I-3419, and subsequent practice summarised in Case C-388/09 *Joao Filipe da Silva Martins v Bank Betriebskrankenkasse-Pflegekasse* [2011] ECR I-5737, 71. Cf also C-619/11 *Patricia Dumont de Chassart v Office national d'allocations familiales pour travailleurs salariés (ONAFTS)*, ECLI:EU:C:2013:92, 40–41.

[84] See Case C-135/99 *Ursula Elsen v Bundesversicherungsanstalt für Angestellte* [2000] ECR I-10409; Case C-227/03 *AJ van Pommeren-Bourgondiën v Raad van bestuur van de Sociale verzekeringsbank* [2005] ECR I-6101; Joined Cases C-225/02 and C-306/03 *Rosa García Blanco Rosa García Blanco v Instituto Nacional de la Seguridad Social (INSS) and Tesorería General de la Seguridad Social (TGSS) and Cristalina Salgado Alonso v Instituto Nacional de la Seguridad Social (INSS) and Tesorería General de la Seguridad Social (TGSS)* [2005] ECR I-523.

[85] Case C-309/96 *Daniele Annibaldi v Sindaco del Comune di Guidonia and Presidente Regione Lazio* [1997] ECR I-7493.

[86] Case C-256/11 *Murat Dereci and others v Bundesministerium für Inneres* [2011] ECR I-11315.

[87] Case C-400/10 *PPU, J McB v L E*, [2010] ECR I-8965.

the entitlement to social security *may* include as the Article states 'in such cases as'.[88] Moreover, as regards the wording, it should thus be a matter of the Member States being free to determine the scope of each respective national social security scheme, even in the future.

In conclusion, due to the wording of Article 34.1, and case law as well as the division of competences between the Member States and the EU, it would be difficult to claim that this article constitutes a right. Instead it should be seen as a principle in accordance with Article 52(5) of the Charter.[89] This principle needs to be supplemented by EU legislation within the social policy area, which requires unanimity among the Member States or an amendment of Regulation 883/2004. The latter piece of legislation entails, however, only a coordination of social security schemes of the Member States. It is therefore still up to the Member States to decide whether to add substance to the Charter's social rights as regards entitlement to social security.

Irrespective of the fact that Article 34.1 should be seen as a principle and not a right in the sense of the Charter, it is interesting to examine whether, *if* Article 34.1 would be regarded as a right, what such a fundamental right might encompass in concrete terms. Article 51.2 establishes that the Charter cannot entail an expansion of the EU's scope. It is thus rather a matter of a reinforcement of the impact on the existing scope. One material right which can certainly be asserted is a ban against gender discrimination in the context of social security, as the EU has competence in this area.[90] As regards other possible areas, it may be difficult to assert these because the Court, as mentioned above, has established in *Annibaldi*[91] and *Dereci*[92] that national legislation not stemming from the EU legal obligations of a Member State cannot fall under the Charter. The above leads to the conclusion that even if Article 34.1 were to be found to be a right and not a principle, it will not be possible to assert the Charter to obtain any substantial rights above and beyond those already included in the social security system of any particular Member State.

A final question is which *ratione personae* could invoke Article 34.1. As stated above, Article 34.2 covers situations where a person moves between two or several Member States and where coordination in accordance with Regulation 883/2004 comes into question. This group of persons constitutes the lion's share of people who are able to assert an EU legal social security dimension. Situations where there is no free movement between Member States would therefore be covered

[88] cf other language versions; 'in cases such as' (EN), ' die in Fällen wie' (DE) or 'f.eks. i tilfælde af' (DK).

[89] cf R White, '*Social Security*' in S Peers and A Ward (eds), *The European Union Charter of Fundamental Rights* (Oxford, Hart, 2009) 318.

[90] P Watson, *EU Social and Employment Law*, 2nd edn (Oxford, Oxford University Press, 2014) ch 26.

[91] Case C-309/96 *Daniele Annibaldi v Sindaco del Comune di Guidonia and Presidente Regione Lazio* [1997] ECR I-7493.

[92] Case C-256/11 *Murat Dereci and others v Bundesministerium für Inneres* [2011] ECR I-11315.

by Article 34.1. However, the remaining *ratione personae* for which EU law comes into question without any crossings of borders are normally already covered by the national social security system. Moreover, the Court of Justice, as mentioned above, has established in *Kohll* that each Member State shall determine the conditions for being insured in its social security schemes. Hence the *ratione personae* who could claim rights under Article 34.1 would be almost no one.

To summarise, the situation is thus that it is difficult to regard Article 34.1 of the Charter as a right, according to the Charter. As a principle resulting from the Charter, it is instead fully dependent on the consensus of the Member States in favour of an expansion of the scope of social security at the EU level, or of national legislative initiatives that expand the substantial social security of each respective state. If the Court of Justice was still to decide that Article 34.1 is a right, the scope would be very limited, as the EU lacks legislative competence in the area. Finally, it has to be said that the *ratione personae* who would be able to invoke these limited rights are almost non-existent.

7.5.2.3. Article 34.2: The Charter in Cross-Border Situations

The second scenario where the national social security systems of Member States might come into question as a fundamental right is in cross-border situations, Article 34.2 of the Charter. The question, however, is whether any substantial rights can be introduced beyond the coordination and equal treatment which are already in compliance with Regulation 883/2004 and Regulation 492/2011. White is doubtful whether anything can be changed, bearing in mind this secondary law.[93] I share these doubts.

The wording in Article 34.2 differs from that in Article 34.1, as compared to Article 34.1 there already exists a right to social security in cross-border situations—which expresses it as a right being dependent on secondary or national law: '*in accordance with the rules laid down in Union law*'. The question, however, is whether the different wording entails a difference in practice, because primary law and the general legal principles can always be said to apply.

To begin with, it can be pointed out that the same line of reasoning as above with regard to Article 34.1 and its standing as a principle or right in accordance with Article 52 (5) of the Charter can be used with regard to Article 34.2. The wording is certainly more direct, as it stipulates a right to social security, compared to the wording in Article 34.1, which states that the Union recognises and respects a right to social security. Nonetheless this right is subject to Union law, and as such is conditional and is not a right on its own. Therefore, Article 34.2 would most likely be regarded as a principle and not a right.

[93] R White, 'Social Security', in S Peers and A Ward (eds), *The European Union Charter of Fundamental Rights*, (Oxford, Hart, 2009) 319.

Unlike the situation in Article 34.1, where the EU lacks legislative competence, the EU does have legislative competence in cross-border situations according to Article 48 TFEU. Thus, the principle is supplemented with secondary law and Article 34.2 of the Charter can therefore be invoked regardless of the fact that it is a matter of a principle. Hence, there is a fundamental right to social security in cross-border situations. However, as follows from the preliminary ruling in *McB*, the Charter can only be invoked in relation to the Regulation and its rules, and not national laws.[94] If the articles of Regulation 883/2004 were to be found to hinder the underlying idea of the Regulation—to strengthen the free movement of persons—it would thus be possible for the Court of Justice to declare such articles as invalid by invoking Article 45 TFEU as well as the Charter. There would thus be a dual order, where Article 34.2 constitutes a lever in the same way that Article 27 was a lever in *Kamberaj*, when the aim of the underlying directive was being interpreted.[95] In addition, however, the Court of Justice established in a subsequent preliminary ruling, *Pfleger*,[96] that a restriction of the freedom to provide services also included the possible restriction that might apply in accordance with the Charter. There was thus no need for a special examination in light of the Charter.[97] The freedom of movement of services thus takes account of the rights that the Charter is set to guarantee.[98] Hence, in the light of *Pfleger*, the Charter should not provide added value in the situations where Regulation 883/2004 is found to restrict the free movement of persons, apart from the fact that this value can be used as a lever.

To sum up, Article 34.2 should not entail any added value to the right to social security in cross-border situations. It should instead simply have a declaratory value; coordination is a fundamental right, as Regulation 883/2004 does not lead to an expansion of the EU's areas of competence—it only coordinates the social security systems of the Member States.

If the Court of Justice nevertheless undertook an expansion of competences 'in the light of' the Charter, the Member States would have the possibility to claim subsidiarity as well as refer to Article 52.1 of the Charter.[99] Here it is possible to envisage a scenario where national restrictions in the right to social security might be introduced as a response to expansive case law, and this response would

[94] See further the discussions as regards the possibility of the Charter expanding both the material and personal scope in the area of social security, above p 165 f.

[95] See above section 7.5.2.2.

[96] Case C-390/12 *Proceedings brought by Robert Pfleger and Others*, EU:C:2014:281.

[97] ibid, 60.

[98] cf the Court's reasoning in Case C-284/15 *Office national de l'emploi (ONEm) v M and M v Office national de l'emploi (ONEm) and Caisse auxiliaire de paiement des allocations de chômage (CAPAC)*, EU:C:2016:220, 31–34. The ruling handed down in the Grand Chamber indicates that the Charter of Fundamental Rights will not be interpreted in an expansionary direction. The Court found that when Art 67.3 of Regulation 883/2004 was intended to reinforce the free movement of the workforce, this was carried out in accordance with Art 45 TFEU. In addition, the article was consistent with Art 15.2 of the Charter of Fundamental Rights.

[99] This does not apply to the fundamental rights classed as absolute rights.

be warranted by the objectively justified reasons to maintain balance in social security system budgets.

7.5.2.4. Conclusion

During the development of the Convention and also in doctrine, it has been claimed that the entitlement to social security runs a special risk with regard to an expansion of competences.[100] After eight years with the Charter and in the absence of case law, it can be said that it remains unclear whether and how Article 34.1 of the Charter will affect the social security systems of the Member States. Similarly, it is unclear whether Article 34.2 means that Regulation 883/2004 may give rise to substantial rights, or may come into question in situations other than those currently covered by the Regulation. Instead, the development of EU competences in the area of social security is more likely to continue through development of case law in the area of free movement of persons—a development that is governed by the principles of the internal market, which in retrospect, through the constitutionalisation of these principles in the Charter, legitimises an expansion of competences.

7.6. SOCIAL SECURITY AND OTHER FUNDAMENTAL RIGHTS AS A WAY TO EXPAND COMPETENCES

7.6.1. Introduction

The EU Charter entails a comprehensive catalogue of fundamental rights, stemming to a large extent from previous case law of the European Court of Justice.[101] The catalogue of fundamental rights includes rights that have already indirectly affected the national social security systems.

As regards the fundamental rights, apart from Article 34, which may have an impact on national social security systems, these are primarily rights closely linked to the internal market, such as the free movement of persons and the equal treatment principle, but also other rights such as those to family life and the rights of the child.

[100] S Coppola, 'Social Rights in the European Union: The Possible Added Value of a Binding Charter of Fundamental Rights', in G Di Federico (ed), *The EU Charter of Fundamental Rights, Ius Gentium: Comparative Perspectives on Law and Justice* (Berlin, Springer, 2011) 209. See also O Zetterquist, 'The Charter of Fundamental Rights and the European *Res Publica*', in G Di Federico (ed), *The EU Charter of Fundamental Rights, Ius Gentium, Comparative Perspectives on Land Justice* (Berlin, Springer, 2011) 12.

[101] Compare D Sarmiento, 'Who's Afraid of the Charter? The Court of Justice, National Courts and the New Framework of Fundamental Rights Protection in Europe' [2013] *CMLR* 1267, 1269–70; see also S Weatherill, 'Protecting the Internal Market from the Charter', in S de Vries, U Bernitz and S Weatherill, *Five Years Legally Binding EU Charter of Fundamental Rights—What is the State of Play in the Protection of Fundamental Rights in the EU?* (Oxford, Hart, 2015).

A fundamental right with significant and complex impact on national social security systems is this latter right—the rights of the child—codified in Article 24 of the Charter. The principle of non-discrimination, which can be found in Article 21.1 of the Charter, is another right that in the context of age discrimination has proven to be directly invocable, with potential impact on national social security systems and in particular pension schemes.[102] The relationship between the Charter and Union citizenship is another delicate issue, as Union citizenship challenges ideas of national citizenship as well as solidarity.[103]

I have decided to exemplify the impact of related fundamental rights on national social security systems by highlighting the rights of the child. The widespread criticism that has been expressed regarding expanding the *ratione personae* as regards social security in an EU legal context can also be put forward regarding CJEU case law as regards age discrimination. Apart from these two groups of people, the codification of the free movement of persons is commented on in more detail, as is the rather less well-developed but related concept of Union citizenship, and how these now fundamental rights can expand the traditional national *ratione personae*.

7.6.2. The Rights of the Child

Children are covered, just as all others, by the general fundamental rights in the Charter. Two Articles in the Charter, apart from these general rights, take a specific children's perspective: Article 24 on the rights of the child and the more specific Article 32 that bans child labour.

Doctrine has been cautious as regards Article 24 being a right,[104] compared to age discrimination, as in Article 21. The Court of Justice points out in *AMS* that the preliminary ruling in *Kücükdeveci*[105] confirms that the Article constitutes a right even in horizontal situations.[106] It may be difficult to draw any conclusions regarding whether rights of the child are designated as rights or principles based on a textual interpretation. Nor do the Explanations in the Charter comment on the status of Article 24 in any detail. *Besselink*, however, finds that certain rights in addition to those mentioned in the Explanations might be regarded as principles,

[102] Cf C Barnard, 'The Silence of the Charter', in S de Vries, U Bernitz and S Weatherill, *Five Years Legally Binding EU Charter of Fundamental Rights—What is the State of Play in the Protection of Fundamental Rights in the EU?* (Oxford, Hart, 2015).

[103] The question of how Union citizenship can generate independent rights originating from the Charter was brought to the fore but not expressed in the groundbreaking preliminary ruling of the Court of Justice in *Zambrano*.

[104] Cf the discussion and referred doctrine in N Jääskinen, 'Fundamental Social Rights in the Charter—Are They Rights? Are They Fundamental?, in P Peers, T Hervey, J Kenner and A Ward (eds), *The EU Charter of Fundamental Rights* (Oxford, Hart, 2014) 1704.

[105] Case C-555/07 *Seda Kücükdeveci v Swedex GmbH and Co. KG* [2010] ECR I-365, EU:C:2010:21.

[106] E Muir, 'Of ages in—and edges of—EU law' [2011] *CMLR* 39; K LeVan Bergman, 'Going Horizontal? Four Possible Interpretations of the Kücükdeveci Case' [2011] *Europarättslig Tidskrift* 88.

albeit not Article 24.[107] The wording of Article 24, however, has not been made dependent on further explanation via Union law or national laws. The indication is therefore that the rights of the child are to be regarded as rights and thus directly invocable. But what are the rights of the child?

Irrespective of the above, the rights of the child entail at least a right to education, as regulated in Regulation 492/2011. Through Court of Justice case law, this right has affected national social security systems in an internal market context in a complex way—derived family benefits can be claimed by parents of children who have an individual right to education in a Member State.

The background is that when Directive 2004/38 was adopted, the parts of Regulation 1612/68 (currently Regulation 492/2011) that dealt with the right to take up residence in the country of work, the right to take up work for family members, and the right to equal treatment were incorporated into the Directive.[108] However, one right regarding migrant workers' family members was not transferred: the right to education of the child of the migrant worker. Thus a migrant worker's child is able to claim, in parallel, a right to education based on Regulation 492/2011 and Directive 2004/38. These rights, however, differ in a decisive way; the right to equal treatment in the Directive is conditional upon the carer of the child having residence, while the Court of Justice has found that the right to education in accordance with Regulation 1612/68 is a child's independent right.[109] This independent right leads to the right to residence for the child, which is not connected with Directive 2004/38 and its requirements of a Union citizen not being a burden on the country of residence. It is a matter of a young Union citizen's fundamental right to studies.[110]

In *Ibrahim*[111] and *Teixiera*[112] this independent right of the child was confirmed, but also put to the test.[113] These two preliminary rulings indicate how the welfare state of a country of residence may be burdened, regardless of the balance struck in Directive 2004/38 between the Union citizen and the state of residence, due to the rights of the child.

The preliminary ruling in *Ibrahim* concerned four minors who were Union citizens, where the two eldest siblings had just started school in the UK. The family

[107] L Besselink, 'The Protection of Fundamental Rights post-Lisbon—The Interaction between the EU Charter of Fundamental Rights, the European Convention on Human Rights (ECHR) and National Constitutions' (2012) 1 *Reports of the XXV FIDE Congress Tallinn*, 63, 109–10.

[108] Regulation 1612/68 Arts 10 and 11 were repealed through Art 38.1, Directive 2004/38.

[109] Joined Cases 389/87 and 390/87 *GBC Echternach and A Moritz v Minister van Onderwijs en Wetenschappen* [1989] ECR 723, 21. Confirmed in Case C-413/99 *Baumbast and R* [2002] ECR I-7091, 50–53.

[110] Compare J Schiratzki, 'Children's rights in the EU—A tool for autonomous citizenship or patriarchy reborn?' [2011] *Europarättslig Tidskrift* 70, esp 82.

[111] Case C-310/08 *London Borough of Harrow v Ibrahim* [2010] ECR I-1065.

[112] Case C-480/08 *Teixiera v London Borough of Lambeth* [2010] ECR I-1107.

[113] For an in-depth examination of these preliminary rulings and their ramifications concerning the British welfare system see C O'Brien, 'Cases C-310/08, C-480/08' [2011] *CMLR* 203. See also J Schiratzki, 'Children's rights in the EU—A tool for autonomous citizenship or patriarchy reborn?' [2011] *Europarättslig tidskrift* 70.

was of Somali origin, and the father Yusuf and the children were Danish citizens. The father started working in the UK in the autumn of 2002 and the family followed him to the UK in early 2003. After May 2003 the father did not work anymore and the family lived instead on social benefits. In 2006 the parents separated and the children stayed in the UK with the mother, who was unemployed.

In January 2007 the mother Ibrahim applied for housing benefit. Her application was rejected because the local administration was of the opinion that Ibrahim as a third-country citizen no longer had a right of residence. The question was whether Article 12 of Regulation 1612/68 on a child's right to education[114] could come to the fore and whether this independent right could lead to derived rights to the mother. The same question was brought to the fore in *Teixiera*, where a Portuguese woman was found not to have a right of residence because she lacked sufficient resources in accordance with Directive 2004/38. Teixiera was a mother to a daughter who went to school in the UK and the Court of Appeal requested a preliminary ruling to decide whether this fact might have any bearing on Teixiera's situation.

The CJEU issued both preliminary rulings in the Grand Chamber on the same day with more or less the same line of reasoning. The CJEU ruled that the right to education in accordance with Article 12 of Regulation 1612/68 was an independent right enjoyed by the children of migrant workers. The CJEU also established, however, that the carer has a derived right of residence in the Member State in order to guarantee the child's independent right to education.[115] Thus, the carer becomes the person who guarantees that the child is able to study, irrespective of whether the carer has a right of residence in accordance with Directive 2004/38.[116]

The latter is important because only in exceptional cases should the independent right to education generate direct social benefits for the child. Normally, as the CJEU observes, it is the carer who is authorised to apply for benefits for him/herself as well as for his/her dependent children. Thus, through the child's independent right to education in accordance with 492/2011, the scheme of social benefits will be burdened; social assistance must be paid because otherwise it would mean that the child's independent right to education would be restricted.

As regards the impact of the perspective of the child on national social security systems, it can be observed that national systems with residence-based elements in their security systems, in light of *Ibrahim* and *Teixiera*, will need to grant benefits as, according to *Brey*, residence-based benefits shall be granted when it is

[114] Art 10, Regulation 492/2011.

[115] Compare the reasoning of the Court of Justice in Case C-200/02 *Kunqian Catherine Zhu, Man Lavette Chen and Secretary of State for the Home Department* [2004] ECR I-9925 and Case C-34-09 *Gerardo Ruiz Zambrano v Office national de l'emploi (ONEm)* [2011] ECR I-1177.

[116] cf Case C-200/02 *Kunqian Catherine Zhu, Man Lavette Chen and Secretary of State for the Home Department* [2004] ECR I-9925.

a matter of residence.[117] In this respect, an assessment should be made based on the residence of the child and not the carer, who if he/she is not a Union citizen cannot be regarded as having residence in accordance with Directive 2004/38.

Ibrahim and *Teixiera* are examples of how the right of the child may have an impact on the social assistance and social security schemes of a Member State. The right to education should be covered by both the first sentence in Article 24.1 of the Charter ('Children shall have the right to such protection and care as is necessary for their well-being') as well as by Article 24.2, which stipulates that the best interests of the child shall be respected as regards 'all actions relating to children'. However, the right to education is not expressly established and therefore one might say that if the Court of Justice is of the opinion that the Charter covers this right, it could have referred to the Charter when the *Ibrahim* and *Teixiera* rulings were delivered—because by then the Charter had come into effect.

However, the British court requested a preliminary ruling only in order to obtain an answer to how the relationship between Article 12 Regulation 1612/68 and Directive 2004/38 was to be understood. It is therefore possible to claim that the legal situation is still open as regards the scope of the rights of the child in accordance with Article 24 of the Charter, particularly when one bears in mind that the rulings in *Ibrahim* and *Teixiera* were entirely based on the internal market perspective.

7.6.3. The Rights of the Elderly

Article 25 on the rights of the elderly should in all probability be regarded as a principle in the sense of Article 52(5), as Article 25 expresses that the Union recognises and respects the rights of the elderly. Furthermore, in the Explanations of the Charter, Article 25 is highlighted as an example of a principle.[118]

To safeguard the rights of the elderly in accordance with the Charter, the understanding of the principle of non-discrimination in Article 21.1 is therefore decisive: 'Any discrimination based on any grounds such as ... age ... shall be prohibited.' In a number of preliminary rulings, among which *Mangold*[119] and *Kücükdeveci*[120] stand out, the Court of Justice establishes that age discrimination can be directly applicable even in horizontal contexts. In *AMS*[121] the Court of Justice took this a step further and established that the set of rights of the elderly in accordance with Article 21.1 in the Charter 'is sufficient in itself to confer on individuals an individual right which they may invoke as such.' In *AMS*, the Court opted to connect

[117] Case C-140/12 *Pensionsversicherungsanstalt v Peter Brey*, EU:C:2013:565, 43.

[118] Amendments to the Charter of Fundamental Rights, [2007] ECR C 303/17.

[119] Case C-144/04 *Werner Mangold v Rüdiger Helm* [2005] ECR I-9981.

[120] Case C-555/07 *Seda Kücükdeveci v Swedex GmbH and Co. KG* [2010] ECR I-365.

[121] Case C-176/12 *Association de médiation sociale v Union locale des syndicats CGT and others*, EU:C:2014:2.

existing case law and the corresponding Article 21.1 in the Charter to establish that a bar on age discrimination is a right, in the sense of Article 52(5). This means that in the future, the Charter could be invoked by individuals in national courts, by combining Articles 21.1 and 34.2, where issues regarding age and equal treatment in relation to Regulation 883/2004 will be asserted in parallel with the more specific articles of the Regulation and the general principle of equal treatment established in Article 18 TFEU.[122]

The actual significance that Article 21.1 will have in relation to Regulation 883/2004 remains to be seen. What is interesting is how the equal treatment in Article 21.1 will work together with the general right to social security in accordance with Article 34.1. The question is whether the combination of these two rights can constitute leverage in the same way that the principle of equal treatment constituted leverage for the Union citizen in *Martínez Sala*.[123] What speaks against this is that the situations covered by Article 34.1 are primarily domestic situations and the competence of the EU covers only the internal market aspects as regards the social security schemes of the Member States.[124] *Barnard* also asks—based on a different perspective—whether the Court of Justice, in its rulings in the area of age discrimination, has started to threaten the delicate balance of national issues that does not stem from discriminatory but rather from economic principles regarding the efficiency of the labour market.[125] According to *Barnard*, this constitutes a legitimate distinction, and one that must be made without being drowned in a flood of individual complaints.

This question is relevant because there is a tendency for the Charter to individualise the fundamental rights at the cost of collective common needs that benefit all at the end of the day. By continuing to assert individual rights, individual rights will also paradoxically be threatened, because in the end if there is no solidarity, it will not be possible to uphold the rights of an individual which result from a public and general system of welfare based on solidarity. The question that politicians in both the national and the EU contexts should answer is therefore: who should foot the bill?

7.6.4. The Charter's Codification of the Free Movement of Persons

The competence of the EU in the area of social security stems from an indirect competence regarding the free movement of persons. The free movement of

[122] Compare S O'Leary, 'The Charter and EU Social and Employment Law', in P Cardonnel, A Rosas and N Wahl (ed), *Constitutionalising the EU Judicial System—Essays in Honour of Pernilla Lindh* (Oxford, Hart, 2012) 317, esp 331.

[123] Case C-85/96 *María Martínez Sala v Freistaat Bayern* [1998] ECR I-2691.

[124] However, compare Case C-212/06 *Gouvernement de la Communauté française and Gouvernement wallon v Gouvernement flamand* [2008] ECR I-1683 where the Court opened up for a broader interpretation of the concept of 'an EU legal dimension', see at 42–60.

[125] C Barnard, 'The Silence of the Charter', in S de Vries, U Bernitz and S Weatherill, *Five Years Legally Binding EU Charter of Fundamental Rights—What is the State of Play in the Protection of Fundamental Rights in the EU?* (Oxford, Hart, 2015).

workers and other economically active persons has been constitutionalised and is guaranteed through Article 15.2 of the Charter, which stipulates: 'Every citizen of the Union has the freedom to seek employment, to work, to exercise the right of establishment and to provide services in any Member State.'

The interesting question in the context at hand is whether Article 15.2 of the Charter could reinforce the free movement of persons and thus indirectly affect national social security systems.

To begin with, it can be said that purely textually, Article 15.2 does not broaden the concept of the free movement of persons as it does not specify how this right can be ensured for the group of entitled persons. Article 15.2 seems rather to 'shadow' the Articles in the Treaty on free movement for persons and services. In line with this, the Court of Justice notes in *Pfleger*[126] that Article 15.2 cannot be understood as independent from Article 56 TFEU on the free movement of services. The Court of Justice decided therefore to respond to the queries of national courts by noting that it was possible to deliver the preliminary ruling based on the principle of equal treatment resulting from the free movement of services.

In situations that are not as straightforward, however, Article 15.2 could possibly be used by the Court of Justice as a lever. In such a case Article 15.2, together with Article 34.2 and its underlying idea of an *entitlement to* social security, could reinforce an interpretation of Regulation 883/2004 in future rulings in the same way that the Court referred to Article 34.3 in its line of reasoning in *Kamberaj*.[127]

The Court of Justice has already made similar market access interpretations in *van Munster*[128] and *Leyman*.[129] In those preliminary rulings, the national pieces of legislation in question were neutral; Regulation 883/2004 was applied correctly but the effect was still to hamper the free movement of persons. With that situation, the Court of Justice ruled in *van Munster* and *Leyman* that the national laws must be overridden and instead the national courts and authorities must apply EU law to resolve the problem outside national legislation in order to ensure the free movement of persons.[130]

A corresponding situation could be strengthened by the fundamental right to free movement of persons in the Charter, as this link could lend further weight to the CJEU's line of reasoning without the area being expanded.

At any rate, an independent expansion of the free movement of persons against the background of Article 15.2 should not come into question because Article 6.1 TEU and Article 51.2 of the Charter underline that the intention is not to expand the competences of the EU. But as *van Munster* and *Leyman* indicate, such an independent development is not actually necessary. The leverage can be seen in an internal market context, where the Charter's corresponding right will be used as a strong argument to interpret a preliminary ruling in an expansive direction based on market access.

[126] Case C-390/12 *Proceedings brought by Robert Pfleger and Others*, EU:C:2014:281, 60.

[127] See section 7.5.2.2.

[128] Case C-165/91 *Simon JM van Munster v Rijksdienst voor Pensioenen* [1994] ECR I-4661.

[129] Case C-3/08 *Ketty Leyman v Institut national d'assurance maladie-invalidité (INAMI)* [2009] ECR I-9085.

[130] See further above section 3.6.4.

7.7. THE EUROPEAN CHARTER OF FUNDAMENTAL RIGHTS AND UNION CITIZENSHIP

The *ratione personae* covered by the Charter are a sizeable group, including (with some exceptions) everyone who resides in the EU.[131] A large part of this group of persons consists of citizens of the Member States who are also Union citizens. This section highlights the issue of whether and when the Charter may be invoked by Union citizens and how this can affect national social security models.

The Charter constitutes a central legal instrument, which leads to expectations not only with regard to Union citizens who assert their right to free movement but also with regard to purely domestic situations for Union citizens.[132] The preamble of the Charter emphasises that the Union: 'places the individual at the heart of its activities, by establishing the citizenship of the Union'. However, according to Article 51.1 of the Charter, the Charter is only applicable vis-à-vis the Member States in situations where the Member States apply EU law.[133] Eeckhout claimed in 2002 that due to the expectations, the Court of Justice would feel obliged to issue extensive interpretations of the term 'applies EU law', covering even situations which appear to be purely domestic, in which case a comprehensive semi-federal catalogue of rights would be introduced.[134] However, as the preliminary rulings in *Zambrano*[135] and *Dereci*[136] indicate, this development has not yet gained momentum.

Zambrano and *Dereci* illustrate in a detailed way the question of *if* and *when* the Charter applies to Union citizens in seemingly domestic situations as regards the right to family life. As opposed to *Zambrano*, the Court of Justice found in *Dereci* that the core rights of Union citizenship are not threatened in a situation where only one parent is threatened by deportation. The child would thus continue to enjoy his/her Union citizenship. However, the Court of Justice continued its line of reasoning in *Dereci* and found that the Charter and its Article 7 might come into question if EU law was being applied by a Member State. The Court remained

[131] Chapter V Citizens' Rights.

[132] P Eeckhout, 'The EU Charter of Fundamental Rights and the Federal Questions' [2002] *CMLR* 945, 970–72.

[133] See further X Groussot and G T Petursson 'The EU Charter of Fundamental Rights Five Years on: The Emergence of a New Constitutional Framework?' and U Bernitz, 'The Scope of the Charter and its Impact on the Application of the ECHR: The Åkerberg Fransson Case on Ne Bis in Idem in Persepctive' in S de Vries, U Bernitz and S Weatherill, *Five Years Legally Binding EU Charter of Fundamental Rights—What is the State of Play in the Protection of Fundamental Rights in the EU?* (Oxford, Hart, 2015).

[134] Compare the Heidelberg Doctrine, which advocates a reverse Solange Doctrine, for those cases where a Member State's legal acts restrict rights that are guaranteed by Art 2 TEU—including human rights—and which could be invalidated by the Court of Justice through a reference to the Charter: A Von Bogdany, M Kottman, C Antphöler, J Dickschen, S Hentrei and M Smrkold 'Reverse Solange—Protecting the Essence of Fundamental Rights Against EU Member States' [2012] *CMLR* 489.

[135] Case C-34/09 *Gerardo Ruiz Zambrano v Office national de l'emploi (ONEm)* [2011] ECR I-1177.

[136] Case C-256/11 *Murat Dereci and others v Bundesministerium für Inneres* [2011] ECR I-11315.

silent, in this interpretation, about whether Article 7 in any way had had an impact on the outcome of *Zambrano*.

It can be noted that the *Zambrano* preliminary ruling was about a situation where a Union citizen would have been fully deprived of his/her rights. The situation in *Dereci* was instead about whether the Charter's respect for family life could be invoked when one parent was going to be deported. Therefore, it might be difficult to draw any far-reaching conclusions as regards the applicability of the Charter in domestic situations. However, the fact of the matter is that in *Zambrano*, the Court of Justice was careful not to open up Union citizenship as a basis for invoking the Charter. Nor does *Dereci* give any guidance regarding how and in which situations the Charter can be invoked, as the Court of Justice chooses to deliver its preliminary ruling against the background that Union citizens continue to be able to enjoy their Union citizenship. It is thus unclear if and how the Charter can be invoked in purely domestic situations.

Barnard refers to the spirit of the Charter hovering over the *Zambrano* case, when the Court of Justice notes that the Colombian parents were the key to the fact that their children, who were Union citizens, might be deprived of 'the genuine enjoyment of the substance of the rights attaching to the status of European Union citizen'.[137] Barnard notes, however, that respect for family life had already previously been recognised by the Court of Justice as a fundamental right in case law.[138] *Iglesias Sánchez*, on the other hand, claims that it is a problem that the Court of Justice did not directly refer in its ruling in *Zambrano* to the Charter's Article on the respect for family life.[139] However, what prevented such a reference to the Charter was the fact that the European Court of Human Rights ruled that deportation was possible in a similar case based on the corresponding article in the ECHR.[140] It is fully possible that the Charter's level of protection is greater than in the ECHR through Article 53 of the Charter, but if the Court of Justice had expressly referred to the Charter, the EU's fundamental rights would have taken a step in a federal direction, as predicted by Eeckhout.[141]

The respect for family life and the child's right to protection and care are actually one and the same right, seen from two perspectives. If you were to take a child's perspective, would Article 24 apply instead for the same situation? Would it

[137] Case C-34/09Case C-34/09 *Gerardo Ruiz Zambrano v Office national de l'emploi (ONEm)* [2011] ECR I-1177, 42.

[138] C Barnard, 'The Charter, the Court—and the Crisis', Legal Studies Research Papers Series, Paper No 18/2013, August 2013, 7 ff.

[139] S Iglesias Sanchez, 'The Court and the Charter: The Impact of the Entry into Force of the Lisbon Treaty on the CJEU's Approach to Fundamental Rights' [2012] *CMLR* 1565, 1593.

[140] K Hailbronner and D Thym, 'Court Case Comments C-34/09, Gerardo Ruiz Zambrano v Office national de l'emploi (ONEm)' [2011] *CMLR* 1260–61.

[141] P Eeckhout, 'The EU Charter of Fundamental Rights and the Federal Questions' [2002] *CMLR* 945.

be possible for this right to lead to another outcome? The situation in *Zambrano* and *Dereci* differs from that in *Ibrahim* and *Teixiera*, in that the children in the former rulings did not apply a right that was the result of secondary law. Despite this, one could view the ruling of the Court of Justice in these cases as a confirmation of a child's right to protection and care in accordance with Article 24.1. The Court of Justice notes in both *Zambrano* and *Dereci* that Union citizenship and its rights cannot be ensured without the primary carer. A child's right to care would thus become the key to the child being able to enjoy the substance of rights that are the result of Union citizenship.

As regards national social security systems, the discussion above is only of theoretical interest: irrespective of whether one asserts that the Charter is applicable in the situation or whether the Court of Justice decides to adjudicate based on the core values of Union citizenship, there will be an impact on the national social security systems of the state of residence. The outcome in these situations will mean, just as in *Ibrahim* and *Teixiera*, that a carer must be able to enjoy the welfare system of the state of residence without being regarded as a burden; the rights of the child must be guaranteed, whether it is a matter of Union citizenship or a fundamental right that is the result of the Charter.[142]

7.8. REGULATION 883/2004 AND THE EUROPEAN CHARTER—ADDED VALUE, OR DOES THE CHARTER STAND ON ITS TWO FEET?

By 2017, the Charter will have been in force for eight years and the question that still needs to be answered is whether it is possible to regard the Charter as only a codification of applicable law or whether the Charter can lead to deeper integration.

Lenaerts, President of the Court of Justice, believes that the Charter fulfils three functions.[143] First, it can form the basis for interpretation when secondary law and national law are interpreted 'in the light of the Charter'. Secondly, it constitutes a legal act which, when applicable, can invalidate EU legislation and national law stemming from EU law obligations, and thirdly when the Court of Justice develops

[142] As a consolation in this context, a child's independent right to go to school or to university is activated when at least one of the parents has been regarded as a migrant worker in accordance with EU law and thus Regulation 492/2011 is activated. On the other hand, the migrant worker does not have to have worked any significant amount of time to be regarded as a worker in the sense of EU law. The Danish father in *Ibrahim* worked for about eight months before he went on sick leave. He subsequently returned to Denmark. This view is entirely in line with the generous case law that has been developed by the Court of Justice in the area of the free movement of workers. For situations like the *Zambraro* case, it will not be possible to request such an introductory link. With *Dereci*, however, the Court of Justice has limited applicability to situations where the rights of a Union citizen would cease entirely.

[143] K Lenaerts, 'The Court of Justice of the European Union and the protection of Fundamental Rights' (2011) XXXI *Polish Yearbook of International Law*, 79, 81.

new general legal principles. Some, like Ward, believe that the Charter will lead to material changes,[144] while others such as Weatherill assert that as yet there has been no material expansion, and nor will there ever be.[145]

Regardless of one's position on the status of the Charter, eight years of case law indicate that the Charter is applicable as soon as an EU law aspect can be asserted. As shown in *Åkerberg Fransson*, and subsequently confirmed in *Pfleger*, EU law is applied even when the measures taken by the Member States are not fully determined by Union law.[146] There has thus been a shift regarding the question of the Charter's status, from whether the Charter can be applied to whether the invoked fundamental right is to be regarded as a right or a principle (the latter requiring further legislation for it to be asserted). Despite this shift, the preliminary rulings in *Zambrano* and *Dereci* clearly indicate that in spite of everything, the Court of Justice is aware of the explosive political issue entailed by a possible evolution of a federal charter of rights.

As regards social security, the monography has indicated that it will not be possible to invoke Article 34.1 of the Charter to any greater extent, as the right to social security is a principle and thus dependent on the legislative initiative of the Member States. Concerning Article 34.2, which regulates internal market issues, the situation is slightly different—this fundamental right, even if it should also be regarded as a principle against the background of the wording, can be asserted only when secondary legislation is present as Regulation 883/2004. In light of Article 6.1 TEU and Article 51.2 of the Charter, however, the Court of Justice could not expand the competences of the EU by referring to Article 34.2, as this would challenge the Member States in two ways; this would lead to an erosion of the sovereignty of national social security systems, and introduce a federal catalogue of rights. An evolution of social security at the EU level has taken place with adjacent rights such as equal treatment and Union citizenship. However, it is not probable, as shown, that the Court of Justice will turn to these provisions of the Charter. Instead, legal evolution will continue in the area of the internal market and the Charter will shadow this development, as has happened in the area of the rights of the child and age discrimination. As regards undesired and unexpected effects despite non-discriminatory national pieces of legislation and a coordination through Regulation 883/2004, the Court of Justice will be able to lean on the

[144] A Ward, Article 51, Field of Application, in in P Peers, T Hervey, J Kenner and A Ward (eds), *The EU Charter of Fundamental Rights; a Commentary* (Oxford, Hart, 2014) 1425; S O'Leary, 'The Charter and the Future Contours of EU Social and Employment Law' in P Cardonnel, A Rosas and N Wahl (eds), *Constitutionalising the EU Judicial System—Essays in Honour of Pernilla Lindh* (Oxford, Hart, 2012).

[145] S Weatherill, 'Protecting the Internal Market from the Charter' in S de Vries, U Bernitz and S Weatherill, *Five Years Legally Binding EU Charter of Fundamental Rights—What is the State of Play in the Protection of Fundamental Rights in the EU?* (Oxford, Hart, 2015).

[146] Case C-617/10 *Åklagaren v Hans Åkerberg Fransson*, EU:C:2013:105, 21, 25 and 26.

rights of the Charter when there is a need to strengthen a line of reasoning, as we have observed regarding social rights in *Kamberaj*. Examples of situations where the Court might resort to such a lever in the future and legitimise the far-reaching impact of EU law on national social security systems could be in situations akin to *van Munster* and *Leyman*. A substantial expansion of the right to social security purely on the basis of the Charter, however, will be long in coming—if indeed it ever does.

8

Conclusions

8.1. INTRODUCTION

The purpose of this monograph has been to examine how the EU law relates to and affects the national social security systems of Member States.

The following three questions have formed the basis for the monograph:

1. How will the internal market and its development affect national social security models over the years, despite the fact that according to Regulation 883/2004 and its predecessor, EU competence in this area is limited to coordination?
2. How has Union citizenship affected the coordination of national social security systems?
3. How has the Charter of Fundamental Rights affected the coordination of national social security systems?

These issues have been highlighted in previous research and more generally from a more limited perspective, but here, a broader overall approach has been taken where all the legal forces are analysed. The knowledge gap intended to be filled by this monograph is particularly important because not only in the wake of the economic crisis, but also through the eastern enlargement of the EU, increasing differences have emerged in levels of economic and social prosperity within the EU. At the same time, the EU promotes the Union as a social market economy. As a result, the tensions between the free movement of people, solidarity and sustainable social protection have increased. This monograph intends to contribute to deeper understanding of the reorientation of national social security models—both the shift that has occurred and the changes taking place in the present.

To answer the three questions of the monograph, more than 400 court cases in the field of social security have been analysed in which the CJEU has issued rulings. In this analysis, I have applied the legal dogmatic method in a broad sense, complemented by EU legal method, and after establishing the relevant case law I have explored the deeper EU legal structures that emerge and which are affecting Member States' national social security models.

When the European Economic Community was created in 1958, the national social security systems were coordinated by Regulation 3/58 in order to support the free movement of workers. This coordination would simultaneously respect the competence of the Member States in terms of the structure of their social security systems. This approach involves conflicting interests: the Member States' understanding of coordination is limited by the perception of state sovereignty, with domestic solidarity within agreed financial frameworks, while the EU's starting point for coordination is based on opening up of the Member States' territorial systems to enhanced freedom of movement for persons. The monograph indicates that these two approaches cannot meet in harmony; the fact that the Regulation operates in an internal market context means that the free movement of workers will have the upper hand when collisions occur.

The monograph shows that the legal landscape in 2017 looks significantly different than in 1958, when the focus was solely on the common market. Today's landscape is characterised by three independent Union legal forces. In addition to the internal market's legal mechanisms, one must take into account Union citizenship and the Charter of Fundamental Rights. This situation derives from an initial legislative development that has led to three parallel forces which interact, reinforce and defend but also change the perception of coordination.

Further, it is noted that the result of this new EU legal reality is an individualisation of social security, which challenges the fundamental idea of solidarity that is the very basis for national social security models. Today, we also see an individual rights perspective, which could open up and even partially dismantle national social security models.

In terms of social security, the legal position described above, with an EU law that restricts national competence with regard to the social security systems, is perceived as either too far-reaching, or as a fully logical result stemming from the inherent power and aims of EU law.

8.2. WHAT IS THE IMPACT OF EU LAW ON NATIONAL SOCIAL SECURITY SYSTEMS?

At the start, let us recall something that can easily be forgotten in a doctrinal discussion. The Member States *are* in agreement that coordination of social security shall take place among the Member States. Therefore, as they are well aware of the importance of coordination for a personal mobility of the workforce, the Member States adopted Regulation 3/58 on social security for migrant workers; this was the very first substantive Regulation for the EU.

The current Regulation 883/2004 generally works sufficiently well. Looking back, however, one notes that Regulation 883/2004 and its predecessor have not kept pace with the developments related to actual migratory movements between the Member States, which have developed much faster. The infrastructure has developed radically since 1958, partly with EU initiatives enabling better roads, more reliable railways, the introduction of low-price airlines and digital highways. This turn of events has enabled citizens to undertake a weekly commute to work in another state, to commute long distances each day, or to simply work on-line with an employer in another Member State. However, legislation is still based on the 1958 idea of a more static migration from one Member State to another. Union citizenship and a rights-based EU are experiencing a trend that would have been difficult to predict in 1958, and the current legislators are encountering difficulties in relating to this trend. In parallel with this development, the national social security systems of the Member States have moved toward increasingly complex welfare structures where interaction with EU legislation and the ensuing result will be even more difficult to predict.

Along with these new movement patterns and unforeseen legal situations, the question is whether the Regulation can deal with the questions that still need to be answered. At these crossroads, the Court has had a choice between more or less of Europe. This is the legal environment in which the questions appear of *how* and *why* the rulings of the CJEU have influenced national social security systems. Section 8.2 explains in more detail the conclusions drawn from the reviewed materials.

8.2.1. Interpretation Methods

Chapter 3 clarifies, through an extensive review of the abundant case law on Regulation 883/2004, that the CJEU applies a textual interpretation method when the Regulation's framework contributes to the Regulation's basic idea of free movement of workers. When the wording of the Regulation does not promote the free movement of people, the CJEU instead works with a systematic interpretation that "bends" the legal framework towards support of the freedom of movement.

According to section 3.5.4, Regulation 3/58 was not a qualitative legislative product as the Court widely used a systematic interpretation and in some cases a teleological interpretation method. Regulation 1408/71 presents an almost opposite picture. However, as concluded by the monograph in section 3.8, this relationship cannot be taken as a pretext for claiming that the EU has respected national social security systems to a greater extent. Regulation 1408/71 was the result of thorough negotiations involving consolidation of the case law in Regulation 3/58. Since Regulation 1408/71 was updated over 30 times, and since recent case law was incorporated, a further consolidated sovereignty erosion has taken place over the years. This involves a textual interpretation, but one that has almost nothing in common with a bilateral coordination agreement. As for Regulation 883/2004, some ten rulings have been delivered so far. It is therefore too early to draw any general conclusions about interpretation tendencies here. As already noted, the groundbreaking preliminary ruling seen in *Brey* indicates a CJEU that is not afraid to put the Regulation in a larger context.

Chapter 3 demonstrates that in coordination situations, the EU law context and basic idea of free movement of persons have thus been decisive in the Court's work.

8.2.2. Equal Treatment

The internal market is based on the principle of equal treatment. Without equal treatment of goods, people, services and capital, no internal market could exist or be sustained. Chapter 4 analyses the development of Union law from equal treatment to market access in the area of free movement. The chapter continues with an analysis of how these different phases of the principle of non-discrimination have influenced national social security models in coordination situations.

8.2.2.1. Impact of Non-Discrimination on Social Security

As shown in section 4.2.2, the most apparent unequal treatment—direct discrimination on grounds of nationality—has not been particularly frequent in the EU social security context. The Member States' legislation, on the whole and after many years of EU membership, is neutrally worded, and citizenship does not constitute a criterion for qualifying for a state's social security system. The cases in terms of direct discrimination which have been brought before the CJEU can therefore be characterised largely as omissions or incorrect application by national authorities.

The doctrine related to indirect discrimination was developed by the CJEU in the early 1970s in terms of free movement of goods. The Court's application of the ban on indirect discrimination has far-reaching effects in relation to national legislation in that domestic rules can be found to prevent free movement of persons despite having no intention to discriminate. The review of the case law in section 4.2.3 shows that momentum grew when the CJEU found that the doctrine of indirect discrimination had application in the context of Regulation 883/2004. EU law and the free movement have a greater impact in terms of the expense related to national social insurance, as the Court retrospectively rejected national social security systems' excessive qualifying periods and calculation principles which were to their own citizens' advantage.

The market access model, termed as the third step in the evolution of the non-discrimination principle, leads to a stronger impact because the CJEU does not need to demonstrate a causal link between different treatment and its outcome. Therefore, one might fear that the market access model will represent a particularly serious threat for national social security systems, but as explained in section 4.2.4, it turns out to be the contrary. The fact that the national social security systems differ will result in a restrictive effect on the free movement of persons. The Regulation was introduced in 1958 as a kind of a market access model. According to section 4.2.4, the many situations where the market access model could be applied found their solution in the rules of the Regulation on aggregation of insurance, residence and/or employment periods from one or more Member States. Regarding the other situations in which the EU applied the market access model, these are cases where the Regulation pointed out the legislation of one Member State or where two Member States' benefits should be aggregated, but the outcome turned out to be unjust. In such situations, the CJEU has stated that the Regulation cannot coordinate all situations. As a result, blind spots have occurred here and there. The market access model is applied when these 'spots' have a deterrent effect on free movement of persons. As a result, the Court has applied the market access model to situations where the outcome of a migrant situation could not be foreseen, or where the result of national rules, in combination with each other or with the Regulation, leads to a clearly unreasonable result. Therefore, the model will not be applied by the CJEU for situations in which an individual has been able to obtain information in advance on how the new competent state system is designed and what the outcome will be. Thus, one can simulate the legal position as one where a potential migrant worker has the duty to investigate, but cannot be blamed for hidden defects.

Section 4.2.5 shows that Regulation 883/2004 neutralises the national legislation of the Member State which could prevent one leaving a Member State. Regulation 883/2004 focuses here on situations in which the aggregation principle prescribes that all insurance periods must be taken into account. Furthermore, the principle of exportability states that benefits shall be paid irrespective of a person's residence. The situations which have arisen in terms of the exit model in the social security context are therefore situations where the Regulation is either not applicable or where the Regulation framework is not able to predict an outcome in a cross-border situation.

When the CJEU notes that unequal treatment is at hand, the principle of proportionality is then applied for the current situation. As shown in section 4.2.6, such an assessment indicates that with very few exceptions, the legislation of the Member States has been found to be disproportionate. This as the national legislation is based on predictability and precise legislation, and as such is automatically disproportionate. Provided unequal treatment is found to be present in a cross-border situation, national social security legislation can be rescued in rare cases by an assessment of proportionality, even if the purpose of the legislation itself could be acceptable. The design of the legislation therefore means that balancing is not possible.

Equal treatment according to EU law means that migrant workers enjoy rights in such a way that they shall be equated with a Member State's own nationals. This means that the Member State must ensure protection systems for individuals who, according to the national rules, would otherwise not be covered by the system. In cases where the principle of equal treatment is extensively applied, the new personal scope would be greater than if the test of direct discrimination had been applied.

8.2.2.2. Equal Treatment of Facts

Previous completed periods from another Member State are of great importance for national authorities when assessing eligibility or the level of a benefit to be granted. This context covers a consolidation, where the Regulation allows taking into account insurance periods from other Member States in an application for benefits in the competent state. Through *Bergström*, the EU clarifies that according to the Regulation, it is enough simply to assert the earned periods from another Member State when applying for benefits in the competent state. Semantically speaking, this strange situation has arisen, as shown in section 4.3, by consideration of residence as a possible basis for determining applicable legislation under the Regulation, while the aggregation principle is derived from earlier times when only work could form the basis. Therefore, aggregation was possible only when work was carried out in both states and it automatically meant (earned) insurance periods from both countries. The new legal situation resulting from *Bergström* is discussed in section 4.3.2. As already stated, the situation is challenging current opinion, according to which a national collective contributes to social security. *Bergström* is an example of increasing individualisation of social security in cross-border movements, where there is no corresponding coverage of the cost.

8.2.3. The Primary Legal Dimension

The monograph shows in Chapter 5 that if Regulation 883/2004 is not applicable in a cross-border situation, this does not automatically mean that the national legislature is free to design and implement its social security system. As shown in section 5.2, the CJEU has stated in the rulings in *Vougioukas, Öberg* and *Rockler* that provided the social security systems are not subject to the coordination rules of the Regulation, the primary legislation shadows the Regulation, when free movement of persons is adversely affected.

Regulation 883/2004 gives rise to a rudimentary solidarity between the Member States, where the result of the Regulation is not always a zero-sum game. When the CJEU applies primary legislation, a more far-reaching loosening of social security territoriality takes place, where a Member State must show solidarity towards groups of people belonging to social security systems which are not intended to be coordinated through the Regulation.

Rulings like *Kohll, Smits Peerbooms* and *Watts* show that the CJEU has broken new ground, as cross-border care was already regulated in the previous Regulation 1408/71. If one turns around the perspective, as in section 5.3.2 of the monograph, this progress appears to be logical. Through Regulation 883/2004, regulation of cross-border care appears as a bonus benefit by the Member States which have not really had anything to do with free movement of persons. Rather, case law developments confirm that Regulation 883/2004 cannot be constructed as a place of refuge where parts of the social protection system are concealed from the free movement of services. Nevertheless, free movement of services is not characterised by a social dimension, but instead focuses fully on enabling the services, service providers and recipients to move freely within the Union. As a result, this individual perspective puts pressure on national health systems, and Member States have previously been able to control this pressure through an adjustment provided by the Regulation.

8.2.4. Union Citizenship

Earlier EU legislation and case law on free movement of persons have focused on migrant workers and ensured their path to the social security system of the working state. As a result of Regulation 883/2004, the legislator has taken account of the evolution of Union citizenship and extended the personal scope to include migrant Union citizens. Even if some doctrine asserts that this does not involve major change, the question is whether this change will create even more erosion in sovereignty for the national social security systems. Chapter 6 describes the background and challenges to be taken into consideration.

The fact that a Union citizen is expressly covered by the Regulation represents, as stated in section 6.3, an opportunity to 'earn a right of residence through residing', provided the rules on the applicable law identify a Member State, to issue residence-based benefits according to their national laws, which leads—paradoxically—to the individual not being a burden on the residence state. As explained in section 6.4, Directive 2004/38 imposes a requirement, that in order to maintain a right of residence, Union citizens cannot be a burden on the residence state in terms of social assistance. Social security and social assistance are two distinct things and the right to social security benefits cannot be made contingent on a right of residence. This has been indirectly confirmed by the CJEU, as concluded in section 6.6.6, in *Brey* and *Dano*. The solidarity and sustainability of social security systems are therefore tested, so that the benefits associated with an individual's residence can give rise to a right to national social security benefits which do not display characteristics of social assistance.

8.2.5. Charter of Fundamental Rights

The Charter of Fundamental Rights is independent of the EU treaty, and because of the reference in Article 6 TEU, it represents binding primary law. The Charter of Fundamental Rights enters the scene only when EU law is applied and therefore, the Charter of Fundamental Rights constitutes the relevant primary legislation in cross-border situations where social security is in question. It has been argued in the work of the convention but also in the doctrine that the right of access to social security, according to Article 34 of the Charter, is at particular risk for competence enlargement. However, according to Article 51.2, the Charter cannot extend the EU's area of competence. In *Dano*, which is analysed from a Charter perspective in section 7.4.2.2, and the subsequent *Poclava*, which is discussed in section 7.4.2.3, the CJEU has adopted a more restrictive view of *when* EU law is applied in accordance with Article 51.1 of the Charter of Fundamental Rights. As the CJEU remains unable to implement the Charter of Fundamental Rights to coordination of social security systems of the Member States, Article 34 of the Charter therefore applies only to the EU institutions. The competence of those bodies is strictly limited because the EU has no real competence in terms of social security. As shown by the concluding analysis in section 7.8, the fundamental rights which approach a form of social security will be used by the CJEU as an extra argument when the Charter of Fundamental Rights shadows an individual-based development in the internal market. In this way, the Charter can stabilise and consolidate the new territory that the CJEU has explored and annexed, and the resulting case law.

8.2.6. The Common Thread

A clear picture of the position of social security within the EU is obtained only when one takes a step back and tries to find the common thread in what may initially seem to be a patchwork of infringement procedures and preliminary rulings.

When the CJEU attempts to mend and extend the EU legal patchwork, this activity emanates from the EU's inherent power: the notion of the internal market. This monograph shows that sovereignty erosion occurs in situations where free movement of persons is restricted by national social security systems, notwithstanding the regulatory framework of Regulation 883/2004. This primordial force has been subsequently complemented by Union citizenship and possibly the fundamental rights in the future which interact and challenge in complex patterns.

The common thread that is revealed when one can take a step back is thus characterised by what may seem obvious, but is still controversial because, on paper at least, it is all about coordination: EU law has priority and is thus restricting the competence of the Member States. This has resulted in an erosion of sovereignty. The regulatory autonomy of the Member States remains, but any chafing edges of conflict have been removed by EU law. This is happening from case to case, and therefore it may be difficult for the individual Member States and authorities to make a preliminary assessment of whether a given situation can be considered a hindrance. This applies in particular as the CJEU, in recent rulings such as *The Commission v Spain*, *Jeltes* and *Dano*, has taken a less expansionary path.

Notwithstanding this more cautious tendency, the review of case law shows that the doctrine of the internal market has led to individualisation of social security in cross-border situations. The question is whether such individual rights challenge the basic idea of collective solidarity present in current social security.

Union citizenship and the Charter of Fundamental Rights have introduced other legal bases than pure market economic considerations. For 40 years, until *Sala*, the internal market and its legal principles developed. Then, Union citizenship developed free movement that was not dependent on an economic activity. The Charter of Fundamental Rights—the third judicial force—is focused on freedoms and human rights. The market economy is certainly one of the foundations of the Charter, but it includes more basic rights and freedoms, such as the right to life, freedom of religion and family life, but also solidarity rights such as the right to social security. *Brey* and *Dano* illustrate in a very clear way the tensions and issues that arise when these three forces meet. The issue in the longer term is understanding the extent to which these two new forces will displace the European legal landscape, and the direction this shift will take. As *Brey* and *Dano* indicate, the legal landscape will become much more open than before. Initially, most indications are that the CJEU has taken a step backwards with regard to free movement, limiting it to the economically active in terms of social assistance and hybrid benefits. The upcoming preliminary rulings must be thoroughly analysed before a debate takes place about a change of course. In this context, is it also important to put *Dano* in its proper context. Will the CJEU continue to be restrictive in its application of the direct rights in the Charter of Fundamental Rights when it comes to social security? As only the Charter is applicable, as indicated in the analysis of *McB* in section 7.5.2.2 and confirmed in *Dano*, in relation to Regulation 883/2004 and its rules, it is difficult to see how a development towards a more free-standing fundamental right to social security benefits in cross-border situations can become a reality. The Charter of Fundamental Rights' regulation of social security benefits, in combination with no apparent intentions of extending competence and the understanding of the application as restrictive, illustrates how the Charter is currently going round in circles.

The common thread indicates that the introduction of a Regulation has led to sovereignty erosion of the Member States' social security systems. Specifically, the intervention of EU law can fluctuate and this will be determined by the CJEU from case to case. Against this background and taking into account the rationality of EU law in terms of the free movement of persons and Member States' wish for clear rules of play, the current legal position appears to counter both EU law and national legal systems.

8.3. HEADED FOR THE CLIFF? OR, WHAT HAPPENS IN CASE OF INDIVIDUALISATION OF SOCIAL PROTECTION FROM THE PERSPECTIVE OF EU LAW?

As noted, the Bismarck model served as the basis for Regulation 3/58 and its successors, and therefore it can be assumed that the Member States that are most affected by the case law developments are those with residence-based social security systems. Paradoxically, Germany—the stronghold of the Bismarck model—has been in focus when the CJEU has handed down preliminary rulings such as *Molenaar*, *Geven*, and *Hudzinski*. These cases have involved residence-based benefits, which one might not have expected in a Bismarck model. This only demonstrates that the division into different welfare models is no longer appropriate, partly because Member States who wish to pursue a national redistribution policy through their social security systems may struggle to assert their residence-based benefits in an EU legal context where individuals can exercise individual rights. However, no individual EU-law social security has developed; instead, these individual rights are fully dependent on the Member States design of national social security systems.

In an open dialogue, it may not seem defensible that EU law is applied to national redistribution policy. Such a policy represents the absolute inner core of a welfare state and the purpose of these benefits is not to promote the free movement of people. It is all about the benefits lying on the fringes of the social security system—benefits that do not require work but instead are based on collective solidarity in the national context. However, from the EU legislation's perspective, individual bridges will appear in these national solidarity benefits, where eligible individuals can hardly claim to belong to the intended target group of the Member State. However, the equal treatment principle in EU law, in combination with national residence-based benefits, will open up the system for migrant persons.

EU law is based on free movement, where redistribution policies can certainly be accepted as overriding reasons but where the proportionality test, as described in section 4.2.6, has so far not been taken into account.

If a Member State chooses to maintain unrestricted national redistribution policies, it risks increased costs along with an influx of Union citizens who might try to 'reside into benefits'. Such a situation may lead to a debate on social tourism, as the nationals of Member States tend only to pay attention to perceived drawbacks of free movement. This perceived erosion can also lead social security systems' loss of legitimacy at the national level, to the detriment of the collective whole.

With *Brey*, *Dano*, *Alimanović* and *García-Nieto*, the CJEU seems to have pressed the pause button as regards the hybrid benefits of the social security system. These benefits can now be subject to a right of residence.

The CJEU chose, in *Commission v United Kingdom*, to respect the essential material differences between Regulation 883/2004 and Directive 2004/38 and decided on the infringement action against the United Kingdom on the basis of Regulation 883/2004. However, the Court accepted the British requirement of a right to reside and has thereby introduced a catch-all principle resembling the right of residence test of Directive 2004/38.[1] Directive 2004/38 contains—in addition to rules on free movement of persons—rules about when Member States can restrict the free movement of persons. The Regulation has no such corresponding rules, but only rules on coordination when a cross-border movement is at hand. As long as this situation lasts, and in terms of pure residence-based benefits, the jurisprudence continues to point in the direction of a new solidarity that is no longer limited to a nation-state population, migrant workers and their families. The Member States may, in this position, either stick to a redistribution policy based on residence-based benefits and thereby risk having also to pay benefits to non-economically active EU citizens, or restrict benefits to migrating workers. However, the negative aspect is then that the redistribution policies are restricted to the working population and not to the more vulnerable national citizens: the incapacitated, unemployed and pensioners. The solidarity of social security must take a back seat and therefore, it may be difficult to defend in a domestic political context. Furthermore, if a Member State chooses to restrict its social security system to just the working population, the impact of EU law on

[1] Cf Cousins, M, 'The baseless fabric of this vision: EU citizenship, the right to reside and EU law' [2016] *Journal of Social Security Law*, p 89.

national social security systems will be obvious. In that case, EU law will drive the development towards a pure social security in the Bismarck spirit, where redistribution policies must be converted to social assistance benefits.

No matter how one looks at it, it would seem that the Member States and the EU must act. This situation will be discussed further in the concluding remarks.

8.4. CONCLUSION

The purpose of this monograph has been to analyse how EU law relates to and affects national social security systems. Has sovereignty erosion occurred? Can one argue that this must be a zero-sum game? As shown in the conclusions, these questions demand a response.

Sovereignty erosion? The answer is yes, as long as we cannot free ourselves from the prevailing sovereignty concept, based on sovereign nation-states. Therefore, provided that the EU gains sovereignty at the expense of the Member States, the issue of sovereignty erosion will continue to be a controversial topic. Zero-sum game? The answer is no, based on the fact that the EU6 chose coordination and not harmonisation (assuming that some solidarity was expected, but that the common market would gradually even out the playing field).

The monograph shows that the national social security systems of Member States are not, and cannot be, unaffected in a European legal context. National social security systems are affected by the internal market, Union citizenship with the right to free movement and perhaps in the future by the Charter of Fundamental Rights, which has not yet shown its full potential. Therefore, the question is whether the further development should be a matter for the EU, or—as has been discussed during the past 50 years—if it will continue to be developed by the CJEU.

The monograph paints a picture where many of the old truths are challenged and questioned. Social security as we know it will change. This new development knocking at the door is shedding new light on prevailing notions of the welfare state and inherent solidarity. Is Regulation 883/2004 able, in such circumstances, to continue to be the main solution for social security in cross-border situations? Can or should the CJEU continue to fill out the Regulation? Or should the Member States agree on new EU legislation based on both the internal market and a common social policy?

The modern social security that constitutes one of the pillars of the welfare state is less than 150 years old. Solidarity between people has changed over time as societies developed, from small village communities to industrialisation. Changes in the concept of solidarity and the various forms of social security are nothing new. Changes in social security have followed when communities have taken new steps in development. From the mid-1800s onwards, the prevailing ideas of a rudimentary state along the lines of a nation-state have been challenged along with growing movement in Europe from the countryside to the cities during industrialisation. The response to the social unrest that arose was the introduction of social security and the advent of territorial welfare defined by each state in light of needs and policy choices. By 2017, the current idea of the welfare state with its territorial solidarity has been challenged by other patterns of movement within the EU that are characterised by movement based on increasingly individual reasons, and where the duration of the mobility is often so short time that no deeper solidarity with the working state can form.

The monograph illustrates an expansion of what Pieters and Verschueren call the solidarity circle, without a development of corresponding financial solidarity at the same pace. A solidarity within the EU, which knows no national borders or national sense of solidarity, can thereby be provocative.

Nationalist winds are blowing in 2017. In the debate that followed the expansion of the EU towards Eastern Europe in 2004 and the bankruptcy of Lehman Brothers in 2008 and the Euro crisis that followed, many have come to see free movement as a problem; many perceive that migrant workers are looking to exploit the welfare system of the state. The focus has shifted from citizens' positive attitudes of free movement of persons as a mean to contribute to their state's welfare through much-needed labour and income that generates growth and increased welfare, to worries that free movement will instead undermine the welfare state. This change of focus was evident in the debate which preceded the British referendum in June 2016.

Nevertheless, the Member States, through the EU Treaty, have pledged to build a 'new' Europe, a Union that will not repeat the mistakes and wars of the past. Article 3.3 TEU describes an internal market where 'The Union must work for the sustainable development of Europe based on balanced economic growth and price stability, on a social market economy with high competitiveness that aims at full employment and social progress'. The Lisbon Treaty talks about a social market economy that is still waiting to be brought into being.

As a starting point in the forward-looking discussions, it is important to note that a case law-driven development towards individualised social security is not sustainable in the long run. History shows us the collective solutions of the social security—the village community, tithes to the church, use of insurance funds, social security contributions. To completely abandon a collective solution is not a fruitful way forward for the EU. The way forward is complex, and the question is how long the CJEU will lead the way, as social security ultimately rests on the issue of who should pay for the social security system.

The CJEU is bound by its mandate and is responsible for ruling on the cases brought before it. Therefore, strictly speaking, the CJEU can only condemn the current national legislation system in an EU legal context, and provide some indications, but it cannot and does not have the mandate to construct a new sustainable system.

As I see it, there are four main ways forward for sustainable National social security systems.

The first involves no change of course, but this path means that Member States must continue to show a certain solidarity with migrant groups of people, while taking the risk that this extended solidarity will be unfunded.

The second way is a federalist direction, in which the EU takes over responsibility for social welfare in a system where national borders no longer correspond to social security and where continued sovereignty erosion can be predicted.

In my opinion, these two directions are not realistic. There is certainly an acceptance of a certain solidarity between the Member States through Regulation 883/2004 during its interaction with other EU legislation; however, this solidarity cannot be stretched indefinitely. Ultimately, this solidarity means that sustainability of the systems is threatened. However, a greater threat, when the free movement is still limited, is the free individual mobility that is unfairly targeted as something that just costs money, and political currents emerge that undermine the internal market foundations. The second choice is not the right way forward because, so far, the marginal free movement of persons cannot be used as a reason for a far-reaching federalisation of the Member State's inner core. In order to tread this path, not only should the politicians be ready; there must also be a common vision and understanding among the Member States' nationals that borderless solidarity is a good thing for the EU as a whole. This does not exist.

However, we cannot be complacent about these findings. Instead, a proactive common policy must be introduced, for which Regulation 883/2004 already has the answer to how free movement can be supported without challenging the autonomous social protection schemes of the Member States or evoking the federalisation spectre. The Regulation is already regulating cash flows arising from cross-border healthcare. In this way, the financial resources of the attending state are not charged, but free movement is supported. The regulation of payment flows is made through a settlement process. To take a full step as a third path towards compensating the state for the provision of other social security benefits by the competent Member State, however, would require a more sophisticated solution because the relatively limited migration still involves significant sums. Furthermore, the poorer Member States with less developed welfare, in addition to trying to sustain such a welfare system, will also have to compensate for their citizens travelling to other Member States. Therefore, a legitimate question would be this: what are the situations in which a state should finance, when its insured persons move to another Member State? Such a structure will result in obvious incentives to change the state's regulations and registration of persons, so that this is lost immediately upon a migrant movement that involves a longer stay in another Member State. This way, the new competent state will take over the full responsibility for costs without corresponding cost recovery.

These comments point to a more nuanced fourth way forward, where a joint fund must be established to defray the additional costs arising from the cross-border movement of persons, with compensation from an EU fund. It is possible that the European Social Fund could take a holistic approach, and not be aimed only at reinforcing and developing national labour market policy. A holistic approach which sees the EU as *one* labour market, where the social fund could compensate Member States for additional costs of social security arising from a more extensive free movement. Thus, the poorer Member States' financial stability would not be challenged, and the Member States with more comprehensive social security would be compensated when migrant workers, but also non-economically active EU citizens, set up residence in the country. It can be argued that such a common fund would serve the purpose of the wealthier Member States, by preventing harm to their own systems, while the poorer Member States would continue to see migratory flows towards the Member States with more extensive welfare, without themselves being able to take advantage of this migration. On the other hand, European mobility has historically been relatively limited, and the reforms and law development are far behind the scope of mobility in the United States. Furthermore, the brain drain occurring today will benefit the states of origin in the form of money transfers sent home to family and relatives. There is also a hope that migrant persons will return home after a few years spent in another Member State, and bring with them new skills and capital. Such campaigns have already begun, for example in Estonia, where the now former President Ilves led the *Talendid koju!* initiative ('Talents, Come Home!').

No matter how one views the constructive suggestions for how to support free movement of persons, while the social security systems of the Member States are being maintained, these proposals contain flaws and unfair measures. The social security systems and their interactions are so complex that a 100% fair new system cannot be achieved. Instead of trying to design comprehensive, complex and opaque systems of compensation, why not ask the fundamental question: threat or opportunity?

Most EU Member States are struggling with population decline, with increasingly ageing populations that will be supported by fewer and fewer economically active. In a few decades, some populations may be insufficient to maintain national welfare systems. In the future therefore, the Member States may come to compete for workers by offering generous terms, including attractive social security systems.

To make this tug-of-war constructive at a European level, the current idea of a nation-state must be revised and migrant workers must (once again) be seen as an opportunity to jointly develop sustainable welfare systems in the long term.

These systems must necessarily have some federal traits in order to remain sustainable. The current situation with struggling solidarity, in the form of national social security without corresponding recovery of costs, has arisen because the EU legal structure is focused solely on supporting the free movement of workers, but where the workers contribute to welfare through work and income. In theory, the uneven playing field will gradually even itself out. The monograph shows that the Member States no longer completely share this view. In addition, free movement now means that not only workers are entitled to move between the Member States, and this gives rise to fundamental questions on solidarity. Therefore, a Union legal structure must be based on the fact that not everyone can or will contribute fully to the social security system of the state. This is particularly important, as the Charter of Fundamental Rights acknowledges an individual fundamental right to social security.

This necessary legal construction is also important from a citizen perspective. The current social security systems and the general welfare structures of the Member States will otherwise be difficult to finance and maintain. If no EU legal construction can be launched that introduces a new kind of solidarity, states risk closing themselves off, to the detriment of the Union, the Member States and the citizens.

Index

www.ingramcontent.com/pod-product-compliance
Ingram Content Group UK Ltd.
Pitfield, Milton Keynes, MK11 3LW, UK
UKHW021907150926
475560UK00003B/236